BETRAYED BY FOREIGN POLICY FAULT LINE 1619–2024, US IN VIET NAM 1865–1975

Brian Douglas Roesch

Copyright © 2025 Brian Douglas Roesch

Nonfiction

First Edition

All rights reserved

briandroesch.com\

This book is fully based on declassified material.

Subjects: foreign policy—US-Viet Nam War, US-Vietnam War—Agent Orange/dioxin—US History—racism—Gaza—school shootings—international relations

On their first appearance in this book, some Viet language terms include accent marks. Later appearances do not use accent marks, except in endnotes and bibliography.

Because of the nature of the internet, web addresses cited herein may have changed and may no longer be valid.

Book cover by Shelley Savoy
Map by Trần Phương Dung

Cover photo Gaza 2024 after indiscriminate airstrike by Israel. Photo by Jaber Jehad Badwan, 2024. See also Gaza in Index. Use permission granted through photographer's notice to Wikipedia. https://en.wikipedia.org/wiki/Gaza_Strip

Cover photo Viet Nam child in 2021 with birth defect from dioxin sprayed during the war. Photo by Daniel Sebold, use permission granted. See also dioxin in Index.

ISBN 979-8-9929448-0-8 (ebook)
ISBN 978-0-9983815-9-6 (paperback)

Interior design by Booknook.biz

OTHER BOOKS BY THIS AUTHOR:

Corporate Tsunami in Countryside Paradise: 1875–1900 Origin of US War in Viet Nam (2020). US: Voter Knowledge Press.

Spirit of Nine Dragons Delta, (Publication summer 2026. A novel of business expansion, romance, politics, and war set in Viet Nam and the US). US: Voter Knowledge Press.

DEDICATION

To people of the US, Viet Nam, and other nations, who are victims of US leaders' business expansion, often by force, from 1619 through 2024

TABLE OF CONTENTS

List of Photographs and Drawings	ix
Map of Viet Nam	xi
Preface	xiii
Introduction	xvii
PART I: Early Start for Business Expansion By Force	1
Chapter 1: Early Business Enabled by Force	3
Chapter 2: Patriotic Ho Leads for Independence	9
PART II: Patterns Targeting Viet Nam & Damaging the World	17
Chapter 3: Simultaneous 1865–1950s Periods of Racism	19
Chapter 4: Ditching Voters from World Order	25
Chapter 5: Targeting Viet Nam in the World Order	35
Chapter 6: Axiom on Control by Force	45
Chapter 7: Signature Techniques Hit Viet Nam & US	51
Chapter 8: Three-Step Analysis Deletes False Claim	67
Chapter 9: 22 Facts Show Pursuit Of Control Not Anti-Communism	121

Chapter 10:	Business Expansion, not Anti-Communism, Has Always Driven Foreign Policy	147
PART III:	US Public Redemption?	169
Chapter 11:	US Civilians Fall Short on Soldiers' Plea	171
Chapter 12:	Imperative for Voters to Transform Foreign Policy Fault Line	175

Acknowledgments	207
Endnotes	209
Bibliography	275
Index	295
About the Author	305

LIST OF PHOTOGRAPHS AND DRAWINGS

Map of Viet Nam	xi
Photo 1: Child dioxin victim 2016	65
Photo 2: US training Niger military in 2007	88
Photo 3: The French colony exported large quantities of rice	89
Photo 4: Child dioxin victim 2021; on book cover & on p. 159	159

Map of Viet Nam

During 1865-1975 Portion of 1865-2024 French-US Mutual "Security" For Resource Control

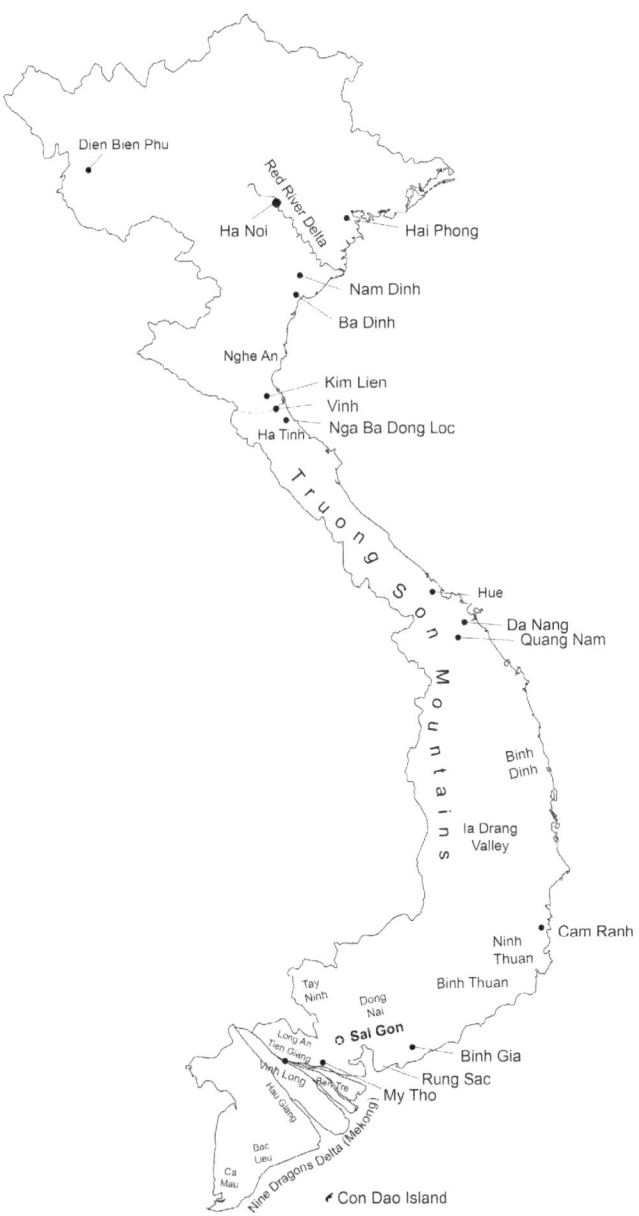

PREFACE

While serving as a US helicopter pilot in Thailand, 1974–75, I read *Bangkok Post* articles about French colonial brutality in Viet Nam during 1860–1954. Our leaders had not told us about that. They said the US entered in 1954, to fight communism. Suddenly, it struck me: Had the US been in Viet Nam during that brutal colony? After all, we had been close friends with France since our own Revolutionary War.

If so, then our leaders had lied in saying we entered in 1954, to fight communism. Would they also lie to our public in the future, about US actions in other countries? Would nice foreigners have to defend their countries against us?

One day in 1975, as I pondered those questions, a two-tour Viet Nam veteran, who had been a door gunner on a Huey helicopter crew in the US with me, my close friend, SSgt Elwood E. (Woody) Rumbaugh, met up with me at an air base in southern Thailand. At about 5 foot 7, Woody was as tough as nails. He had a throaty laugh and grin. A tough guy, with a heart as big as the sky.

Part of our conversation was:

'Woody, some *Bangkok Post* articles say that long before 1954, the French colony brutalized Viet Nam,' I said,

'That would anger the people of Viet Nam. Maybe that's what started the French war. If so, maybe our war, too, is not really about communism.'

'Oh, we're fighting Communists alright,' Woody replied in a strong voice. He leaned forward, no laughter this time. 'That's what we're fighting. Tough Commies.'

'Yes, some of them are tough Commies, but still, brutality makes people fight back,' I said. 'Maybe they see the US as an invader, too."

Woody looked at me.
I continued, "When I get back to the US, I'm going to dig and find what really happened. We are US soldiers. Our own government can't send US soldiers to die for a lie.'

'Goddam right," Woody nodded. "*IF* you find out that's why these people fight us, then write it. Tell it to the public. *IF* you find that.' Out came his deep-throated laugh, with his tough guy grin full of heart.

A few weeks later, on May 16, 1975, Woody was a Flight Engineer/door gunner on the Mayaguez Incident at Koh Tang Island, Cambodia. The following was described to me later that day on the airbase flight line, by MSgt Bounds, a Flt Engr/door gunner on a different helicopter in the fight at Koh Tang. Bounds had previously served as a Huey crewmember with Woody and me. Under heavy machine gun fire, Woody's helicopter, with Woody firing his machine gun, landed U.S. Marines on the beach. Heavily damaged, one engine out, the helicopter turned, limped away, and crashed into the sea, 1.6 km from the island. Main rotor blades were slamming into the ocean as some crewmen jumped into the water. Woody made it to the door, ready to jump. He turned. He scrambled back to the cockpit. He freed the trapped copilot, threw him into the water, and jumped, only to sink under the surface of the sea. Woody never resurfaced.

While completing my duty in 1975, I regularly heard Woody's voice saying to find the truth and write it. I returned to the US and began digging. A surprising answer turned up in 2003 in the U.S. National Archives: Thousands of declassified reports were there, sent by US government business consuls in Viet Nam beginning in 1889. More digging showed that US businesses had operated there during 1865–1954, enabled by French violence.

The *IF* that Woody and I had pondered was now a proven fact. This search for more evidence became a decades-long effort on behalf of US soldiers endangered to this day by the false premise of a noble foreign policy. It is created by the false claim of a noble entry in 1954 into Viet Nam. Indeed, the soldiers came from an endangered US public.

My search included reading in hundreds of books in the Viet language in the University of Washington Library, reading many US histories, and eight trips to Viet Nam. The first trip there, in 1990, included original interviews and site visits. Later trips included Viet Nam National Archives materials, more interviews, and travels. This volume recounts the findings and conclusions. They form clear proof of US business expansion by force not only specific to Viet Nam, but also continuing worldwide through 2024.

As this volume demonstrates, 58,281 US soldiers died in Viet Nam without knowing the true reason for the war. More have died through 2024, not knowing of the business expansion by force. Millions of Viet people died as their nation defended. More foreigners have died through 2024. US civilian voters have a duty to prevent any more from dying under the false claim of a noble, 1954 entry into Viet Nam.

Helping me keep this dream alive for the US public to know and begin redirecting foreign policy are Tomas Heikkala, who served in Viet Nam, and Gregory Laxer, who refused to go, was court-martialed, and wrote *Take This War and Shove It! : A Most Unwilling Soldier 1967–1971.*[1]

Along the way, as a criminal defense lawyer, I saw that about 15 percent of defendants in criminal cases actually had not committed a crime. Sometimes a witness made a false statement, or even lied, or sometimes the police and prosecutor had a wrong view of the evidence or had failed to find some evidence. In such cases, if the defense attorney dug hard, often sweating blood, to find the real facts, and the evidence of the facts, and get them into court, the truth would most often prevail. Juries appreciated solid proof like that. They generally recognized and agreed in cases where the government had missed the truth. This book presents such a case, of digging for the real facts and real evidence of the government presenting a false claim. This book is the result of 50 years of finding and marshalling evidence for You the Jury.

This volume uses the two-word names, "United States" and "Viet Nam," rather than one-word names, "Unitedstates" and "Vietnam." Like the two words, "United" and "States" have content meaning rather than being jumbled together, the word, "Viet" means the Viet race of people, and "Nam" means "South." The two distinct words in "Viet Nam" are a proud statement that Viet people south of China have long defended their nation's independence.[2]

INTRODUCTION

Adding to many people's knowledge about US leaders' imperialism, a recently uncovered, real reason for the US-Viet Nam War exposes a long-term fault line that has created conflict in the world for hundreds of years into the 2020s.

A pervasive false belief hiding the real reason for the US-Viet Nam War—to continue hidden early decades of US business by force—misleads many US voters. So they don't realize that in the decades since that war (the biggest US war since World War II), US leaders have continued to pursue business by force in many other countries.

US leaders falsely claim that the US entered Viet Nam in 1954. Virtually 100 percent of US voters believe that false claim. The false 1954 entry is presented as a noble effort to fight communism. But during 1889–1954, US businesses and government officials operated in Viet Nam enabled by a violent French invasion.

Trying to continue that hidden, early business by force, after Viet Nam defeated France in 1954, US leaders attacked. That was the real reason for the US-Viet Nam War—the biggest US war since 1945.

The false claim of a noble entry in 1954 has long allowed US leaders to escape blame for that real reason. They continued business expansion worldwide, often by force, through 2024.

That pursuit has angered much of the world. This is a chief cause of conflict. Over 50 years after the US-Viet Nam War, the US public has a duty to stop its government from business expansion by force.

The early US commerce in Viet Nam, enabled by force, included large and small items. For example, sales of US tire repair kits and California fruits were important, along with sales of Standard Oil kerosene and purchases of rubber. The small manufacture of tire repair kits employed US workers. Although on a smaller scale than Standard Oil operations, little enterprises helped make the US economy robust.

An additional small percentage of voters realizing the real reason for the US-Viet Nam War, hence the foreign anger at US force worldwide, would affect US national elections. For, the nation is evenly divided. A five percent shift of voters, for example, would add to an already existing bloc of US voters who see that US leaders have long been imperial. Augmented by voters who accept the proof in this volume, these voters could elect leaders who would pursue diplomacy for mutual development, not business expansion by force.

Many fact patterns identify the real reason

Massive evidence establishes various fact patterns that, individually and together, illustrate that the US-Viet Nam War was for US business expansion by force, rather than for fighting communism. And, they show that US leaders have never informed voters about that.

Business Expansion in Viet Nam during 1865–1954, Enabled by Force. Thousands of long-silent, declassified

Introduction

reports in the U.S. National Archives reveal the US business and the French force.

22 Facts Many facts placed together in one chapter leave no doubt of commerce-by-force in US economic growth. For example, a **406-year practice of business expansion by force started in 1619 with slavery** in North America. Over 200 years into this practice, **US ships entered Viet Nam in 1865. They began transporting rice that the French stole** by violence. The thefts of rice caused widespread malnutrition. Force was needed to dominate like that. For example, a French governor general objected, was fired, then wrote in 1895:[3]

> I can cite one district in Ha Noi Province, in which they decapitated, in fifteen days, seventy-five notables who were unable or did not want to—who can know in such a case what was the truth—say which roads a band of rebels followed who had passed through their villages.

More than 300 years into this practice of business by violence, a **State Department report in 1943 said "a long and disastrous period of repression"** would be needed if the West wanted to control Viet Nam any longer.[4,5]

Using **Signature Techniques** worldwide is evidence of a common plan for business expansion by force. For example, US leaders have long **misled the public** to think the 1954 Geneva Accords led to Viet Nam being two countries. That false belief is "an absurd concept," Joseph Buttinger wrote. The Accords "recognized Viet-Nam as one state," Prof. Quincy Wright, editorial board, American Association of International Law, explained in 1965. The plain words of the Accords, Article 14(a), recognize it as one nation.[6]

Into this nation, US soldiers entered the southern half, thinking it was being invaded from the north. But the vast majority in the southern half, angry at the century of Western invasion, fought the US. The northern half supported them. The US leaders' claim that the south was a separate nation was deceptive and foolish.

The US public and US soldiers did not know of the loyalty those villagers held for their single nation, Viet Nam. Indeed, in the 1960s, a US general lamented that he had no idea how the southern forces were able to consistently replenish their units after losses. The answer is that when some died fighting against the violent US invasion, more villagers joined.

Breaking the Golden Rule. Wrongfully taking other people's property—including much of Viet Nam's food—harms them. Some fight back. This makes it understandable and reasonable that Viet Nam's people fought back.

Three-Step Analysis. Exposure of the false claim of a noble, 1954 entry destroys the presumption that actions elsewhere were also noble. In the absence of that presumption, facts emerge that show the real US intent.

On Gaza, for example, without the presumption of a noble US intent, the spotlight falls on a 1943 State Department report that said a one-state solution injected "racial opposition" and "hatreds" that would take "statesmanlike guidance" to diminish. Superpower US leaders knew that principle all along. But they failed to succeed with "statesmanlike guidance." In 2024, despite nearly all the world's nations favoring a two-state solution—a condition ripe for US "statesmanlike guidance," US leaders supplied Israel with weapons as Israel killed about 14,000 children in Gaza.[7]

Another pattern is the **Creation of Cruelty to children** in various countries and areas. Gaza is a prime example. In Viet Nam, some children are born with birth defects caused by Agent Orange. And on climate change, as nature's 2030, 1.5C degree deadline to curb future devastation approaches, some children realize with horror that US leaders have long failed to take appropriate emergency action.

Seeing the US leaders' model of violence overseas (for business expansion), some troubled students choose violence and do school shootings.

Cruelty to children impacted **The Sequence and Logic of the Life of Ho Chi Minh**. When Ho was five years old, the French beheaded one of his relatives in young Ho's village. Many colonial abuses gave Ho a lifelong desire to rid his country of Western invasions.

A 1921 consensus of about 100 US foreign policy leaders, historian Michael Wala says, was that **"Access to raw materials and markets of the whole world should be *secured* for the United States."** (Italics added.)

Harm to US and World

The ignoble foreign policy of business expansion by force has harmed the US as well as much of the world. For, more and more of the harmed world rejects US leadership and trade. Recent articles in *Foreign Affairs*, say the US is in "America's Last Chance With the Global South," has "diminishing capacity" to "sustain fights," and (on the Middle East), "Washington enjoys far less influence and credibility in the region than it did in the 1990s."[8]

Democracy and justice

Foreshadowing a possible sea change, "the American people still cling to a basic sense of fairness, that once they understand the facts, they rarely permit injustice to stand," Juan Gonzalez says in *Harvest of Empire*. But many people say that US voters cannot have an effect on foreign policy: They lament that the Republican and Democratic parties, not the voters, control what is happening. However, that is not the traditional relationship.⁹

The traditional role of US voters has been to guide the general direction of foreign policy. A senior fellow in foreign policy, Walter Russell Mead wrote in 2004:[10]

> And while American foreign policy is studied in great detail by professionals and scholars, it must ultimately be debated and decided by tens of millions of voters."

The US public has the time and ability to learn about foreign policy. For example, on most weekends the public devotes countless hours of time and hundreds of millions of dollars on sports teams. So, public energy exists for voters to guide the nation to live by the truth on foreign policy.

Such a public outlay of time and energy pales before the sacrifice of US soldiers who go in harm's way.

Example of Changes in domestic debate

Some people say that 'one dead US child killed by an undocumented immigrant is one dead child too many.' But now, the revelation of a lack of a noble reason in the US attack on Viet Nam exposes the lack of a noble reason in Gaza. So, 64,000 dead and maimed children of Gaza are 64,000 too many.

Professor Noam Chomsky and Professor Angela Davis urge the US public to learn about foreign affairs, not just domestic matters. The truth that the US did an imperial attack on Viet Nam is known worldwide—except among much of the US public. On April 30, 2025, the 50th anniversary of Viet Nam's 1975 victory over the US, Viet Nam's General Secretary, To Lam, spoke to attending world leaders about a strategic partnership

Introduction

with the US, and also about the US having done an imperial invasion of Viet Nam.[11]

But the US government continues to deny the destructive imperial attack and the similar policy worldwide through 2024. Now, with the extensive proof in this volume, will the US public finally guide foreign policy based on truth? Or will much of the public choose to bask in a Matrix-movie-style mollycoddling of minds to acquiesce in business expansion, often by force?

They tell me the fault line runs right through here.

—John Hartford lyrics
sung by Cass Elliott[12]

PART I

EARLY START FOR BUSINESS EXPANSION BY FORCE

Tomorrow is the most important thing in life
Comes into us at midnight very clean
It's perfect when it arrives and it puts itself in our hands
It hopes we've learned something from yesterday.

> — Epitaph, John Wayne.[13]

CHAPTER 1

EARLY BUSINESS ENABLED BY FORCE

President George Washington urged in his 1796 Farewell Address: "Observe good faith and justice towards all nations. . . ." But the US business community followed a different rule on Viet Nam. In 1858, The *New York Times* reported on a French invasion earlier that year in Viet Nam:[14]

> . . . The enterprise can have but one result. The bayonets of allied commerce and Christianity will open Annam [Viet Nam] to the world. The missionary and the merchant will press in. And the history of an extinct people will be written by the historian of two or three generations in the future.

In 1865, US merchant ships began arriving at Sai Gon harbor, about 10 ships per year. Around the late 1860s, some US ships loaded cargoes of rice the French stole, for sale overseas. (See Endnote 14.)

After 1865, "as American economic production grew, domestic markets became glutted, leading to new American economic interest in burgeoning markets in East Asia, Latin America, and Africa," Professor Harold Hongju Koh observes in 2024.[15]

In Viet Nam, the French invasion was violent. Viet Nam put up a strong resistance. In April 1859, The *Michigan Farmer* reported "a loss of 900 men on the French side."[16]

Viet Nam had an ancient tradition of defeating all invaders. The Mongol Empire invaded in the 13th century, and Viet Nam became the first nation to defeat it. Three Mongol invasions met three defeats by Viet Nam. And, Viet Nam defeated repeated invasions from China. Some Western academics say Viet Nam has a Tradition Of Heroic Resistance Against Foreign Invasion (TOHRAFA).[17]

Viet people fought to defend their enjoyable way of life. A deeply spiritual religion led them to strive for harmony with nature and with other villagers. Professor Tran Ngoc Them describes in detail. Spirits of ancestors and of nature made worship an honored part of everyday village life.[18]

But by the 1860s, the French began exporting much of the nation's rice. Widespread malnutrition struck in the 1880s and lasted the entire colonial period. Viet Nam had reasons to fight back. The US loading of rice cargoes by the late 1860s meant the US played a part in this early cause of the later war.[19]

In 1873 and 1875, trying to restore peace in this beautiful, spiritual land, Viet Nam sent emissary Bui Vien to Washington, D.C. US leaders rejected these overtures.[20]

By 1884, Standard Oil was selling US kerosene oil in Viet Nam. In the ensuing decades before World War II, Standard operated throughout Southeast Asia, and China.[21]

The first real oil strike in the US had occurred in 1859. By the early 1860s, oil refined as kerosene was being exported into Asia and elsewhere by John D. Rockefeller. Using native agents, his Standard Oil Company distributed free or low-cost lamps known as the Light of the World, which used kerosene.

By 1865, Rockefeller was exporting large quantities of kerosene; Standard Oil controlled 90 percent of the refineries in the US.²²

In 1884, ships carrying oil from the US began sailing direct to Sai Gon, rather than to regional ports such as Singapore. By 1888, "Direct imports of American petroleum into Sai Gon had indeed become large," the US consul in Singapore reported.²³

By 1885, an estimated 70 percent of Standard's business was done abroad. "Had we been dependent solely upon local business, we should have failed long since," John D. Rockefeller later said. "We were forced to extend our markets into every part of the world."²⁴

US consulate

Two New York oil men, Mr Carleton and Mr Moffatt, told the US State Department that appointment of a consul in Viet Nam would assist in compiling trade statistics and in promoting US goods. In 1889, the State Dept appointed Aimee Tonsales as the first US consul in Viet Nam. Tonsales was managing partner of Denis Freres, the largest commercial firm in Sai Gon. He was already in touch with the oil men.²⁵

Denis Freres, at 4 Rue Catinat in the heart of Sai Gon and near the port, served as an agent for Standard Oil and initiated imports of US "oil on an extensive scale," US Vice Consul Edouard Schneegans of Denis Freres observed in 1894. He assured State: "Preference is given to American oil over Russian oil."²⁶

Business was competitive. In the 1890s, consulates were in Sai Gon from Austria-Hungary, Belgium, Denmark, Germany, Great Britain, The Netherlands, Italy, Portugal, Spain, and Siam (Thailand). Through 1939, the US consular office either had one consul, or a consul and a vice consul, or occasionally two consuls.[27]

By the 1890s, oil and flour imports from the US "enjoyed great favor" in Sai Gon, a Denis Freres report said. Imports also included Oregon pine and smaller items.[28]

The imports of flour and Oregon pine by the colony evinced the colonial purpose of making profits for foreign investors, even at a cost of harm to natives. Importing wheat flour but exporting most of the nation's rice, causing widespread malnutrition, showed the goal of profits amid harm to the natives. Importing pine wood in a nation of vast forests violated common sense, except on the principle of foreign profits even though the natives had no need for US wood.

US cotton to Viet Nam amid virile racism

As US business in Viet Nam increased in the 1920s and 1930s, after a 1921 recession, cotton and oil ranked first and second in imports from the US. Their rankings changed back and forth. The US produced about three-fifths of the world's cotton and exported about half of that (1928 figures). Small manufacturing in Viet Nam produced cotton goods. In 1934, the US exported $1,699,000 in cotton to Indochina. In 1936, US cotton to Indochina increased to $2,040,000.[29]

The US cotton trade had grown through the enslavement of human beings, and this played a key role in the industrial revolution. Prof. Edward E. Baptist points out:[30]

> Their practices rapidly transformed the southern states into the dominant force in the global cotton market, and cotton was the world's most widely traded commodity at the time, as it was the key raw material during the first century of the industrial revolution.

After 1865, US black people freed from slavery were denied land ownership. The land went back to the whites who had been slave owners, and who had rebelled against the US. Without land, having little food, black US citizens died in large numbers. Most blacks who survived returned as laborers in the cotton fields, often for the same whites who had held them as slaves. Low wages to blacks working in cotton fields were enforced by 6,500 reported lynchings, including burnings alive, during 1865–1954, with no criminal convictions. (Chapter 3)[31]

In 1921, France granted favored-nation status to the US. That year, US autos led sales in Viet Nam. But the US autos used too much gas and were in danger of losing their lead, Consul Leland Smith cautioned in 1922. Similarly, US Consul Karl deGiers MacVitty reported in 1922 that the US had led in tire repair kit sales but had lost the lead in 1921. These reports illuminate a consular method of fostering large and small business opportunities in a competitive world. After the consulate facilitated a 1921 visit to Sai Gon by the San Francisco Chamber of Commerce, miscellaneous goods shipped from San Francisco to Viet Nam increased. In the late 1920s, expensive brands of canned fruits from California were stocked in grocery stores in towns. After the Great Depression hit, these gave way to cheaper brands and smaller quantities. US exports of canned sardines decreased.[32]

In 1926, "Noteworthy increases" in exports and imports were made with the Far East (Southeast Asia and a much larger area), the US government's *Foreign Commerce Yearbook* reported. Exports that year increased from $699,000,000 to $771,000,000. This was largely due to increases in sales of machinery, automobiles, mineral oils, iron and steel, and lumber. But then, the Great Depression decreased commerce with IndoChina. The 1930 *Foreign Commerce Yearbook* said it "was believed to have been the lowest since the war." Rebounding, post-Depression recovery showed increases in IndoChina exports to the US:[33]

> Export values to US:
> 1934 $2,489,000
> 1935 $5,704,000
> 1936 $6,368,000

Small items were important. Along with sardines and canned fruits, Denis Freres made an agreement in 1930 to import Remington typewriters. Remingtons were manufactured in the US.[34]

Between World Wars I and II, rubber and exports from Viet Nam were important in the US economy. Viet Nam rubber in the 1930s helped meet an almost vertical curve in US demand for rubber. Viet Nam rubber production was far higher per acre than in Singapore and Indonesia, though Viet Nam's total rubber production was far less than from vast rubber plantations in some other colonies.[35]

During the 1930s, the US led all European nations, except France, in the value of imports from Viet Nam. Viet Nam was France's most lucrative colony. In 1939, the US received 12 percent of Viet Nam's exports.[36]

CHAPTER 2

PATRIOTIC HO LEADS FOR INDEPENDENCE

Ho Chi Minh's childhood (born 1890, childhood name, Nguyen Sinh Cung) experienced what Professor William Duiker illuminates as: "The brutalities perpetrated by Western colonialism that he observed during his early years deeply offended his sensibilities."[37]

In 1895 in his village, the French beheaded one of his relatives. In 1901, young Ho's infant brother died of the colonial malnutrition. Without adequate medical care in colonial poverty, his mother died of blood loss from that childbirth. The French were building the Road of Death in nearby mountains, so some frightened roadworkers hid in young Ho's home. Of men from Ho's area forced to work on that road, Duiker wrote: "The lucky ones returned home broken in body and spirit."[38]

Young Ho's father and teachers showed him sites where people of Nghe An, Ho's home province, had helped save Viet Nam from past invasions. Ho developed pride in the country, to accompany his emotions about invaders causing misery.[39]

In the early 1900s, Ho learned a lifelong, guiding lesson. It came from Phan Boi Chau, a famed patriot leader. Chau visited Ho's father and young Ho from time to time. Chau lived only 4 kilometers from Ho's village. Chau told them that many patriots as fervent as Ho had fought back and died. For, the French had superior firepower. By the 1890s, they were able to surround any uprisings and defeat them piecemeal. Viet Nam's only chance was if someone found a way to avoid piecemeal defeats.[40]

That lesson from Chau guided young Ho for the rest of his life.

During this period, young Ho's father (Nguyen Sinh Sac) renamed him Nguyen Tat Thanh, meaning Nguyen Who Will Succeed. In Viet Nam culture, names can show a person's aspirations or moral qualities. True to his name, Nguyen Tat Thanh sailed from Viet Nam in 1911 at age 21, searching for a way to save his country. He would spend 30 years abroad, 1911–41.[41]

In 1918, young Ho changed his name to Nguyen Ai Quoc (Nguyen Who Loves His Country). It fit his lifetime of devotion to save his country.[42]

Nguyen Ai Quoc continued Viet Nam's overtures to the US for peaceful trade. At the Versailles Peace Conference in 1919, he and two other leaders filed a petition that Duiker says was "fairly moderate in tone." It accepted French control, while calling for election of natives to the French Parliament, equal judicial protection, and the abolishment of "special tribunals that were instruments of terrorizations." The senior advisor to President Wilson at Versailles wrote two notes to Nguyen Ai Quoc, acknowledging receipt of the petition and saying it would be brought to the attention of President Wilson. But no further communication was made to him or to Viet Nam on that petition. US leaders also rejected petitions from other colonies.[43]

Nguyen Ai Quoc realized he would need to continue searching for a way to fight back. For, he saw that severe racism, as well as greed, powered the US and France. Stopping an invasion powered by those would not be easy. Of US racism, he wrote:[44]

> A June 26, 1919 *Jackson Daily News* article was headlined: "Negro J. H. To Be Burned by the Crowd at Ellistown This Afternoon at 5 P.M." And, he observed that *The Chattanooga Times*, February 13, 1918 reported: 15,000 people, men, women, and children, applauded when petrol was poured over the Negro and the fire lit . . . Two of them cut off his ears while the fire began to roast him. . .

One night during July 1920, in his Paris hotel room at 9 Impasse Compointe, Nguyen Ai Quoc began reading a work by the communist leader, V.I. Lenin. It was the *Theses on the National and Colonial Questions.* It said the "overwhelming mass of the population in backward countries consists of peasants" and that for a revolution to succeed required "educating and organizing the peasantry and the broad mass of the exploited." That, Nguyen Ai Quoc suddenly realized, could fulfill Phan Boi Chau's lesson. The millions of suffering farmers in Viet Nam would be an unstoppable force, if they were educated about the invaders, and if a national organization was created to back them. If so, when a resistance war started, the resistance would be large enough to prevent the French from isolating areas and defeating them piecemeal.[45]

"I was excited to tears," he later described. "Sitting alone, I spoke loudly as if to a crowd, 'People suffering, this is what we must follow. It is the way to liberate us!'"[46]

Nguyen Ai Quoc believed that "He now had laws of history, and that he had a mission as a history-maker," said Pham Van Dong, later one of Ho's highest leaders. Dong added that "The spark of truth burning in Lenin's theses caused the ideas in Ho Chi Minh's thinking and soul to flare up into a fire. . . ."[47]

What have they done?

But in Paris, most socialists said a revolution must start in European capitals, the center of capitalism. Nguyen Ai Quoc replied that colonial farmers could do an uprising. That, plus his effort at Versailles, built a reputation for him as the best spokesperson for colonial peoples. So, he was invited to the Soviet Union to study Karl Marx and work at Communist headquarters. He arrived there on June 30, 1923.[48]

In Moscow, Nguyen Ai Quoc ran into the same problem: Moscow communists said the revolution against capitalist exploitation must begin where capitalism was—in industrial cities of Europe. It could not start in colonies, because they were pre-capitalist, even though colonial farmers were seen as allies.[49]

Nguyen Ai Quoc replied that the capitalists were in the colonies stealing the resources that supported European cities. Trying to stop that in Europe was like "trying to kill a snake by stepping on its tail." He criticized the Communist Party in a June 23, 1924 speech at a major meeting in Moscow:[50]

> What have they done from the day they accepted Lenin's political programme to educate the working class of their countries. . . . I am very sorry to say that our Communist Party has done hardly anything for the colonies.

Nguyen Ai Quoc felt like a "voice crying in the wilderness," says Duiker. To pursue his vision—a nationwide organization in Viet Nam—he asked for a position in southern China. Refugees were streaming there from Viet Nam, as the French denied all requests for meaningful reform.[51]

He received an appointment and arrived in Quang Chau (Canton), China on November 11, 1924, as a representative of the Farmer's International, and as an interpreter for communists openly on the staff of the Nationalist Party. Also, he began working among Viet Nam's refugees to set up a nationwide revolt. In 1928, he began sending his first leaders into Viet Nam to begin secretly building leadership for his organization. On February 3, 1930, Ho established a unified Communist Party of Viet Nam. And on February 24, it became part of a Communist Party of Indochina.[52]

By 1940, urgency increased. In September 1940, Japan invaded Viet Nam across the northern border with China. That same month, Japan forced French colonials to agree to run the colony for Japan. Proving their worth to Japan, in November 1940, the French quelled a planned uprising in southern Viet Nam. They strung some prisoners together by forcing wire through their hands, bombed, imprisoned thousands, and executed over 100.[53]

That blow reinforced Nguyen Ai Quoc's guiding lesson: uprisings without a national organization would suffer piecemeal defeats. He continued building to answer that.

On January 28, 1941, Nguyen Ai Quoc returned to Viet Nam for the first time in 30 years. On May 10, 1941, in the northwest mountains, he set up the Viet Nam Independence League (Viet Nam Doc Lap Dong Minh Hoi) [Việt Nam Độc Lập Đồng Minh Hội]. The core meaning was *Viet Nam Independence* (Viet Nam Doc Lap). The abbreviation, *Viet Minh,* became the name for its army.[54]

By late 1943, in guerrilla war against Japan, the League controlled parts of the mountains and western Red River Delta.

They assisted US soldiers in rescuing US pilots shot down by Japan over Viet Nam.[55]

As the end of World War II neared, Japan seized most of Viet Nam's rice to make fuel. That caused a famine in the north region. "It can be taken as established that the population lives at the borderline of famine and misery," observed Professor Pierre Gourou, at a 1945 Virginia conference.[56]

During August 1944–45, about two million people starved to death in Viet Nam's northern half.[57]

During August 14–25, 1945, after the atomic bombs on Japan, the Independence League and army moved into power throughout nearly all of Viet Nam.[58]

On September 2, 1945, Japan signed surrender documents ending World War II. Also on September 2, 1945, Ho Chi Minh stood in Ba Dinh Square, Ha Noi and declared independence in front of half a million people in and around the square. In the nation's South Region, more than 1 million people gathered in central Sai Gon and listened by radio broadcast. Ho read a Declaration of Independence composed largely from his memory of the US Declaration of Independence.[59]

In 1947, Viet Nam diplomats spent four months offering the US a tax-free monopoly on Viet Nam's lucrative rice exports. The offer included other trade advantages, like a Ford plant in Ha Noi. That offer opened the door to US diplomats to establish some capitalist relations with Viet Nam. But US leaders rejected it. They tried to gain control. In some 1939–45 Studies, five reports by the Council on Foreign Relations (CFR) called to attack Viet Nam:[60]

- A June 20, 1941 report. "The Economic Organization of Peace in the Far East," said Indo-China presented "no great problems" to being included in a regional economy with Japan and Thailand. Japan needed "important political and social changes." The changes came fast in 1945, after the massive violence of two atomic bombs.

- A Sept. 11, 1942 report, "Postwar Security Arrangements in the Pacific Area," called to hold a port in Viet Nam in order to control the South China Sea (Viet Nam's Eastern Sea). It reported that Southeast Asia was a "cheap source of vital materials." US national interest required, "placing political and economic control in hands likely to be friendly to the United States."
- A Sept 14, 1943 report, "Regionalism in Southeast Asia," called "to *secure access* to the trade and raw materials of the region." (Italics added.)
- A Nov. 16, 1943 report, "The Future Status of Indo-China as an Example of Postwar Colonial Relationships" contravened the 1941 report. Mainly on Viet Nam, this 1943 report said "a long and disastrous period of repression" would be required if a new United Nations wanted to control peoples of the East any longer. For, "disaffections which were evident in Indo-China" showed "It is impossible" that the people would accept a return to colonial control.
- A year-end review by the CFR Steering Committee said that the Nov. 16, 1943 report meant "there should be a continuance of the French Colonial Regime in Indo-China."

Instead of telling the public about that attack, US leaders spoke of a Cold War on communism:[61]

In 1947, America emerged from World War II only to find itself emmeshed in a Cold War, the ideological and historical dimensions of which have been thoroughly examined. The Truman Doctrine, the Marshall Plan, military alliances such as NATO, SEATO, CENTO, and ANZUS, the Inter-American Defense System, and the Mutual Defense Assistance Program all formed inter-related substantive planks of President Harry Truman's foreign-policy response.

PART II

PATTERNS TARGETING VIET NAM & DAMAGING THE WORLD

CHAPTER 3

SIMULTANEOUS PERIODS OF RACISM

In Viet Nam during 1865–1954, US business was enabled by violence against yellow and brown people, and in the US during 1865–1950s, white racists murdered at least 6,500 black US citizens for white economic advantages. That economic purpose was highlighted in a 1951 petition titled, *We Charge Genocide*. African American leaders of the US in the Civil Rights Congress presented it to the United Nations:[62]

> This genocide of which your petitioners now complain serves now, as it has in previous forms in the past, specific political and economic aims. Once its goal was the subjugation of American Negroes for chattel slavery. Now its aim is the splitting and emasculation of mass movements for peace and democracy, so that reaction may perpetuate its control and continue receiving the highest profits in the entire history of man. . . .

Examples of murder in both nations include: The *New York Times*, July 27, 1946, reported that last night in Georgia [US], "Two young Negroes, one a veteran just returned from the war, and their wives were lined up last night near a secluded road and shot dead by an unmasked band of twenty white men." And, on November 20, 1946, about 20,000 civilians were killed when the French ship *Suffren*, along with tanks, artillery, and aircraft, shelled the northern port city of Hai Phong [Viet Nam] including residential areas.[63]

Sources in Viet Nam say close to 20,000 perished. That is corroborated by the *Suffren* commander who admitted to international journalists: "No more than 6,000 killed, insofar as naval bombardment of fleeing civilians was concerned." His statement was about the navy. Additional killings were by tanks, artillery, and aircraft.[64]

The *New York Times* article said: "After the men were taken from their car and walked down a side road, their wives started screaming. So, "some of the men then came back and dragged the shrieking women from the automobile." Of Hai Phong, Philippe Devillers wrote:[65]

> "In the pungent and dark smoke through which the odor of blood began to rise, the slaughter among the columns of fugitives that streamed over the routes to Doson and Kien An was horrible."

Some US leaders on Viet Nam backed racism in the US. In 1919, US Secretary of State Bert Lansing refused passports for ten black leaders to travel to the Versailles Peace Conference to present a petition about US race discrimination. Lansing had been the beloved "Uncle Bert" to John Foster Dulles and Allen Dulles when they were children. He had taken them on regular fishing trips at their parents' resort on Lake Ontario. "Uncle Bert" and other leaders guided the young brothers to pursue careers in foreign policy.[66]

The US delegation at Versailles was headed by President

Woodrow Wilson. President Wilson's racism was "significant and consequential, even by the standards of his own time," said Princeton University's president in 2020, upon removing Wilson's name from its prestigious public policy school, in the aftermath of the murder of a black citizen, George Floyd, by a white police officer. At Versailles, John Foster Dulles and Allen Dulles "fell fully under the spell of Woodrow Wilson," reports Kinzer. Wilson had been the favorite professor of John Foster Dulles at Princeton.[67]

John Foster Dulles as secretary of state (1953–59) threw obstacles in the way of US black leaders who asked government to end the violent race discrimination. Paul Robeson, his wife Eslanda—a distinguished anthropologist—and his son were among 94 leaders of the Civil Rights Congress, who signed *We Charge Genocide,* the 1951 petition to the United Nations. Its Introduction said:[68]

> Here we present the documented crimes of federal, state and municipal governments in the United States of America, the dominant nation in the United Nations, against 15,000,000 of its own nationals-the Negro people of the United States. These crimes are of the gravest concern to mankind.
>
> A sample of its contents included:
>
> And on Norfolk, Virginia, on May 28, the Reverend Joseph Mann was burned to death by a mob, which drenched his clothing in gasoline before igniting them, for preaching a sermon against segregation. . . .

Opposing that petition and other civil rights efforts, the State Department denied a passport to Robeson during

1952–58. An international opera star, he had 86 performances scheduled abroad, including in London in the title role in Shakespeare's *Othello*. All 86 appearances were cancelled. This crippled Robeson financially, as well as harming his opera career.[69]

Robeson challenged Secretary of State John Foster Dulles in 1956 in written testimony to a US Senate committee: "I have been denied these freedoms because Dulles, Eastland, Walter, and their ilk oppose my views on colonial liberation, my resistance to oppression of Negro Americans. . . ."[70]

The problems we face today cannot be solved by the minds that created them.

—Albert Einstein[71]

CHAPTER 4

DITCHING VOTERS FROM WORLD ORDER

In 1921, US leaders formed a Council on Foreign Relations devoted to business expansion and securing access to resources worldwide. But by the 1940s, they realized that Viet Nam and others would fight back. So the leaders set up a system for the US to pursue control worldwide, by force if needed.

The Council on Foreign Relations (CFR) formed in New York. Members were primarily owners of wealthy corporations operating overseas, and Wall Street lawyers. Founders included John Foster Dulles and Isaiah Bowman. Both had been at Versailles. The 1921 CFR founding consensus, Michael Wala describes, was: "Access to raw materials and markets of the whole world should be secured for the United States."[72]

The CFR and post-World War II foreign policy

During 1939–45, the CFR prepared the War and Peace Studies, 682 reports and memoranda for post-World War II US foreign policy. The CFR donated them to the State Dept. Setting the stage for pursuing control of resources, Memorandum E-B19 said the US needed:[73]

> to secure the *limitation of sovereignty* by any foreign nations that constitutes a threat to the minimum world area essential *for the security and economic prosperity* of the United States and the Western Hemisphere. (Italics added.)

These materials outlined a world order. In 2017, US Senator John McCain talked of a "world order which was established after World War II." Professor Laurence Shoup calls these reports and memos "blueprints" for a "world order." Henry Kissinger, in his 2014 book, *World Order*, wrote about "the American vision of world order." In *The wise men*, Walter Isaacson argued that in the "world order," the US was "defending freedom." On the other hand, the 2004 book by CFR Senior fellow Walter Russell Mead pointed out that the "world order" brought "inequality, instability. . . ." and eventual condemnation in much of the world in a "majority verdict."[74]

The world order continues into 2025. Chomsky points out:[75]

> . . . in the **unfolding new world order . . . control of the incomparable energy reserves of the Middle East would yield "substantial control of the world."** And correspondingly, they believe that loss of control would threaten the project of **American global dominance that was clearly articulated during World War II and that has been sustained in the face of major changes in world order since that day. . . .** (Emphasis added.)

Ditching the public

In 1939, a CFR founding director, Isaiah Bowman, stated at the outset of the War and Peace Studies that outlined the world order: "The matter is strictly confidential, because the whole plan would be 'ditched' if it became generally known that the State Department is working in collaboration with any outside group." Other members agreed. So, the studies were not shared with the public.[76]

Without public approval, a so-called National Security Council (NSC) was set up in 1947, to pursue the plan set up in the 682 reports and memos. Its name is a misnomer. It has actually operated as a National ***Securing*** Council: (Emphasis added) Its main function has been *securing* resources. This implements the 1921 CFR founding consensus that "Access to raw materials and markets of the whole world should be *secured* for the United States."

An informal grouping called a foreign policy force, conducts most US foreign policy. This force consists of corporations, government institutions, the NSC, associations, the CFR, officials, international lawyers, experiences overseas, experts, reports, and many other components. Under it, foreign policy developed its own inertia. Presidents inherited the foreign policy. They did not invent business expansion by force. Rather, they put their personal stamp on it.

"Securing" resources was the goal in Viet Nam. From 1865 onward, US leaders operated there for decades with resources "secured" by French military force. So, the goal there was not "security." For, Viet Nam never threatened the "security" of the United States. Viet Nam was smaller in area than the US State of California. Viet Nam had no capacity to attack the US across the ocean. Far from that, Viet Nam made repeated overtures for friendship, friendly trade, and adoption of US-style institutions.

In 1948 the misnomer was confirmed: The function of this National *Securing* Council was explained by CFR member George Kennan, head of the State Department Policy Planning Staff:[77]

> **We have about 50 percent of the world's wealth, but only 6.3 percent of its population** . . . In this situation, we cannot fail to be the object of envy and resentment. Our real task in the coming period is to **devise a pattern of relationships which will permit us to maintain this position of disparity** . . . We need not deceive ourselves that we can afford today the luxury of altruism and world-benefaction . . . The day is not far off when we are going to have to deal in straight power concepts.

That was a claim of a freedom to rob and exploit, as Prof Chomsky points out.

Voters' role of guiding general direction

Prior to the setting up of the world order, the US public had a role of debating and guiding the general direction of US foreign policy. A general question for US foreign policy is: Should the US use "straight power" like Hitler, or should the US pursue fair trade and mutual economic development?

Before World War II, US democracy placed a role on voters to debate and guide such questions for the general direction of foreign policy. That makes common sense. For, it is a decision about the general character of the US. Such questions should not be decided just by the very wealthy of society. Thus, the public took part in a national debate around 1900, on whether the US should do imperial attacks. "This was a debate over the very nature of freedom," says Stephen Kinzer in *The True Flag*. (Although the public decided to go along with imperialism, it was hotly debated. Moreover, the public did not relinquish its role. But after World War II, US leaders unilaterally took that power away from the public.) [78]

With the public "ditched" upon the setting up of the world order, no public "debate over the very nature of freedom" occurred on whether the US should attack Viet Nam. The public was not told of a 1943 CFR report on Viet Nam, titled, "The Future Status of Indo-China As An Example Of Postwar Colonial Relationships." It said France had "politically and economically tended to strangle" the country and "It is impossible" that Viet Nam would accept more colonial control.[79]

The report continued:[80]

> The new and vital demands which will be insistently voiced by the colonial peoples of the East can be ignored only if the United Nations are prepared to undertake **a long and disastrous period of repression**. It is impossible that these people will regard a mere return to the old established forms of colonial government as an adequate satisfaction of their demands...." (Emphasis added.)

Even millions of US veterans returning from World War II were denied the role of debating whether the US should attack Viet Nam for business gain. They, who had sacrificed greatly against invasions and coups, were not allowed to vote on a few wealthy US leaders profiting from invasion and coups, while misleading the US public.

This historical evidence shows a probability that, if informed, many World War II veterans would have voted against the US running such Hitler-style invasions and coups. A probability exists that they would have voted "no" to invading Viet Nam to cling to "Colonial Relationships."

The "ditching" undercut democracy. For, the proper role of US voters is pinpointed in 2004 by a CFR Senior Fellow, Walter Russell Mead:[81]

> And while American foreign policy is studied in great detail by professionals and scholars, it must ultimately be debated and decided by tens of millions of voters."

Because such voter decisions require the truth, the US Supreme Court quickly upheld the 1971 newspaper publication of the top-secret *Pentagon Papers* on Viet Nam. Supreme Justice Hugo Black explained in a concurring opinion: "Only a free and unrestrained press can effectively expose deception in government."[82]

New York Times writer Anthony Lewis explained this as protecting the role of "the citizen-critic of government." Likewise, Supreme Court Justice Lewis Powell (appointed to the Court in 1972), observed:[83]

> no individual can obtain for himself the information needed for the intelligent discharge of his political responsibilities.... By enabling the public to assert meaningful control over the political process, the press performs a crucial function in effecting the societal purpose of the First Amendment.

That standard was not followed on Viet Nam.

Systemic change needed

Prof Koh, cited earlier, says the US "plainly" needs a systemic change in how the checks and balances of the three branches of government operate in foreign policy:[84]

some key modifications needed to revise the laws on use of force. But plainly, we need a better overall system of checks and balances to govern war making. After half a century, the War Powers Resolution of 1973 must be replaced.

This current volume extends his point, by showing that the public is still "ditched" from its traditional role. So, the new evidence of the pervasive false claim on Viet Nam its false guidance of foreign policy through 2024 means that Koh's "key modifications" must necessarily include a return to voters guiding the general direction.

Without public guidance, the NSC runs policy for the wealthy

During 1945–68, Council on Foreign Relations members held from 42 to 57 percent of government's major foreign policy posts, Prof. Laurence Shoup demonstrates. These included National *Securing* Council (NSC) members serving as secretaries of state, presidential advisors, and other key positions.[85]

Newsweek Magazine observed in 1971: "The foreign policy establishment of the US was the CFR leadership."[86]

That concentrated control has continued. A 2005 article by Lawrence Jacobs states that "U.S. foreign policy is most heavily and consistently influenced by internationally oriented business leaders." The article—cited with approval by Chomsky in 2024 in *The Myth of American Idealism : How U.S. Foreign Policy Endangers the World*–says that "public opinion" has "little or no significant effect on government officials.[87]

A 2015 study, *Wall Street Think Tank*, by Prof Shoup reports on:[88]

the close interconnections between the CFR and the U.S. government. In fact, the single institution that appears to be most interpenetrated with the CFR is the federal government of the United States, which has hundreds of members of the Council working in it. As of July 1, 2011, for example, the CFR had 529 of its members serving in "government." Given the CFR focus on foreign policy, one can safely assume that the great majority of these members are working in the federal government.

Similarly, *White House Warriors: how the National Security Council transformed the American way of war*, a 2019 study by John Gans explains that: "the NSC has exerted more influence over presidential decisions than any single institution or individual over the last seventy years . . ."[89]

A 2024 article in the CFR's journal, *Foreign Affairs*—"the leading forum for serious discussion of American foreign policy and global affairs," says Prof. Shoup—admits that the US still conducts the world order system set up after World War II: "U.S. foreign policy is made in an institutional ecosystem conceived during World War II, expanded during the Cold War, and maintained through the post–Cold War period of American hegemony."[90]

In this "institutional ecosystem," David Talbot points out in *The Devil's Chessboard* on Allen Dulles, "the creation of the World Bank and International Monetary Fund, two linchpins of the world financial order." Talbot cites criticism of "the heavy social and economic costs that IMF arrangements often impose on debtor countries."[91]

Further defining that "institutional ecosystem," a 2024 observation in the CFR journal says: "For decades, American presidents have waged illegal wars. . . ." Indeed, much of those illegal wars have been set up not by presidents, but by other officers in foreign policy posts, as this volume and *Corporate Tsunami* show.[92]

More than wars, historians document 100-plus coups, destabilizations, and invasions. During 1947–89, as the 2018 book, *Covert Regime Change* points out, at least 56 regime changes were authorized by Democratic presidents, and at least 62 by Republican presidents. Noam Chomsky observes that during 1946–2000, "the United States undertook more than eighty election interferences around the world." A list of 24 coups during 1945–76 appears in Appendix III of *Corporate Tsunami in Countryside Paradise* by this writer. As if stating a right to dominate, Henry Kissinger asserted in 1973, upon illegally overthrowing Chile's democracy: "The issues are much too important for the Chilean voters to be left to decide for themselves."[93]

Among such election interferences, Viet Nam was scheduled to have a 1956 election. But Ho Chi Minh, whom US leaders knew would win in a landslide, wanted fair trade with the US. US leaders decided—like on Chile later—that they couldn't permit Viet Nam's voters to elect him for that. US leaders wanted the business, but like Macbeth, they also wanted one more thing: control.

Viet Nam and Chile were among 100-plus coups, invasions, and destabilizations by foreign policy force leaders during 1945–2024. This force's existence and operation were no surprise: Bertrand Russell lambasted both in 1967 (see quote following this chapter).

. . . the system which has taken control of the United States and perverted its industrial life into a grotesque arsenal for a world empire . . . regarded by the people of three whole continents as their main enemy in life and the source of their misery and hunger.

—Bertrand Russell, 1967[94]

CHAPTER 5

TARGETING VIET NAM IN THE WORLD ORDER

In 1945, Ho and Viet Nam declared independence, however during 1939–45, US officials had named Viet Nam to stay in "Colonial Relationships" in the world order.

Keeping control of Viet Nam for US business expansion fit the centuries-long US practice of racial violence for economic gain. For seven decades, US business operations in Viet Nam, enabled by force, had been part of the US economy.

Targeting Viet Nam as the prime example
Extraordinary violence and persistence were known to be necessary. For, the 1943 CFR report that called to keep Viet Nam in "Colonial Relationships," said "It is impossible" that the country would accept more colonial control. Seizing it by force would require "a long and disastrous period of repression."[95]

That CFR forecast proved accurate. A 1949 Joint Chiefs of Staff (JCS) report said Viet Nam's nationalism "cannot be reversed" and "could not be crushed by force." That same year, Paul Mus told the State Department that the full support of the people, except a tiny minority, was behind their nation of Viet Nam. It was the Democratic Republic of Viet Nam (DRV), from the northern border with China to the southern tip in the sea south of Sai Gon. In 1950, The *New York Times* described "universal resentment of the Far East against the colonialism that oppressed Asiatics for decades before the Japanese war." In 1951, Congressman John F Kennedy (JFK) visited Viet Nam. He returned, saying the "Fires of nationalism . . . are now ablaze."[96]

Nevertheless, a July 3, 1951 State Department press release about the new Colombo Plan said that the US had a deep interest in Viet Nam's economic development and that security would be important. Security meant military force against the DRV.[97]

National *Securing* Council commits to extremes

By telling the Colombo nations that the US would provide security, US leaders committed on the world stage to try to prevail despite their own warnings in 1943, 1949, 1950, and 1951 that Viet Nam's nationalist resistance would put up a major fight. Thus, US leaders were committing to extremes of violence and persistence.

Moreover, the commitment was for "securing," not for "security." Viet Nam did not threaten US security. "Securing" matched the 1921 consensus goal of US leaders for resource access to be "secured."

So, the correct name of the NSC was National *Securing* Council.

Pointing to extreme violence, the 1941 War and Peace report titled, "The Economic Organization of Peace in the Far East" said Japan and Viet Nam were to be included a regional trading relationship. Japan needed "important political and social changes." By 1945, samurai Japan was losing the war but gave no sign of those internal changes.[98]

In August, 1945 in Japan, opposition to change ended in an elapsed time of about two minutes. This was the explosion and initial destruction time of the two bombs dropped on Hiroshima and Nagasaki in August 1945.

In Viet Nam by 1975, the US used about 100 times more explosive power than in the two atomic bombs dropped on Japan. In Indochina, the US used more than three times, by weight, of the bombs and explosives used by the US in all of World War II.[99]

Extreme violence and persistence

Having committed on the world stage to defeat that small country, US leaders escalated force whenever Viet Nam was getting the upper hand. The escalations not only showed commitment, they also showed the racial animus of US leaders. For, racial violence for white economic advantage had been done for centuries, from 1619 through the 1950s. That kind of perseverance was mirrored in the perseverance against the yellow and brown people of Viet Nam.

US escalations of force included:

1. Viet Nam declared independence in 1945, so US leaders funded most of the 1945–54 French re-invasion. France, weakened by World War II, could not have invaded on its own. France estimated that it killed 500,000 people.[100]
2. Viet Nam defeated the invasion, so US leaders attacked by January 1955. They used a proxy army that had fought for France against Viet Nam. US civilian leaders ordered it to do "pacification." But no one was fighting back. In 1955–60, this army killed at least 70,000 defenseless villagers. The US and its proxy leader, Ngo Dinh Diem, canceled the elections in August 1955 and claimed on

October 26, 1955 to set up a "South Vietnam" nation. But Viet Nam (DRV) still existed in the south.[101]

After those actions, Ho Chi Minh, began a land reform campaign in November 1955, but he stopped it after nine months, on August 17, 1956. For, many people used it as a tool to settle personal grudges. In it, Buttinger says, it is "generally believed that the number killed was between 10,000 and 15,000. . . ." In contrast, the US-backed murders in the southern half continued for five more years, killing over 70,000. The US was still the invader. (See Endnote 101.)

3. In 1960, reacting against the killings, villagers seized control of 90 percent of the villages in Viet Nam's southern half. This "deteriorating situation" caused alarm "among officials at the highest levels of the American government," a USAF report said.[102]

So, US civilian leaders escalated in late 1961 by spraying dioxin, dropping napalm, and starting a new kind of helicopter warfare to counter millions of villagers all over Viet Nam's southern half. The new usage of helicopters illustrated another side of the business expansion goal in the US pursuit of control by force.

In 1957, the vision appeared of using helicopters in Viet Nam like cavalry. Air cavalry helicopters could ferry soldiers and drop them off for fast ground assaults. This tactic would require speed and reliable power, for which jet engines were far superior to piston engines. That meant sales by General Electric Company. GE was the nation's largest supplier of jet engines for aircraft. GE had been a defense contractor since 1896. The company emerged from World War Two about three times as large as it had been before the war.[103]

The decision to spray dioxin was by the National

Securing Council (NSC) led by civilians. Control over dioxin spraying was to remain with civilians: National Security Action Memorandum 115 (NSAM, Nov. 21, 1961) said, "There should be careful prior consideration and authorization by Washington of any phase developed."[104]

4. NSAM 115 contemplated spraying dioxin in areas inhabited by humans in War Zone D or on the border, if there are "realistic possibilities of immediate military exploitation," and it must be in consultation with Washington. War Zone D was "a hotbed of Viet Cong strength, 25 miles northeast of Saigon . . . Its population is totally Viet-Cong controlled. . . ." The memo said "inhabitants of affected areas will be advised that the spray will have no harmful effects on humans, livestock, or the soil." The chief USAF scientist on dioxin later said, "Did we spray where the enemy was? You're damn right we did."[105]

On August 10, 1961. the first test spraying used a US-supplied helicopter and chemicals, and a proxy aircrew of Viet nationality. Over the next few months, about 20 such missions were by proxy aircrews.[106]

On November 6, 1961, a radio broadcast from Ha Noi said that the US was spraying poison gas that made people sick. The "poison gas" complaint is referred to in the Nov. 21, 1961 NSAM 115.[107]

The air floating down was a gas, which some people on the ground breathed. It contained the dioxin. The dioxin was a solid, not a gas (in some conditions it could be a liquid). So, the US was using poisoned gas—the air into which the US sprayed solid dioxin and which people feared enough to run away—though not technically spraying poison gas.[108]

The US public received no explanation denying a 1959 report by Dr Friedrich Hoffmann of the Army Chemical Corps, that minor exposure to dioxin, in some cases, killed people or caused serious internal disease. In 1959, some Corps scientists were told that the Corps was stopping its development of dioxin. The cessation, scientist Ronald Kassel said, was "because of its insidious effects, its chronic toxicity." But shortly after the stop, the work on dioxin continued. The USAF's James Clary, scientist, wrote after the war, "When we initiated the herbicide program in the 1960s, we were aware of the potential for damage due to dioxin contamination in herbicides."[109]

The US public also received no explanation denying the history of three deaths from chloracne around 1936, along with 50–60 chloracne cases (dioxin caused chloracne), having led to a 1937 meeting at Harvard University; attending were Harvard scientists, the US Public Health Service, Massachusetts and Connecticut health officials, Monsanto's medical director, and General Electric Company. This is reported in 2018 a major work by Gerard Tilles. After that meeting, chloracne continued to occur. During World War II, war production resulted in additional cases of chloracne in workers for the US Navy and in civilian factories producing for the Navy. Chloracne was also observed in some of their family members. Two deaths occurred. A study published in the Journal of the American Medical Association in 1944 said that due to war production demands, "Workmen cannot be transferred or laid off in numbers which interfere with production schedules and must be studied on the job as humanly as possible."[110]

5. In 1964, the DRV scored repeated successes, and US leaders significantly escalated the dioxin spraying:[111]

   - February 1964 intelligence report said that the southern government had only a 50–50 chance of surviving the next several months.[112]
   - On February 26, 600 DRV soldiers held off 3,000 southern proxy soldiers who surrounded them but failed to attack.
   - In repeated battles (shown in *Corporate Tsunami*, Ch. 38), Viet Nam scored victories. On April 20, many US military leaders said the proxy army was ineffective; desertions and low enlistment were factors.[113]
   - During July 11–12, in the war's largest battle to date, at least 1,000 guerrillas twice attacked a proxy force, then ambushed the relief force, killing 200 and seizing 100 weapons.
   - On July 13, guerrillas ambushed a convoy south of Sai Gon, killing 3 US soldiers and 16 of the proxy force. During July 15–16, another 16 clashes showed stepped-up activity.

   Escalating in 1964, US leaders tripled the dioxin spray per acre to three gallons and nearly quadrupled the number of acres sprayed. One gallon per acre was enough, some army scientists believed. They were overruled by the Department of Defense (DOD). DOD was controlled by the civilian government, as shown above. Dioxin concentrations were much too high, some Army Chemical Corps scientists later testified. Nearly quadrupling the nearly 25,000 acres sprayed in 1963, the US sprayed just under 94,000 acres in 1964.[114]

At the start of 1965, despite prior US escalations, the DRV controlled most of the southern countryside and scored a resounding victory in a six-day battle at Binh Gia, east of Sai Gon. Five US advisors died—the most yet in one battle. A Southern zone report said:

"The battle of Binh Gia was a warning . . . the Viet Cong forces were capable for large battles. They began to combine guerrilla and conventional warfare."[115]

The US effort had failed. As Prof Chomsky points out:[116]

Leading U.S. government scholar Douglas Pike, in his book Viet Cong [1966], said that "aside from the NLF there has never been a truly mass-based political party in South Vietnam." John Paul Vann, widely regarded as the U.S. official most knowledgeable about the situation in South Vietnam, wrote in 1965 that "a popular political base for the Government of South Vietnam does not now exist. . . ."

6. In July 1965, a group with seven CFR directors as members met with President Lyndon B Johnson (LBJ) and supported him in escalating. LBJ directed the military to "kill more VC."[117]

Civilian deaths became "widespread, routine, and directly attributable to U.S. command policies," Nick Turse shows in *Kill Anything That Moves*.[118]

In September 1965, The *New York Times* reported: "No one here seriously doubts that significant numbers of innocent civilians are dying every day in South Vietnam. . . . US air raids . . . have resulted in widespread destruction of hamlets and mounting civilian casualties." The attacks on the South included "large-scale application of chemical weapons, and napalm. . . ." Chomsky later pointed out. Bernard Fall observed in 1967, that "Vietnam as a cultural and historic entity . . . is threatened with extinction" as "the countryside literally dies under the blows of the largest military machine ever unleashed on an area of this size."[119]

A USAF officer explained, "When we are in a bind . . . we unload on the whole area to try and save the situation. We usually kill more women and kids than we do Viet Cong. . . ."[120]

Despite photographs in newspapers in 1967 showing a child born with a duck-like face, the spraying of dioxin continued into 1971. "Monster" births also occurred by 1967. Mothers were left in shock.[121]

By the end of the war, dioxin had been sprayed on between 2.1 million and 4.8 million people in 3,181 hamlets.[122]

Viet Nam's response to the wrongful US attack on Viet Nam for years killing millions of Viet citizens, compared with the US response to the Sept 11, 2001 attacks in the US that killed 2,977 US citizens, provides a measure of the feelings with which Viet Nam fought against the wrongful US invasion.[123]

Blessed are those who hunger and thirst for righteousness, for they will be filled.

—Jesus[124]

CHAPTER 6

AXIOM ON CONTROL BY FORCE

The simple Golden Rule forms the basis of an axiom on control by force: Wrongfully taking other people's property often causes them to fight back. Many children understand that. Nevertheless, US foreign policy has "applied one standard to Europeans and another to everyone else," a 2025 *Foreign Affairs* article reports. Indeed, Secretary of State John Foster Dulles said in 1956: "For us there are two sorts of people in the world: there are those who are Christians and who support free enterprise and there are the others."[125]

The axiom on control by force is formed by historical events and literature. It includes the Golden Rule, articles in Andre Malraux's Sai Gon newspaper *L'Indochine Enchainee*, Viet Nam's classic *Tale of Kieu* by Nguyen Du, Shakespeare's *Macbeth*, colonial people's statements, black Americans' statements, a comparative observation by Noam Chomsky, and an urging by George Washington.

The Golden Rule is in all major religions and ethical systems. In Hinduism the Golden Rule is: "This is the sum of duty; do naught onto others what you would not have them do unto you."[126]

Andre Malraux's Sai Gon newspaper, *L'Indochine Enchainee* (1925–26), criticized the French colony for violating "the most elementary principle of justice and good sense, [which] requires that each nationality have forever that territory traced by its ancestors back to time immemorial."[127]

In Viet Nam's classic *Tale of Kieu* by Nguyen Du, powerful people separated two lovers for 15 years. But the power of love endured, so that when they found each other again and stayed together, their bonds included "strong friendship's powerful chain."[128]

In Shakespeare's *Macbeth*, hero Macbeth saved Scotland, so a grateful King Duncan offered riches and everlasting gratitude. But Macbeth wanted the riches and more: He wanted control. So, he killed Duncan. Sons and friends of Duncan fought back and killed Macbeth.[129]

In Asia after World War II, 500 million colonial people clamored for independence and economic justice, a US planning report observed. They were citizens of nations, including Viet Nam, in which European colonialism had long stolen property, enabled by violence.[130]

In the 1950s, Paul Robeson and Dr. Martin Luther King, Jr. peacefully posed the principle that black people were equal to white people. But through 2024 in the US, racism has preserved a 12-to-1 average asset ratio favoring white families over black. Despite that, some whites falsely say the playing field is level.[131]

Those examples support an observation by Professor Noam Chomsky:[132]

> It would be interesting . . . to see the argument explaining why we should disregard elementary moral principles in thinking about U.S. involvement in foreign affairs . . . We have no difficulty demanding that our enemies follow such principles.

Urging the US to follow an elementary moral principle, George Washington stated in his 1796 Farewell Address: "Observe good faith and justice towards all nations. . . ." (See Endnote 14.)

Reactions against US leaders violating the axiom

The US leaders' use of the false claim to fool the US public into unwittingly supporting the wrongful pursuit of control doesn't fool the foreign people whose property and resources it takes. Such foreign people react. Some of their nations are forming groups, seeking to establish their own international trade and to reduce their trade with the US. Key ones are illuminated in a Nov. 12, 2024 *Foreign Affairs* article:[133]

> great powers have become more active in creating and bolstering their own structures independent of the United States. These range from the BRICS+ to OPEC+ to the Shanghai Cooperation Organization. More informally, one can see a "coalition of the sanctioned," in which China, North Korea, and Iran are happy to help Russia disrupt global order.

The list is growing. US hegemony is challenged by the Community of Latin American and Caribbean States (CELAC). In 2024, it and the European Union (EU) work together for sustainable development on poverty, social cohesion, and climate change. These seek to change damage done by the US. The Asian Infrastructure Investment Bank joins the list, shown in a January 2025 article.[134]

The US belief the US could rely on superior military force and succeed failed in Viet Nam. Likewise, a 2024 CFR *Foreign Affairs* journal article observes:[135]

Washington finds itself embroiled in conflicts it has **diminishing capacity** to resolve. Many analysts are thus calling for a major strategic reorientation—whether, for example, by enlarging the U.S. military so that it can **sustain fights** in multiple theaters or by handing off some <u>burdens</u> to U.S. allies and partners. . . . (Emphasis added.)

Prof. Andrew Bacevich wrote in 2013, "As for global hegemony, we can kiss it goodbye." In 2015, Nick Turse wrote, of Africa, ". . . American operations serving as a catalyst for blowback." In 2018, Prof. Richard Falk said the reactions were against US "erroneous hard-power." Thus, on the Middle East, an article in 2024 in *Foreign Affairs*, the prestigious journal of the CFR, observed, "Washington enjoys far less influence and credibility in the region than it did in the 1990s." This has been coming for a long time. In 1968 Chomsky pointed out of the US terror in Viet Nam, that it was up to US people "to save our own country from becoming an object of hatred and contempt. . ." The US terror reached further than Viet Nam. It struck throughout the system of US force for resource control. Prof Colleen Woods describes it in 2020: "the reality of state-sanctioned political terrorism today."[136]

Viet Nam's 10 young heroines of Dong Loc risked all against the terrorism. In 1965, 17-year-old Vo Thi Hoi wrote to her mother: (See prior endnote & *Corporate Tsunami*.)

> Bombs and bullets pour down on Dong Loc . . . But all of my squad is unafraid. As soon as the bombs stop, we go out and make the roads so the vehicles can keep up their job of traveling the roads to the South, oh Mother dear!

I think Americans have tried, we've all tried very hard, to escape what we've learned in Viet Nam, to not come to the logical conclusions of what's happened there.

—Randy Floyd, former US pilot.[137]

CHAPTER 7

SIGNATURE TECHNIQUES HIT VIET NAM & US

Despite the Golden Rule and Viet Nam's impassioned 1945 Declaration of Independence, US foreign policy force leaders targeted Viet Nam for continuing colonial control. Trying to defeat Viet Nam, US leaders used Signature Techniques worldwide, in Viet Nam, and in the US on Viet Nam.

An overarching Signature Technique was: Destabilizing a nation or region created opportunities to gain control for business expansion and secured access to resources, often by force. When choosing to use this technique, US leaders often rejected diplomacy for fair trade and mutual development.

This combination of destabilization and force was used early against black people and Native Americans.[138]

Signature Techniques inside US, on Viet Nam after 1941 Coup eliminating policy of independence and fair trade.
In the 1944 "Pauley's Coup," **opponents of President Franklin D. Roosevelt (FDR) knew he was dying, so they removed Vice President Henry Wallace from the re-election ticket.**

Wallace had just achieved an international agreement with China to honor Viet Nam's Declaration of Independence. They replaced Wallace with Harry Truman, a foreign policy novice. On April 12, 1945, FDR died. Truman became president.[139]

On April 13, two advisors from the CFR briefed Truman. He followed their view, blamed communism, and reversed FDR's policy of independence for Viet Nam. US leaders backed France to re-invade Viet Nam.[140]

If FDR had continued living, no US-Viet Nam war would have occurred, Buttinger says.[141]

Some US presidents were novices at foreign policy, so NSC and CFR foreign policy leaders led them to go along with the world order for US business expansion and access to resources. Some others knew some about foreign matters, but still believed in the false claim of a noble entry into Viet Nam, so they were also led in the world order pursuit of control. Novices included Harry Truman (1946–53) and Ronald Reagan (1981–89). Barack Obama (2009–17) had more knowledge of foreign cultures, but being a conciliator and not knowing of the false claim on Viet Nam, he accepted advisors from the world order system. President Truman said, "I may not have much in the way of brains, but I do have enough brains to get ahold of people who are able and give them a chance to carry out responsibility." CFR members held 42 percent of top foreign policy posts during his two terms as president (1945–1953).[142]

President Ronald Reagan relied on advisors for his decisions, including to conduct terror wars in Central America (Chapter 8, Section 6, "American hemisphere"). For, *The Education of Ronald Reagan,* an extensive study friendly to Reagan, is devoid of any mention of Reagan learning about countries like Guatemala for their history, social structure, and Western corporate domination. Instead, *White House Warrriors* by John Gans shows that Reagan's limited knowledge as an actor-turned-politician meant that he relied on advisors:[143]

> Reagan's style. The actor-turned-governor-turned-president preferred, according to one close observer, to have 'the boys,' as Reagan called the older, and even elderly, men who were his advisors, settle any disagreements and then give him a consensus recommendation to approve.

Barack Obama had more knowledge of foreign countries, but he became a conciliator, says *The Education of Barack Obama*. He was born in Hawaii in 1961 of a white American mother and an African father, and he moved during 1967–71 to post-1965 coup Indonesia with his mother and an Indonesian stepfather, a member of the Indonesian Army. After the 1965 US-backed bloodbath coup, the "unsavory deals Soetoro [Obama's stepfather] brokered between the Indonesian government and American businessmen" created a rift with Obama's mother, and their different values gave Obama a sense of skepticism, *The Education of Barack Obama* reports. This window shows the young Obama close to this stepfather who, this evidence shows, must have been on the side of the US world order for business expansion—in Indonesia by exceptionally brutal force. In 1971, Obama returned to Hawaii as a young teenager at an excellent private school. An excellent student, he became editor of the *Harvard Law Review*.[144]

During Barack Obama's presidential administration, CFR influence continued heavily in government. As noted above Shoup reports that "As of July 1, 2011, for example, the CFR had 529 of its members serving in government." Obama's three national security advisors have been CFR members, with Susan E. Rice and Thomas E. Donilon being "especially close to the CFR." From various influences, Obama had learned to listen to other viewpoints, and to compromise between views. He listened to advisors from the world order governed by the false claim of a noble 1954 entry into Viet Nam. During Obama's administration, US drone strikes greatly increased, killing many civilians.[145]

1950–54 Signature Techniques in Viet Nam
The 1945 re-invasion ran into serious defeats in battles during 1950, so foreign policy force leaders pursued the 1950–54 Alternative Plan to take over the war. In this plan, **Signature Techniques included: Cutting out the real Viet Nam from development by the Griffin plan for "economic rehabilitation" and by the Colombo Plan for economic development; by US soldiers preparing for war by traveling in Viet Nam; and by US officials and soldiers meeting collaborators to prepare proxies for war.**[146]

1954 onward, Signature Techniques included:

- **The US broke the 1954 Geneva Accords, a Signature Technique of disregarding treaties and pursuing expansion by force.**

    The Accords left Viet Nam as one nation, with France having a duty to administer the south half, southern "regrouping zone," until elections. Articles 1 and 14(a) say that in plain words. But US leaders applied pressure, so France withdrew. And, no "South Viet Nam" existed. Viet Nam remained one country, with over 90 percent support, that had defeated France. This Viet Nam defeated the US.[147]

The departure ended France's administration of the southern half, thereby breaking the main operative mechanism of the Accords. By causing this result, US leaders played a main role in breaking the 1954 Geneva Accords.[148]

The results came swiftly and deadly. As shown in Chapter 5, a proxy army directed by US civilian leaders started killing villagers. A February 1, 1955 State Department telegram said the army had killed "large numbers" of civilians. Violating the Nuremberg Ruling by entering and doing large-scale killings, this used the Signature Technique of disregard of international law and instead pursuing US economic goals.[149]

The Nuremberg Judgment said that it is a crime to do:

> Planning, preparation, initiation or waging of a war of aggression. . . . To initiate a war of aggression, therefore, is not only an international crime; it is the supreme international crime differing only from other war crimes in that it contains within itself the accumulated evil of the whole.

- The Nuremberg Ruling against aggressive invasions applied to all nations. It was independent of the US claim that Geneva did not bind the US. The US takeover of the war violated Nuremberg.
- **The violation of Viet Nam's sovereignty was a Signature Technique used in the other three coups of 1953–54: Iran, Brazil, and Guatemala**.
- **Illegal alliance payments** to Ngo Dinh Diem (Diem), the proxy for US leaders, who was too weak to even be in Viet Nam without US military backing.[150]

- **Central Intelligence Agency (CIA) false rumors**, such as a leaflet showing the North Region in an atomic bull's-eye. Such actions influenced about 900,000 Catholics to move to the South Zone and support the illegal presence of the US.
- **Diem passed a law permitting a death sentence for 'supporting communists.' Summary executions were done by military forces entering villages.**[151]

Signature Techniques in US against Viet Nam 1950s and 1960s

- **Ditching the public from knowledge** about the 1865–1954 US business enabled by force.
- **Ditching the public from knowledge** about the War and Peace reports that set up the world order for US control, often by force.
- **Ditching the public from knowledge** that the 1954 Geneva Accords recognized the nation as one country, Viet Nam. The Accords never said "North Viet Nam" or "South Viet Nam." No nation called "North Viet Nam" ever existed. No purported "South Viet -Nam" even existed at the time of the 1954 conference. The US did not purport to create it until October 1955. That was illegal under the 1954 Accords: France had the duty to administer the southern half.[152]

Attacking for control for business, but falsely blaming the people attacked by US leaders. As proven throughout this volume, US leaders claimed to back "South Viet Nam" against a communist invasion, but instead, US leaders invaded to seize control, to continue the 1865–1954 US business enabled by violence.

- **Ditching the public from facts by CIA book publishing** in association with major publishers during the 1950s and 1960s. This **assisted in cultivating the belief that Viet Nam was wrong.** Prof. Ray Price says in a 2020 Counterpunch article: **"CIA backed narratives championed global democracy while ignoring American CIA interventions undermining democratically elected governments promising greater distribution of wealth."** Susan Williams says in 2021 in *White Malice* that **over 1,000 books in the 1950s and 1960s were published with CIA funding, rather than having to rely on the free market for book sales as did other authors.** In this method, **"the US government secretly corrupted scholarship and warped academic freedom in ways that left the American public uninformed."**[153]

Some presidential advisors ignored key, available information. Walt Rostow, a professor of economic history, ignored Viet Nam's centuries of economic history, including organization and performance. Rostow's 1960 book erroneously said, Viet Nam was among "countries that have not yet attained self-sustained growth." That book also mistakenly categorized Viet Nam as one of colonized areas that often were "incapable of self-organization. . . ."[154]

However, in 1288 CE, Viet Nam's third victory over the Mongol Empire invasion "was the strength of the socio-economic system established under the Ly and Tran, and the successful military policy followed by the Tran command," observed Nguyen Khac Vien. During the 15th century, Dai Viet exported high-quality glazed ceramics and other goods throughout Southeast Asia, as well as to Turkey and Persia; by the 16th century, ceramics were exported to Europe.[155]

Moreover, the 1945–54 victory over the US-backed French invasion required national unity and self-organization. Eminent historian Le Thanh Khoi explained in 1955, "A national union was indispensable for reconquering independence." That is because, as a practical matter, fighting invasions requires a spirit of unity, belief in independence (love of country), community spirit, spirit of autonomy, eminent Professor Tran Ngoc Them explained later, in 2001.[156]

In accord with that historical record, even hawkish columnist Joseph Alsop, who traveled in southern Viet Nam, wrote in 1954:[157]

> The Vietminh could not possibly have carried on the resistance for one year, let alone nine years, without the people's strong, united support.

So, Rostow erred, saying Viet Nam was "incapable of self-organization. . . ." "Rostow displayed myopia toward the aspirations and cohesive nationalism" of Viet Nam, biographer Milne concludes.[158]

Isaiah Bowman had been only an assistant professor, when he was picked to lead The Inquiry preparing US positions for the 1919 Versailles Conference. At Versailles, the advice of Bowman and the Dulles brothers led the US delegation to deny the petitions of Viet Nam and other colonies for gradual independence.

Although Bowman later wrote that unfair territorial settlements violated "*fairness* which is one of the essential elements of a stable peace" he used strained reasoning support the US control by force. He said small nations had no right to control what large nations did.[159]

Foreign policy force leaders ditched the US public from

learning that JFK had been testing a withdrawal, which would have ended the decades of US business by force in Viet Nam. In 1951, after JFK visited Viet Nam, his statement that the "Fires of nationalism . . . are now ablaze" directly opposed the false claim that the US entered to save those same people from communists. Indeed, JCS had said the West could not crush Viet Nam, and the 1943 CFR report said further control would require "a long and disastrous period of repression." In 1963, JFK was taking steps to withdraw from Viet Nam, though he was riding the fence as he was being labeled soft on communism. His effort to withdraw was well-known.[160]

The Armed Forces' *Pacific Stars and Stripes* reported October 4, 1963, "White House Report: U.S. Troops Seen Out of Viet[nam] by '65". The *New York Times*, reported on November 16, 1963, "1,000 U.S. Troops to Leave Vietnam." In 1963, Diem floated the idea of a coalition government for unification following the Geneva Accords. Ho and Viet Nam (DRV) responded favorably.[161]

If Diem and JFK had persisted and the US had withdrawn, that would end the long run of US business in Viet Nam since 1865, enabled by force.

Very extensive evidence in other works supports the conclusion of the House Select Committee that JFK was killed in a crossfire, which means a group conspiracy planning between two or more shooters. That evidence is beyond the scope of this book. But the House Select Committee analyzed acoustical evidence of a crossfire. The earlier Warren Commission failed to examine that evidence. And, the Warren Commission further relied on a falsified x-ray that purported to show the back of JFK's head was still in place. But at the Dallas emergency room, doctors saw it the back of his head was missing. That meant a crossfire.[162]

JFK had angered some powerful NSC civilian and military

people, as well as big business people on other matters. Similarly on Viet Nam, his steps toward withdrawal angered powerful people.[163]

False reporting by CIA to the new president. One month after JFK was killed, a December 21, 1963 "report" was presented to LBJ, purporting to be written by Secretary of Defense (DOD) Robert McNamara during a recent inspection trip to Viet Nam. While he was in Viet Nam, however, the "report," was prepared in Washington, D.C. by an office that connected the CIA and DOD. Upon returning to Washington, McNamara presented it to LBJ as if it were the results of his inspection trip. The opposite of JFK's steps toward withdrawal, it said, "We also need to have major increases in both military and USOM (United States Operations Missions) staffs."[164]

Destruction in Viet Nam preparing for industrial development. A new industrial heartland, planned in the 1960s by John D. Rockefeller III and others, could use hydroelectric lines from the Mekong River. In the 1960s, anthropologist Jules Henry would say: "The destruction of the Vietnamese countryside is the first, and necessary, step to the industrialization of Vietnam. . . ." Industrial labor was planned to come from farmers displaced by the US-Viet Nam War. Bernard Fall said, ". . . the countryside literally dies under the blows of the largest military machine ever unleashed on an area of this size." [165]

During 1960–75, in Indochina, **the US did the heaviest bombing and use of explosives in history, much of it in Viet Nam**. A research study shows the US used more than three times, by weight, of the bombs and explosives used by the US in all of World War II:[166]

The United States Air Force dropped in Indochina,

from 1964 to August 15, 1973, a total of 6,162,000 tons of bombs and other ordnance. U.S. Navy and Marine Corps aircraft expended another 1,500,000 tons in Southeast Asia. This tonnage far exceeded that expended in World War II and in the Korean War. . . .

US leaders **hit Indochina with about 100 times the combined explosive power of the atomic bombs dropped on Japan in 1945.**

Giving illogical reasons for using dioxin. (*See Corporate Tsunami,* Ch 30, 34, & Ch 49.) 1. Illogical on its face. US leaders stated that a legal precedent for the US to use dioxin in Viet Nam was that during 1951–53, the British had used "herbicides" in Malaysia against rebels. But that is like saying that Bonnie and Clyde robbing banks was a legal precedent for others to rob banks. Two wrongs don't make a right.[167]

Illogical on the facts. Leaders said that dioxin was an herbicide to destroy leaves that hid the enemy. But during the war "at least 2.1 million people but perhaps as many as 4.8 million people in 3181 hamlets were sprayed." (Stellman study). Spraying dioxin on that many people is illogical, when the claim is that it was sprayed on leaves. [168]

Signature Technique of intimidation by spraying dioxin:

- Photographs in newspapers in 1967 showed a child born with a duck-like face. In 1969, monster births occurred but the spraying of dioxin continued into 1971.[169]
- Dioxin poison floating down in the air was known to be intimidating, a different purpose than use as an herbicide. The chief USAF scientist on dioxin later said, "Did we spray where the enemy was? You're damn right we did." Asked if the spray frightened the enemy, he

replied that they ran:[170]
- **Intimidation is shown by the wrongful use on people, a decision a network of professional people whose job included finding and acting on facts.** The Chemical Corps, NSC, CIA, and Advanced Research Projects Agency (ARPA, later DARPA for Defense ARPA) worked closely together. High NSC policy makers had long directed the common plan for a world order, often using force. ARPA was created in 1958 to coordinate the development of weapons. In the 1950s, Chemical Corps scientists conducted the poison program of Allen Dulles of the CIA and NSC during 1953–61. Dulles was famed for ferreting out facts, details, and issues. Such topics to ferret out included the insidious nature of dioxin.[171]
- Spraying dioxin on people was a form of straight power, reflecting diplomat George Kennan's statements in the 1940s.[172]
- Dioxin spraying supported the "long and disastrous period of repression" in the 1943 report.
- Racism was a factor in spraying dioxin. Dioxin was not authorized to be sprayed on people in the US.
- US leaders claimed they did not know dioxin would cause birth defects, but they knew it was dangerous to people. The dangerousness was known in 1959 as "its insidious effects, its chronic toxicity" precluded the authorization of spraying dioxin on millions of people in the US. The Chemical Corps 1959 stoppage of work on dioxin, was, as Chemical Corps scientist Ronald Kassel said, "because of its insidious effects, its chronic toxicity."[173]
- Extensive environmental effects from dioxin are detailed in *Corporate Tsunami in Countryside Paradise,*

Chapter 34. This includes:

"Dioxin is extraordinarily destructive and persistent. It can last for decades, both in the environment and in our bodies," reports Sills in Toxic war. K. R. Olson pointed out that dioxin's half-life is ". . . as long as 20 to 50 years or more when buried in tropical subsoils, and more than 100 years in river and sea sediments." Viet Nam is a nation of myriad waterways. A US government report in 2009 stated: "Dioxin is not water soluble, but an unknown amount of dioxin has washed into the rivers, streams and coastal and ocean beds."

Signature Technique in the US of ditching the public, by the *Pentagon Papers* not disclosing the real reason for the war. As *Corporate Tsunami in Countryside Paradise* states:[174]

However, **despite the assertion that the *Pentagon Papers* revealed how the war started, they did not**. Even the title said "1945–1967." The *Papers* failed to mention the 1889–1954 US empire activity. They did not mention the 1943 report titled, "The Future Status of Indo-China as an Example of Postwar Colonial Relationships."

Postwar Signature Techniques against Viet Nam Destabilizing by financial pressure. The 1973 Paris Peace Agreement said: "In pursuit of its traditional policy, the United States will contribute to healing the wounds of war and to postwar reconstruction of the Democratic Republic of Viet-Nam." The US had led reconstruction of wartime enemies, Germany and Japan. **But US leaders destabilized Viet Nam, by (1) failing to pay under the 1973 Paris Peace Agreement, (2) doing**

the opposite by applying a trade embargo, (3) using US military technicians in civilian clothing to continue operating technological warfare weapons for continued, illegal attacks by the South Zone, (4) supplying artillery shells which the south fired at the same rate as before to the extent that US stockpiles were depleted, (5) pressuring Viet Nam to "repay" $140 million that had been US aid to the illegal proxy "South Viet Nam," and (6) not compensating dioxin victims into 2024. In economic trouble from devastation by the US invasion, Viet Nam agreed to pay the $140 million on a 20-year schedule.[175]

Destabilizing by not compensating the living Agent Orange/dioxin/toxin victims, though having sprayed dioxin in furtherance of the aggressive attack that violated Nuremberg. The victims include approximately more than 100,000 children in 2024 (150,000 in 2021 estimate) living with birth defects caused by the US sprayings. Quality of life payments for them have long been called for in a Barbara Lee congressional bill. As US leaders spend about 60–70 billion US dollars per month on military matters, a one-time payment of such an amount to Viet Nam's dioxin victims could be doable.[176]

Many of these victims are helpless and are cared for at home by parents and relatives providing care 24 hours a day, 7 days a week. The legislation proposal describes how caregivers, counselors, education facilities, and other measures are needed to add to their quality of life.

Young dioxin victims in 2016 needing 24-hour care, and General Tran Ngoc Tho, Chairman, Viet Nam Association of Victims of Agent Orange/dioxin (VAVA), Ho Chi Minh City. Photo by VAVA

Using a different standard of diagnosis than in the US, US leaders wrongly say Viet Nam's birth defect victims can't prove they are dioxin victims. Before the war, Viet Nam had no high rate of birth defects such as after the war. That matches a dioxin diagnostic inquiry in the US, which asks if the child's family had a history of birth defects. However, for a child victim in Viet Nam, it says each must show dioxin was the cause.[177]

Come Mister tally man, tally me banana
Daylight come an' we wan' go home.
> —"Day-O." [178] Song of banana workers American Hemisphere

We have come, treading our path
through the blood of the slaughtered.
> —"Lift Every Voice and Sing" [179] Black National Anthem in US by James Weldon Johnson

"I cannot accept the assumption from, that the Palestinians do not belong to Palestine. This is ridiculous."
> —Professor Ilan Pappe[180] Israeli dissident, former Israeli soldier.

"The power of a theory is exactly proportional to the diversity of situations it can explain."
> —Elinor Ostrom, Nobel Prize[181]

CHAPTER 8

THREE-STEP ANALYSIS DELETES FALSE CLAIM

Overwhelming evidence destroys the false claim of a 1954 entry into Viet Nam for a noble cause. Removing that false claim, a three-step analysis clarifies diverse foreign policy matters worldwide. They include nations, regions, and topics.

The false claim gone, it no longer creates a presumption of a noble purpose in the diverse other matters. In the void, real facts emerge. They show what really happened.

The variety of matters this chapter analyzes is: (1) Thailand, Viet Nam, & Japan; (2) Gaza, Palestine, & Israel in Middle East; (3) Viet Nam and Africa under US-France mutual "security" 1865–2024; (4) Afghanistan; (5) Syria; (6) American hemisphere; (7) Cruelty to Children of Dioxin, Gaza, & Climate Change; (8) Creation of unpayable debts by force on nations as plantation economies; and (9) Ukraine and Russia.

The Three-Step Analysis is:

1. How does the false claim of noble purpose against Viet Nam create the false presumption of noble purpose in a later action?

2. Without the false presumption of a noble purpose, what real purpose emerges, considering any common plan report, Signature Technique or other fact?
3. Do the facts show any Signature Techniques for control for business expansion and access to resources like used against Viet Nam?

Many real facts have not been told to the public. Some are stated in the 682 common plan reports and memos of 1939–45. Some are Signature Techniques, which US leaders use to gain advantage. And, some facts are specific to a particular country or topic.

The essence of post-colonial controls was described by Indonesian President Sukarno, in his opening address at the 1955 Bandung Conference:[182]

> Colonialism has also its modern dress, in the form of economic control, intellectual control, actual physical control by a small but alien community within a nation. It is a skillful and determined enemy, and it appears in many guises. It does not give up its loot easily.

(1) Thailand, Viet Nam, & Japan. Three-Step Analysis

1. How does the false claim of a noble purpose in Viet Nam create the false presumption of a noble purpose in the other action?

When US newspapers were full of the 1975 US defeat in Viet Nam, the public was not told of US-backed coups in 1947 and 1976 in nearby Thailand.

2. Without the false presumption of a noble purpose, what real purpose emerges, considering any common plan report, Signature Technique or other fact?

Two CFR-State common plan reports show the real purpose to be two-fold: A trading system and use of Thailand bases to bomb Viet Nam to set up the trading system. The 1941 report, "The Economic Organization of Peace in the Far East" said, "in a new ordering of the Far East. . . Thailand and French Indo-China offer no great problems. . ." Exports from Thailand and Viet Nam would support a reconstituted Japan. In turn, this system would support the US at the top.

This system would require severe force on samurai Japan and on Viet Nam. That 1941 report called for "basic changes . . . an overturn in the Japanese government, perhaps accompanied by important political and social changes . . . necessary changes." And for Viet Nam, the 1943 report said that forcing it back into "Colonial Relationships" would require "a long and disastrous period of repression." (See Chapter 11)[183]

Another 1943 report, "Thailand," said: "The quislings who actively aided Japan were in many instances men who had already been discredited among the Thai themselves."

3. Do the facts show any Signature Techniques for business expansion and access to resources like used against Viet Nam?

With two reports, **US leaders chose to back the use of force in a 1947 coup by quisling, right-wing** General Phibun (Luang Phibunsongkhram). That was despite him having earlier declared war against the US, siding with Japan. Backing military rule had two purposes:

- It supported the US plan to attack Viet Nam, shown in the 1943 report on disastrous repression to keep Viet Nam in "Colonial Relationships." From air bases in Thailand during the 1960s, the US would do heavy bombing of Viet Nam. And, Thailand became important in a vision of a Mekong River Basin regional hydro-electric and industrial system reaching into Viet Nam.[184]
- It applied the overarching Signature Technique of **US leaders rejecting diplomacy for fair trade, democracy, and mutual economic development, instead choosing to back military control for US business expansion and access to resources.**[185]

After World War II, US air corps advisors, technicians and similar people stayed in Thailand. And in March 1961, the US started adding a combat-oriented reconnaissance detachment in Thailand.[186]

The US **granted $10 million aid to the Phibun coup government, which strengthened the coup generals. Phibun and others then disregarded the Foreign Ministry.** US military aid and money were Phibun's main sources of power, Prof Chomsky reports in *The Washington Connection and Third World fascism*.[187]

In the early 1950s, the US strengthened its relationship with Thailand's military rulers, as the US Alternative Plan developed in Viet Nam from 1950 onward for the US to take over the war if the French invasion was defeated (*Corporate Tsunami*, Chapter 26).

By 1950, **Sea Supply Company, a CIA front, dummy corporation in Miami, funneled money, arms, and supplies into Thailand for Thai generals. Willis Bird, a CIA agent, worked for Sea Supply in Thailand. In 1950, Sea Supply opened a paratrooper camp north of Bangkok to train 50 police a year in airborne and guerrilla operations.**[188]

During 1951–52, **Phibun sought to enhance his reputation with the US, so he, along with US pressure, led the Thai government to crackdown on leftist elements in the government and army**. This aligned Thailand strongly with the US and ended any real relations with China and the Soviet Union.[189]

However, the 1943 CFR report, "Thailand," provided evidence that there was little or no communist influence. The report said, "But the Thai are not an excitable people; on the contrary, they are inclined to be conciliatory and even indifferent and lazy with respect to politics and economics." It said most countryside people were rice farmers. Very few cared about national elections.[190]

During 1954–59, **Thai military spending increased 250 percent, while per capita income substantially decreased during 1950–59. During the early 1960s, no substantial threat was posed by any rebels. But US aid to the military government increased markedly as the US bombed Viet Nam, as Chomsky observes.**[191]

In 1973, a revolt in Thailand threw out the US-backed military rule and established a democracy. However, as Chomsky observes, **the US gave no encouragement to this democracy; rather the US increased aid to the military and decreased economic aid**. Chomsky points out that in the prelude to **overthrows of democracy in both Thailand and Chile during this period, "the intent was clearly hostile to the new democratic forces and supportive of the anti-democratic military-police establishment."**[192]

Ditched from the facts, the US public had virtually no ability to guide the general direction of policy to support the 1973–76 democracy in Thailand for fair trade and development.

During 1975–76, oil drum burnings by right wing militia-thugs occurred in the countryside. Victims were beaten unconscious or semi-conscious, then placed in oil drums, in which the lower part held wire mesh, over a fire below. **Oil drum burnings and other tortures and shootings were led by two right-wing terrorist organizations, whose leaders had been in a US-run Communist Suppression Operations Command.**[193]

In 1976, soon after the US effort in Viet Nam failed, a **CIA-backed coup that used torture overthrew Thailand's democracy and restored military rule.** [194]

"During the 1980s . . . **the Thai upper middle class formed its attachment to authoritarianism and openly rejected the electoral rights of the rural poor**," a 2019 book, *After the Coup*, reports. **Over the years, major export markets for Thailand developed in the US, Japan, and Europe.**[195]

(2) Gaza, Palestine, & Israel in Middle East. [196] Three-Step Analysis.

1. How does the false claim of a noble purpose against Viet Nam create the false presumption of a noble purpose in the other action?

The false claim creates a false presumption that the US needs to back a one-state solution in a world of hostile Arabs and terrorists.

2. Without the false presumption of a noble purpose, what real purpose emerges, considering any common plan report, Signature Technique or other fact?

Two facts showing real purpose appear in the light:

First, the idea of a proxy force for access to oil appears in a 1944 CFR report, "The Oil Situation in the Middle

Three-Step Analysis Deletes False Claim

East": "a policing problem in Palestine, Transjordan, and Saudi Arabia which could only be solved by the use of American troops or by agreement with some foreign power or group."[197]

The reason, Chomsky points out, is:[198]

> . . . in the unfolding new world order of that day. . . **control of the incomparable energy reserves of the Middle East would yield "substantial control of the world"**. . . Washington anticipated that it would end with the United States in a position of overwhelming power . . . **a "Grand Area" that the United States was to dominate. . . .** (Emphasis added.)

Second, British documents show that an 1840 origin of Zionism in the original British conquest of the eastern Mediterranean gave Britain a hope for a Jewish settlement in Palestine to extend British capital expansion tied to the cotton trade.[199]

Three 1940s CFR reports identify why a two-state solution could occur, and why a one-state solution is a powder keg, but the State Dept has overridden those concerns through 2024.

One 1943 report said a one-state solution injected "racial opposition" and "hatreds" that would take "statesmanlike guidance" to diminish. ("The New Zionism and a Policy for the United States"). But US leaders acquiesced in what Rashid Khalidi calls a Jewish "para-state."[200]

The second, a May 31, 1943 report, said perhaps just "tell the Arabs to come to terms with the Jews. . . ." That one, "Future of the Jews in Europe with Special Relation to Palestine," missed the realities that (1) in bargaining, a side with little or no power can expect to receive little or no compromise, and

(2) it eliminated the "statesmanlike guidance" that the State Dept said was needed.[201]

The third report, (1944), contains **faulty reasoning, asserting that since Palestinians live in a tribal culture, they are incapable of having their own nation**. But they had long lived successfully in a tribal culture. So, an Arab part of a two-state solution would not need to meet a US definition of a nation. This report is, "Palestine: A Solution of Its Immediate Problem."[202]

Another part of this "Solution" report said it was up to the British to decide a solution, as they controlled the area under international mandate.

This third report, "Palestine: A Solution of Its Immediate Problem" said "no inherent 'promise' of an independent Jewish state in Palestine can be evoked out of the wording of the 1917 Balfour Declaration itself." (Palestine: A Solution p. 2) And, it said: "nothing shall be done which may prejudice the civil and religious rights of existing non-Jewish communities in Palestine." (Palestine: A Solution, p. 4) This **report thereby establishes a strong, logical basis for the US to join the 149 nations that recognize Palestine. This would produce a situation of skillful diplomacy working to accomplish a two-state solution. The US has failed to do that, despite claiming skill at diplomacy. The strength, logic, and prospect of skillful diplomacy appears as the only realistic way to get Israel to the bargaining table.**[203]

Rejecting the US leaders' violations of their own reports, 149 nations recognize Palestine in 2024. Recognition is a step toward a viable two-state solution.[204]

In early October 2024, *Foreign Affairs* reports: "The reputational damage to the United States, as well as to Israel, is also steadily building, with negative consequences for other global priorities shared by both countries."[205]

3. Do the facts show any Signature Techniques for business expansion and access to resources like used against Viet Nam?

Destabilization of Palestine included the 1948 *Nakba*. Zionists forcibly removed 750,000 Palestinian Arabs from 500 of the 1,000 villages and erased any trace of them having living there. This was an ethnic cleansing. It started in February 1948, and by May it had virtually depopulated five major towns and much of West Jerusalem. It moved 130,000 people to Arab nations before May, when Arab soldiers started arriving to fight back.[206]

Efforts for two states were limited to pronouncements, not structural action, while the foreign policy force pursued business expansion by force, such as destabilizing the region by a 1953 coup in Iran. President Obama (2009–17) said Israel and Palestine each had a right to a state. To do that, he could have (a) given military aid to Israel but conditioned it on Israel accepting Palestinian statehood; (b) joined about 130 nations in 2009 that recognized Palestinian statehood; and (c) with them, conducted the "statesmanlike guidance" that a State Dept report said was necessary to avoid prolonged conflict.[207]

Instead of "statesmanlike guidance," the foreign policy force had destabilized the region in 1953 by overthrowing democracy in Iran. In 1949, Allen Dulles had negotiated what Kinzer calls "the largest overseas development project in modern history." It was for 11 engineering firms in Overseas Consultants Inc. It was set up after a 1949 dinner for Iran's shah at the Council on Foreign Relations. But in 1951, Iran's parliament democratically elected Mohammad Mossadegh as Prime Minister. He led parliament to reject the deal as a major give-away that would "break the back of future generations." Also, Iran nationalized the oil industry after electing Mossadegh.[208]

In 1953, Secretary of State John Foster Dulles and CIA Director Allen Dulles, organized a coup with the British. It installed what Blum reported as a regime "of grinding poverty, police terror, and torture" and thousands of executions. After the coup, 40 percent of Iran's oil went to US oil companies. The coup followed the War and Peace memo that had recommended disregarding sovereignty where US economic interests were at stake.[209]

The coup in Iran, and the position that Palestinian Arabs had no right to a sovereign state in Palestine, though Jewish immigrants had such a right, have branded the United States as unfair and criminal.

The destabilization of Palestine included a Signature Technique that Professor Ilan Pappe describes as "**ideological moral assumptions, the assumption that Palestine belongs only to the Jewish people the assumption that dehumanizes the Palestinians and does not see them as equal people as the Israeli Jews.**" Pappe observes, "I cannot accept the assumption from, that the Palestinians do not belong to Palestine. This is ridiculous."[210]

Massive force including genocide has been used during October 2023–October 2024, when Israel killed over 40,000 Palestinians in Gaza, about 14,000 of them being children. See front cover of this book for photo of destruction in Gaza. During these attacks, US leaders continued supplying Israel with weapons. This support of Israel and of harming Palestine is the Signature Technique of developing an advantage to gain power.[211]

Prof. Pappe was labeled as a traitor and forced out of teaching at Haifa University. He says that recently, Israel's education system has become "more racist." US support of Israel but not Palestine as a state reflects the virulent racism in the US.[212]

Using cruelty to intimidate or weaken reflects in a report by some US doctors: "As Surgeons, We Have Never Seen Cruelty Like Israel's Genocide in Gaza." Many children with wounded limbs but no antibiotics to stop infections have had to have amputations. Prof. Pappe labels Israeli actions in Gaza as genocidal. (*See* Endnote 215.)

Violation of the Nuremberg Ruling against aggressive invasions The attack on Gaza was illegal under Nuremberg, given that the backing of the one-state solution was known to cause conflict.

In 2024, US ally Israel is pursuing oil and gas production in the eastern Mediterranean, in an area that had been under control of the Palestinian Authority. This furthers the US goal of access to fossil fuels.[213]

Failure to use "statesmanlike guidance" marks a US diplomatic failure to work with Arabs and the 149 nations that back them to accomplish the very thing many want. In early October 2024, *Foreign Affairs* reported: "The reputational damage to the United States, as well as to Israel, is also steadily building, with negative consequences for other global priorities shared by both countries."[214]

(3) US-France Mutual Security 1865–2024 in Viet Nam, sub-Saharan Africa, and the Sahel Three-Step Analysis

1. How does the false claim of a noble purpose in Viet Nam create the false presumption of a noble purpose in the other matter?

That **false claim ditches the US public from knowing of the 1865–1954 US period of business in Viet Nam, enabled by French violence. So, the public cannot see it as part of a longer period, 1865–2024, of US-French mutual security for each other.**

2. *Without the false presumption of a noble purpose, what real purpose emerges, considering any common plan report, Signature Technique or other fact? .*

In the light, an unbroken 400 years of US racism against Africa emerges. It started with the 1619 use of slaves taken by force from Africa. Reliance on the slaves by force continued through 1865. After that, the violence continued as shown below. It was no coincidence that America relied on violence against Africa starting in 1619 for slaves and again in the 1960 Congo coup for the purpose of retaining Western control throughout sub-Saharan Africa and the Sahel. That control has lasted through 2024.

The following facts show **an 1865–2024 system of US-French mutual security for control for business expansion and access to resources**:

(1) **The 1865–1954 French "security" by violence for US businesses in Viet Nam now appears.**

(2) **In the second period, during 1955–75, the US provided "security" for US and French business in Viet Nam, and the US backed the 1960 Congo coup that stopped economic development in much of sub-Saharan Africa and the Sahel.** (*See* below.)

(3) The **second period began when US leaders sent no message to the December 8, 1958 opening of an All African People's Conference (AAPC) of major African leaders. Its theme was, "Hands off Africa,"** as their nations neared independence. **By sending no message, US leaders used the Signature Technique of destabilization: It signaled that the US opposed real independence and instead looked for dictators to give US and Europe control over resources.**[215]

Three-Step Analysis Deletes False Claim

(4) That destabilization gained force, being during the US leaders destabilizing Viet Nam by the 1955–60 murders of 70,000 citizens.

(5) Earlier in 1958, Ghana had become the first African nation to win independence from colonialism. Ghana trained and helped Pan African and freedom movements across the continent. In 1960, 17 nations won their independence from colonialism.[216]

(6) But the opposite of "Hands off Africa," US leaders were **concerned "to ensure and protect US imports of uranium from the Congo,"** Susan Williams reported in 2021 in *White Malice*..[217]

(7) **In 1959, the CIA formed its Africa division. It funded CIA front organizations.**[218]
In Africa, the CIA conducted activities but left little or no record on paper, a 2021 study, *White Malice: The CIA and the Covert Recolonization of Africa,* by Prof Susan Williams says.[219]

(8) **In 1960, the NSC and CIA used the Signature Technique of rejecting the use of skillful diplomacy where good possibilities existed for mutual development, instead pursuing control for business expansion and access to resources by force by backing a coup in the mineral rich Congo.** In 1960, the Congo was one of the 17 nations in Africa that gained independence.[220]

Prime Minister Patrice Lumumba of **the democratically elected government of the Congo** traveled to the US and spoke at the United Nations. He asked for help in getting Belgian troops out of the country. But some wealthy Americans had investments in Katanga in uranium and copper. That was Lumumba's "fatal mistake," says Gerard Colby. And, he said the Congo was now a sovereign nation and thus had a right to a fair percentage of profits from its own mineral wealth. The children could then attend decent schools, and the people could have a higher standard of living[221]

Diplomacy for fair trade and mutual development could have led the US to act like Ghana, which in 1960, acted "to send to the Congo some of the professionals it so badly needed: doctors, nurses, policemen, engineers, electricians, civil servants and other trained personnel. . . ." Williams recounts in *White Malice: The CIA and the Covert Recolonization of Africa*.[222]

But on January 14, 1960, in an NSC meeting on Congo's impending independence, CIA chief Allen Dulles stated the **CIA view, that just about no chance existed that Africa could accomplish orderly development**. VP Richard **Nixon said some Africans had only been out of the trees about 50 years**. Another NSC member said some were still in the trees. Neither **President Eisenhower nor anyone else on the NSC** opposed these remarks. Nixon said the US needed to **rely on local strongmen, or in some cases to develop strongmen. Eisenhower agreed. He saw Lumumba as a mad dog**.[223]

The NSC said Lumumba might turn toward the communists for aid. **At an NSC meeting, President Eisenhower gave an order that could only be interpreted as to kill Lumumba**. A CIA agent later testified that this meant that Allen Dulles, CIA chief, had approved the killing. A CIA officer, Dr Sidney Gottlieb, arrived in the Congo carrying poison with which to kill Lumumba.[224]

The **CIA targeted Ghana**, as **President Kwame Nkrumah** helped found the Organization of African Unity in 1963, promoting economic growth and nonalignment. And Ghana wanted a nuclear reactor. US leaders, denying Africa's right to growth, toppled Nkrumah in a **1966 coup**. See prior endnote.

The third period of US-French **mutual security covered**

1975–2024 in Africa and in Viet Nam, which US leaders tried to destabilize.[225]

By 1978, the CIA had 40 stations and bases in Africa, as well as many **front organizations.**[226]

To keep its ties, **France set up three pillars of power:**

1. 14 nations used an African franc tied to the value of the French franc,
2. French experts remained in financial, institutional, and educational roles, and
3. French troops remained in many nations, with the right to intervene as France saw fit..[227]

But in the late 1990s, domestic politics in France led it to reduce the size of its military, and it backed away from some unilateral action in Africa. By 2002, French troops in Africa were reduced to 5,300. France began to look to the UN and US for multilateral efforts.[228]

3. Do the facts show any Signature Techniques for business expansion and access to resources like used against Viet Nam?

The third period of US-French mutual security continued during 1975–2024, as a Signature Technique of applying US force wherever destabilization created opportunities.

Similar to Viet Nam in 1954, the **CIA backed the coup in the Congo in 1960 by Belgium and local forces.** The coup overthrew the democratically elected government. Lumumba was executed, despite not having committed any crime, and the coup government being illegal.

The Congo coup and killing also showed the US racism since 1619 for economic advantage for whites by murder of black people.[229]

The Congo plunged into decades of **bloodbaths for control of valuable minerals, rather than decades of US-Congo-Ghana cooperation in development based on fair sales of minerals**. That could have been a model for sub-Saharan Africa and the Sahel. But **other African nations also suffered destabilizations, used by the US, France, and other Western nations to secure access to resources** while majorities lived in poverty. **This Signature Technique gave the US access to Congo copper during the 1960s, in high demand for military use in the war in Viet Nam.**[230]

In the Congo, five years of war erupted. Didier Gondola points out that **the 1960–65 war shows the West has responsibility for turning the Congo into a place of chaos rather than of peaceful development of rich resources. "Mobutu is screwing up the country pretty good. He has no idea how to run a country," said Bill Avery, a CIA senior paramilitary expert, in 1975, after meeting with Joseph Mobutu on sending Congo arms into Angola to start a US presence in a war there.** [231]

Ludo de Witte writes:[232]

> the assassination of Lumumba and tens of thousands of other Congolese nationalists, from 1960 to 1965, was the West's ultimate attempt to destroy the continent's authentic independence development.

A UN Security Council Panel of Experts reported:[233]

> The conflict in the Democratic Republic of the Congo has become mainly about access, control and trade of five key mineral resources: coltan, diamonds, copper, cobalt and gold. The wealth of the country is appealing and hard to resist in the context of lawlessness and the weakness of the central authority.

Three-Step Analysis Deletes False Claim

Godfrey Mwakikagile wrote in 2019 of how that effect spread, so rich foreign nations have continued to profit from Africa, but postcolonial Africa remains poor:[234]

> To a very large degree, their very prosperity depends on perpetuating the status of African countries and other underdeveloped regions of the world as plantation economies for the provision of cheap raw materials to the industrialised world, and as a source of cheap labour for the manufacture of consumer goods for the metropolitan countries.

A senior CIA officer who became a whistleblower, John Stockwell writes in his book, *In Search of Enemies*:[235]

> The Congo covert action cost American taxpayers a million dollars a day for a sustained period. The CIA claimed to have won that one, although it was by no means clear ten years later what we had won—Mobutu was energetically running the country into the ground and he had turned on his American benefactors.

Some Congo minerals were shipped to the US through neighboring Angola to a Pacific Ocean port. In Angola, US leaders carried on similar efforts to destabilize and move for control. Stockwell, points out on Angola in late 1975:[236]

> Frustrated by our humiliation in Vietnam, Kissinger was seeking opportunities to challenge the Soviets. Conspicuously, he had **overruled his advisors and refused to seek diplomatic solutions in Angola.**

Diplomacy in Angola had concrete possibilities, but Kissinger relied on the US public and Congress being ditched from the facts on Angola. Stockwell, a manager in the CIA program in Angola, resigned and reported:[237]

> the CIA "lied to Congress and the 40 Committee, which supervised the CIA's Angola program . . . we actively propagandized the American public . . . Our secrecy was designed to keep the American public and press from knowing what we were doing—we fully expected an outcry should they find us out.

A civil war in Angola had erupted in July 1975, upon independence from Portuguese colonial control. From then onward, the MPLA (Movimento Popular de Libertação de Angola; People's Movement for Liberation of Angola) held the upper hand.

On October 22, 1975, the MPLA arrived in Washington to plead Angola's case to continue major business deals and friendship with the US. Boeing Company had a contract to deliver two 737s to Angola. A down payment of $30 million had already been made, and 12 Angolan pilots were in the US training to fly them. Since 1968, Gulf Oil had been pumping 150,000 barrels of oil a day from Angola's Cabinda oil region waters in the Pacific. (The Cabinda area, 2,800 square miles, had tribal ties to both Angola and the Congo.) By 1975, Gulf Oil in Cabinda was pumping was $500 million per year worth of oil from 120 oil wells there. Mobil and smaller Western companies also operated in Angola.[238]

A CIA station chief in Luanda, Angola, Bob Temmons, flew to Washington and joined Boeing's president in pleading to continue US business deals there with the MPLA. Temmons stated, as recounted in Stockwell's words, that "the MPLA was

Three-Step Analysis Deletes False Claim

best qualified to run the country, that it was not demonstrably hostile to the United States, and that the United States should make peace with it as quickly as possible."[239]

However, Angola was a nonaligned country in the spirit of the 1955 Bandung Conference. US leaders had boycotted Bandung and opposed its principle that called for emerging nations to be independent of Western control. That US opposition had led to US support for the 1960 Congo coup. As shown above, that coup was designed to destroy real independence throughout sub-Saharan Africa. But an independent Angola posed a real challenge to that US purpose in mineral-rich Africa. For, Angola was not only doing business with US companies, it was also asserting a right to do business with the Soviet Union.[240]

Angola's independent attitude ran squarely against the 1619–2024 US policy to pursue control for business expansion and access to resources by force. That policy had produced the US attack on Viet Nam—an effort to continue decades of business expansion by force Though US leaders had failed there, they had demonstrated that small nations would face US violence if they tried to break away from US control. So, Kissinger and the NSC pursued control of Angola. They sided with an invasion force from the apartheid racist nation of South Africa. It backed a different faction in the Angola civil war. Stockwell wrote, "There was nothing the Lusaka station could invent that would be as damaging to the other side as our alliance with the hated South Africans was to our cause."[241]

Such alliances, this volume shows, have damaged the US reputation worldwide. Yet, many in the US public are unaware of the wrongful policy of US leaders. On Viet Nam, Angola, and many other regions, the US public has never been told the real facts.

85

So, the business deals that could have led to capitalist-style relations and friendly development for the Angola public were lost. Instead, Kissinger committed the Viet Nam error, saying the US needed to fight communism in Angola.

That pursuit of control led to a build-up of US military providing so-called "security" for Western power, not for the impoverished millions.

It includes the 1975–2024 part of the US-French system of US-French mutual security for control for business expansion and access to resources. For, in 1975, France kept a hand in wars in the Congo for minerals and Angola for oil. In Angola, France convinced the CIA to pay France $250,000 to prove CIA "good faith" to France's actions. That matched the mutual security purpose—though some people, unaware of the false nucleus of foreign policy related to the long US-French mutual security during and after Viet Nam—wondered why the CIA needed to prove anything to France. France reciprocated by delivering for CIA use in the Congo civil war, or for CIA delivery to the Congo coup government, antitank missiles, 120 mm mortar rounds, ammunition, and four missile-firing helicopters.[242]

In 1996, the US started a military presence called African Crisis Response Initiative (ACRI) in 1996, training militaries in 9 countries. During this period, a 1996–2005 war in the Congo killed 5 million people.[243]

Around 2002 or 2003, Turse reports, US "security assistance" began in Niger, a former colony of France. In 2004, ACRI expanded into African Contingency Operations Training Assistance (ACOTA) that began training militaries in 24 countries. Other military programs were also involved.[244]

France worked closely with the US to develop a multilateral approach to "security." **Vallin reports that France still used** two main tactics: coercion by force and "mastery of irrational violence."²⁴⁵

The US and France closely coordinated efforts. But France intervened in Africa 42 times during 1997–2001, with only 8 times being multilateral. ²⁴⁶

By 2007, the US was training Niger soldiers. This followed the **US leaders' Signature Technique of avoiding skillful diplomacy for fair trade and mutual development, instead proceeding as if military control was the required method in largely black, impoverished Africa that happened to be mineral rich.**

By 2008, the US had military agreements with 18 African countries. China had military agreements with 15 African countries.²⁴⁷

Next door to Niger, France launched military operations in Mali and Chad in 2008, both against so-called jihadists. In French actions in those former colonies "the major weakness was the colonial origins of those same relationships," a 2023 article in *Military Review* points out.

(4) Local resistance to Africom military action
In 2007, **Africom, a US military command was created, but it is for the US-created war on supposed terror that follows from the false claim on Viet Nam. For, in Africa, US leaders provided security for France, not for the nations whose resources it used. In Niger, for example, the US provided "security" as France paid 1/250 the value of Niger uranium.**²⁴⁸

US leaders falsely labeling of opponents appears. For example, US leaders say that on Nigeria, the name "Boko Haram" designates an Islamic group labeled as "radical terrorists." But its origin is in disaffections, like in Viet Nam. Disaffections in Africa are against economic abuses by the West. The Royal African Society's weekly newsletter, *African Arguments*, said in 2011 of Boko Haram:²⁴⁹

Betrayed by Foreign Policy Fault Line

US training Niger military in 2007. Under the false claim on Viet Nam of a noble effort, US leaders have provided security in Africa for Western access to resources, while black Africans resided in poverty.
Public domain photo[250]

Three-Step Analysis Deletes False Claim

In Viet Nam, the French colony exported large quantities of rice from fields like in this photograph. The exports led to widespread malnutrition from the 1880s through the entire colonial period.
Photo credit: Kieran Barry

It is a local political movement now fighting a national campaign to pursue its ends. Its recruitment of predominantly unemployed, poorly educated young Muslim men is made possible by the national political failure to provide jobs, health or education. When northern primary school teachers were recently given a national primary-level exam, nearly all of them failed it. Unemployment in northern cities is extremely high. Without a decent future, young men are easily drawn into fanatical movements. . . .

The only long-term solution is the development of the region.

That description of Boko Haram matches the fact that US leaders chose destabilization of the entire region, when they rejected Ghana's 1960 overture to work for development in the Congo, as a model for the region. Instead of development, military power has thus been the determining factor of whose businesses expand here and who uses the rich mineral resources. Western leaders have ignored or opposed social and economic causes of unrest throughout Africa. This explains why local citizens would join Boko Haram.

Boko Haram is a Muslim society on both sides of the Nigerian-Cameroon border.

An Africom spokesperson said that **Africom troops are deployed around the year "to train local armies at battling insurgencies and rebellions."** In 2012, Africom conducted 14 major joint-training exercises, including in Botswana, Cameroon, Gabon, Lesotho, Morocco, Nigeria, Senegal, and South Africa. In 2015, Turse revealed that the **US military was in "a string of shadowy forward operating posts. . . ."** The US was doing **military actions opposing so-called "terrorism."**[251]

In 2017, four US soldiers were killed **fighting in Niger. The US public did not know they were there, much less why they were fighting.** Recently revealed facts now show that US "security" from a base in Niger has included reconnaissance drones, armed drones and combat soldiers. The drones also operated in surrounding countries.[252]

That shows the importance of the observations above by Gondola, de Witte, Mwakikagile, and the UN Security Council Panel of Experts. As Mwakikagile wrote in 2019 of Western domination: "To a very large degree, their very prosperity depends on perpetuating the status of African countries and other underdeveloped regions of the world as plantation economies. . . ."[253]

The Signature Technique of US leaders paying a small group to gain access to resources cast a strong control over much of Africa. A Ghanaian professor of economics, George Ayittey quoted by Mwakikagile says: "(Africa's economies will remain crippled) as long as you have these mafia governments, these predatory states. In Nigeria, in Zaire, all over the continent, the people in government are just looters."[254]

Thus in the 2020s, **France paid Niger 1/250th of market value of Niger uranium while backed by US security**, while most people in Niger lived in poverty. That guaranteed conflict. It came from the system Mwakikagile described:[255]

> Rich nations dominate the world economy, hence the world market. They are not interested in changing terms of trade to their detriment in order to enable Africans and other Third Worlders have access to markets in metropolitan countries and sell their products to Western consumers on fair terms; nor are they going to allow them to have control over the prices of the goods they produce and sell on the global market.
>
> That is not how the profit system works; not at the national level or at the international level. You can't reform the price system for the benefit of the underdog because the only way it is meant to work is to serve the interests of the rich and the powerful;

Amid such exploitation, President Ibrahim Traore of Burkina Faso in western Africa says, "Africa is a continent blessed with natural resources, water, and food, yet it is categorized as one of the world's poorest continents. . . ." He calls for Africa to find other partnerships to replace **exploitative Western controls**.[256]

In 2019, Mwakigagile outlined an answer needed for Africa:[257]

> Multinational corporations can help accomplish both goals: In exchange for being granted licences to grow food for export, corporations should be contractually required to invest in local agriculture and offer technical assistance and infrastructure improvements for small landholders. For this to happen, however, the playing field between local and foreign interests must be levelled. Binding rules need to be established by international bodies — and agreed to by African governments and multinational corporations — which will protect the rights of indigenous farmers, as well as ensure the integrity of Africa's environment, soil and water. Otherwise, the hastily negotiated land deals will continue to shortchange the long-term interests of millions of Africans, leading to more hunger, displacement, even turmoil.

That points to real opportunity for the US to join Africa and support fair trade and mutual economic development as shown in the final chapter.

But in case the US public continues to fail to change the direction of foreign policy, Ghana and Burkina Faso announced peace talks in October 2024, which could lead to joint economic efforts. These include expanded trade routes, agricultural innovation, and focusing on cooperation. A goal is to support economic growth on both sides. This is an experiment in Pan African unity. If the US fails to change to support fair trade and mutual economic development, the US could continue to suffer loss of leadership, shrinking economy, and destabilization in the US.[258]

(5) Afghanistan. Three-Step Analysis.

1. How does the false claim of a noble purpose in Viet Nam create the false presumption of a noble purpose in the other action?

It created a presumption that the 2001–2021 US war was for noble, stated goals of (1) capturing Osama bin Laden of Al Qaeda, as mastermind of the 9/11/2001 attacks in the US, and (2) ejecting the Taliban government.

2. Without the false presumption of a noble purpose, what real purpose emerges, considering any common plan report, Signature Technique or other fact?

For example, in Afghanistan, with the presumption of noble intent gone, two real facts emerge.[259]

First, a 1942 report in the State Department said that transport difficulties made Afghan oil much less usable than oil of Qatar, Saudi Arabia, and others. That situation existed into 2021. So, control of oil was not a major goal.

Second, Afghanistan did not plan the 911 attacks on the US, and it offered to turn over Osama bin Laden who did, but US leaders refused. President George W. Bush said the US wanted to "show muscle." Secretary of Defense Donald Rumsfeld said, "We don't negotiate surrender."

Those statements meant, as Prof Noam Chomsky points out in a 2022 study, that the best statement of the real US goal was: "We just want to show our muscle, intimidate everyone, go on to further goals."

Indeed, the Taliban offered to surrender Taliban forces, as well as to turn over Bin Laden with no war. But US leaders refused both offers.[260]

The admission by Pres Bush that the US went to Afghanistan to "show muscle," supported by the common plan report on unusable Afghan oil, shows the damage from voters being "ditched" from giving real guidance over the policy of business expansion by force in Viet Nam and later.

That stated purpose reflected the faulty Wolfowitz Doctrine. Paul Wolfowitz (foreign policy positions 1981–2007) advocated military superiority and unilateral use of force to prevent other nations from being real competitors. The "Wolfowitz doctrine" is superficial. For, as the axiom on control by force shows, the pursuit of resources by force violates elementary moral principles. It causes foreign citizens to fight back.[261]

This NSC and CFR world order was inherited by a conciliator, President Barack Obama (2009–17). Although he exuded hope as he started his presidency, he was limited in foreign policy by the false presumption of a noble intent, created by the false claim of a noble entry into Viet Nam in 1954.

With those influences, Obama followed NSC and CFR advisors, many who followed the Bush and Wolfowitz view. *Wall Street Think Tank* points out of drones under Obama.[262]

> In 2003 the Pentagon had only fifty drone aircraft, by 2013 it had about 7,500. During this period, but especially since 2009, when the Obama administration came into office, the JSOC, along with the CIA, have jointly operated a murderous program of drone strikes against targets in several third world nations as mentioned below. These attacks have killed thousands of people, some on "kill lists" of supposed terrorists personally vetted by President Obama, often based on questionable intelligence, and an unknown but large number of them completely innocent civilians.

Wall Street's Think Tank asks of these drone strikes, "are these actions 'defensive measures,' or are drone strikes simply terrorist attacks and war crimes via remote control?" The drones killed many innocent civilians in strikes that "killed thousands of people, some on 'kill lists' of supposed terrorists. . ."[263]

The "supposed terrorists" question reflects on the world order of US pursuit of control for business expansion. As it often violates the Golden Rule, it angers reasonable citizens of foreign nations. When they fight back, US leaders label them as "terrorists."

Such strikes were the Signature Technique of **intimidation**. **Intimidation in Afghanistan** is described in *The Myth of American Idealism* by Noam Chomsky:[264]

> A Human Rights Watch account from the end of October documented horrific bombings of remote Afghan villages, where residents "were adamant that there were no Taliban or Al-Qaida positions in the area." One forty-year-old mother lost her husband and all six of her children in one of the U.S.'s "carefully targeted" bombing raids.

Not only did the bombing intimidate, it also caused obvious resentment of the US. Chomsky further points out:[265]

> The leading Afghan women's rights organization, Revolutionary Association of the Women of Afghanistan (RAWA), issued a declaration on October 11, 2001 . . . , strongly opposing the 'vast aggression on our country. . .' by the United States. . . . a murderous assault. . ."

The failure of US methods is shown in a 2021 article by Graeme Herd about the Taliban government since the US withdrawal: "It does welcome and shelter radical groups and the territory of Afghanistan does become a sanctuary allowing for the resurgence of transnational terrorism."²⁶⁶

3. Do the facts show any Signature Techniques for business expansion and access to resources like used against Viet Nam?

The **avoidance of diplomacy for peace and fair trade appears in the wish to "show our muscle, intimidate."**

This use of force **further violated the Nuremberg Ruling and elementary moral principles by massive bombing in a sovereign nation,** by use of **proxies (rendition) for torture**, and by **paying into rampant corruption of US contractors in the course of upsetting Afghanistan's sovereignty**. A US Inspector General found, **$2 trillion in supposed US aid went to a "gallery of greed" that "fattened the wallets of the rich in the United States, Pakistan, and Afghanistan."**²⁶⁷

(6) Syria. Three-Step Analysis

The Three-Step Analysis includes:

1. How does the false claim of noble purpose against Viet Nam create the false presumption of noble purpose in a later action?

The false claim created the presumption that US actions had a noble intent and that opposition was "terrorists."

2. Without the false presumption of a noble purpose, what real purpose emerges, considering any common plan report, Signature Technique or other fact?

The purpose emerges of mislabeling reasonable reactions as terrorism. In "a prescient 2020 essay" (a 2021 *Foreign Affairs* article says), Marc Lynch explained the popular Arab uprisings of late 2010 and early 2011:[268]

> The fact that dictators once again sit on the thrones of the Middle East is far from evidence that the uprisings failed. Democracy was only one part of the protesters' demands. The movement was engaged in a generations-long struggle that rejected a regional order that had delivered nothing but corruption, disastrous governance, and economic failure.
> By that standard, the uprisings have profoundly reshaped every conceivable dimension of Arab politics, including individual attitudes, political systems, ideologies, and international relations. . . .

3. Do the facts show any Signature Techniques for business expansion and access to resources like used against Viet Nam?

The Signature Technique mislabeling local unrest as terrorist opposition, so US leaders could maneuver for opportunities to control Syrian oil fields, by force if necessary. Lynch writes that crackdowns were "marketed in the West [as actions] by the regimes partly as a response to an alleged Islamist takeover." However, Lynch observes that Syria was in a "long struggle that rejected a regional order that had delivered nothing but corruption, disastrous governance, and economic failure."[269]

Indeed, the region remembers that the only nation to overthrow democracy in Iran was the US. Lynch writes that US actions failed to address the frustrations of the masses. This has led to a:

> newly multipolar Middle East . . . . The United States' inability to compel its allies to resolve their differences

and cooperate against Iran shows just how far its influence has fallen since 2011.

(7) "American hemisphere" Three-Step Analysis

1. How does the false claim of a noble purpose in Viet Nam create the false presumption of a noble purpose in the other action?

The false claim of noble anti-communism in Viet Nam supported a presumption of a noble purpose of anti-communism to justify US-backed coups, destabilizations, dictators and torture.

2. Without the false presumption of a noble purpose, what real purpose emerges, considering any common plan report, Signature Technique or other fact?

Widespread proof by documents, eyewitnesses, and scholars has been made of US-backed dictators and violence in this area, while reactions have frequently occurred. With the removal of the presumption of a noble intent, the US-backed violence was from the overarching Signature Technique of rejecting diplomacy, instead pursuing control, often by force, for US business expansion and access to resources.

Because of that proven record, a 1944 War and Peace report, "The Inter-American System in the Postwar World" admitted that: "Pan Americanism is still under suspicion as a vehicle for the furtherance of United States policy and influence throughout the Americas."[270]

An excellent short summary of 1960–1990 in this hemisphere appears in *Who Rules the World?*, by Chomsky. Citing some original sources and scholarly works, he writes of critical US decisions in the early 1960s: [271]

One was to shift the mission of the militaries of Latin America from "hemispheric defense" (an anachronism from World War II) to "internal security"—in effect, war against the domestic population, if they raised their heads. Charles Maechling Jr., who led U.S. counterinsurgency and internal defense planning from 1961 to 1966, describes the unsurprising consequences of the **1962 decision as a shift from toleration of "the rapacity and cruelty of the Latin American military" to "direct complicity" in their crimes, to U.S. support for "the methods of Heinrich Himmler's extermination squads."** One major initiative was a **military coup in Brazil, backed by Washington and implemented shortly after Kennedy's assassination, that instituted a murderous and brutal national security state** there. The plague of repression then spread through the hemisphere, encompassing the 1973 coup that installed the Pinochet dictatorship in Chile and later the most vicious of all, the Argentine dictatorship—Ronald Reagan's favorite Latin American regime. Central America's turn—not for the first time—came in the 1980s. . . . (Emphasis added.)

Chomsky points out that "This is merely the briefest sketch of terrible crimes for which Americans bear substantial culpability, and that we could at the very least have easily ameliorated."[272]

Because that terrible history violates the Golden Rule, continual reaction has occurred. For example, Chomsky's 2022 book with Vijay Prashad and Angela Y. Davis, *The Withdrawal*, observes:[273]

. . . reversals of the US-led coups in Chile, Honduras, and Bolivia. The regime of the 1973 coup in Chile is being undone by the drafting of a new constitution and by the 2021 election of a post-coup political coalition. The 2009 coup in Honduras has been reversed by the 2021 election of the political forces that had been overthrown in the coup. The 2021 election in Bolivia of the leftist forces is a reversal of the 2019 coup against the government of Evo Morales.

Guatemala presents a case history of US-backed dictators and violence for more than a century. Guatemala's main resource for export was bananas, not a vital resource. That shows that rather than coveting bananas, US leaders coveted control for business expansion and access to resources.

In Guatemala, a dictator friendly to US business, Manuel Cabrera, ruled from 1885 to 1931. In the summer of 1907, Lt. Joe Stilwell (later, General "Vinegar Joe" Stilwell) traveled Guatemala in civilian clothes, under an assumed name, and mapped the country, including topography, political conditions, physical features, weather, and many other topics.[274]

Following a 1922 coup that protected American monopolies, United Fruit Company controlled Guatemala's railroad, electrical utility, and much of Guatemala's land. In *Doing business with the dictators*, Paul Dosal reports: "Democracy and prosperity adversely affected United Fruit's political relations with the host government; it always obtained more generous concessions from the dictator of an impoverished or economically stagnant country."[275]

By the 1930s, United Fruit dominated Guatemala's economy, mainly in banana plantations. A lawyer for United Fruit, John Foster Dulles wrote contracts with dictators, favorable for

United Fruit. In 1931, Jorge Ubico took over and ruled with violence. John Foster Dulles negotiated contracts for United Fruit Company in 1936 for a "ninety-nine-year lease with exceptional tax benefits."[276]

In 1944, a revolution established democracy. Guatemala called for redistributing unused land that United Fruit owned. CFR board member John J. McCloy, "Chairman of the Establishment," sat on the United Fruit board. Earlier, as president of the World Bank, he denied Guatemala loans "after reviewing its agrarian reforms and liberal labor laws."[277]

In 1954, McCloy, the Dulles brothers, and a committee with 15 other CFR members, decided on a coup. They argued that communism threatened Guatemala. But their main evidence was Guatemala's attempt to redistribute land. In the coup, in about 15 days, 9,000 Guatemalans were killed, about 7,000 were jailed, and over 18,000 workers were fired. An estimated 1,000 workers were machine-gunned on United Fruit land at Finca Jocotan (Jocotan Plantation).[278]

In Guatemala, the 1954 coup led to civil war until 1996. During 1964–74, 25 US officers with experience in Viet Nam were transferred to Guatemala. The US-backed government killed any opposition leaders–no matter how responsible, patriotic, or nonviolent. In 1972 'political' deaths averaged 30–50 a month, by 1980, 80–100 a month, and by 1981 after President Ronald Reagan took office in January, 250–300 a month. **As president, Reagan (1981–89) soon used a policy of international terrorism, Chomsky points out. This Signature Technique was used to intimidate and gain control.** During 1980–85 the US-backed government used a scorched earth method. They killed 100,000. A dictator name Rios Montt ruled during 1982–85. His scorched earth policy wiped out an estimated 626 Mayan villages. Tortures, disappearances, mutilations, and rapes were committed against the Mayans. The government also tried a practice of killing a quota of 30 percent in an area and providing food to the other 70 percent. In December 1996 a peace agreement was signed with a return to a democratically elected government.[279]

Of the "American Hemisphere" in the 1950s, *The Devil's Chessboard,* exposing NSC member Allen Dulles and his CIA, shows that 13 dictators "allowed U.S. corporations to exploit their nations' people and resources, and they cracked down on labor agitation and social unrest as Communist-inspired." The dictators used savage tortures and pocketed millions from the US. During 1945–76 US leaders backed 23 coups, most of them in this region.[280]

During the 1980s US-backed savagery against Guatemala, El Salvador, and other Central America nations, the **Signature Technique appeared of the NSC and CFR setting foreign policy for a president who lacked knowledge of the countries he claimed were threatened by communism.** (An earlier example was on President Truman on Viet Nam. Chapter 7) *The Education of Ronald Reagan,* a 2006, extensive study friendly to Reagan (president 1981–1989), is devoid of any mention of Reagan learning about countries like Guatemala for their history, social structure, and Western corporate domination. Reagan's education was within the US, from where he saw the USSR as evil. Reagan is credited with accomplishments in a Strategic Defense Initiative for missile defenses. And, Reagan opposed the USSR in four summits. But he knew nothing about history, culture, and US domination of small nations, like Guatemala.[281]

So, ditched like the rest of the US public, Reagan voiced the false assumption that the US had entered Viet Nam in 1954 for a noble effort. That created the false belief that US policy in Central America in the 1980s was noble.

Three-Step Analysis Deletes False Claim

With that false belief, he developed anti-communist zeal. He blended that with skill in talking smoothly from his days as a Hollywood actor. Evans notes that the AFL-CIO said in 1962 that Reagan had become a "right-wing zealot."[282]

In *White House Warrriors*, John Gans shows that Reagan's limited knowledge meant that he relied on advisors to decide how to handle matters:[283]

> Reagan's style. The actor-turned-governor-turned-president preferred, according to one close observer, to have 'the boys,' as Reagan called the older, and even elderly, men who were his advisors, settle any disagreements and then give him a consensus recommendation to approve.

Among Reagan's top foreign policy officials, 14 of 19 were CFR members. His vice president, George H.W. Bush, had been a CFR director and a director of the CIA. Both of Reagan's secretaries of state were longtime CFR members. The 682 reports and memos drafted by CFR members had formed the basis of the common plan for the world order for US business expansion and access to resources, often by force. So, Reagan's lack of knowledge, but his anti-communist zeal, and his reliance on the world order, led him to conduct terror in Central America.[284]

In Guatemala, terror had been so bad that the prior president, Jimmy Carter, had cut off aid in 1977. President Reagan restored aid, even though, as Chomsky points out, "The government was in fact carrying out one of the worst acts of genocide in the modern history of the Americas, with the close collaboration of U.S. military and intelligence units."[285]

3. *Do the facts show any Signature Techniques for business expansion and access to resources like used against Viet Nam?*

US leaders relied on killings by proxy for stability for investors and profits. In 1930–31 in Viet Nam, the French killed over 10,000 while US companies operated, and in 1932 in El Salvador, US companies operated while a US proxy killed between 10,000 and 30,000. US warships with Marines waited offshore as US financial leaders threatened to cut off bank loans, unless strongman Maximiliano Martinez would protect American coffee prices and other exports from worker demands for higher wages. Martinez used his army to do the killings. He then ruled El Salvador with an iron hand.[286]

The signature Technique of use of local militaries took force in March 1945. The US committed to train, supply, and indoctrinate the militaries of the rich elites of all "American hemisphere" nations except Argentina, when Undersecretary of State Nelson Rockefeller **signed**, in Mexico, **the Act of Chapultepec.** Those **forces generally supported US businesses against poverty-ridden majorities**. Rockefeller said that no kind of socialism would be tolerated, as it could open the door to communism. This strategy **overrode the policies of the gravely ill FDR**.[287]

In 1803, Haiti became the only country to successfully revolt and end a European slave colony, but the **US and France saddled Haiti with unpayable debts**. Today, many Haitians say the US tries to make it "a platform for export to the US market."[288]

In June 2024 a US jury verdict found Chiquita Brands International liable for eight killings in Colombia by a violent paramilitary group that it funded in the 1990s and 2000s. That verdict is based on proof beyond a reasonable doubt.[289]

Nevertheless, the false claim on foreign policy, ignoring the US attack on Viet Nam, has prevented the US public from seeing the US leaders' extensive pursuit of control for business expansion and access to resources.

(8) Cruelty to Children of Dioxin, Gaza, and Climate Change into 2024 by the common plan pursuit of control for economic power.

<u>Dioxin</u>. Approximately more than 100,000 children (150,000 in 2021 estimate) children in Viet Nam live with birth defects from US spraying of Agent Orange/dioxin/toxins in the attempt to seize control over 50 years ago. **Failing to compensate them for quality of life, US leaders use Signature Techniques of (a) Destabilization by placing an economic burden on a smaller country, (b) Intimidating by showing the US is capable of inflicting extreme damage.** Payments equaling, for example, one month ($60 to $70 billion) of the US military budget would help these kids in their desperate struggle for quality of life.

Ditched, the US public is not told by US leaders about these children and their struggle for quality of life.

<u>Gaza</u>. As described above, **US leaders supporting Israel in a one-state solution violate their own common plan reports.** In 2024, 149 nations recognize Palestine as a country, but US leaders fail to follow their own reports that say "statesmanlike guidance" is needed for a two-state solution, without which conflict is certain. Instead, **during October 2023 into 2024, US leaders supplied weapons to Israel in genocide against Gaza, bombing, and killing at least 14,000 children. These are the Signature Techniques of (a) Reducing Palestine's relative economic and political power, with the US much more powerful, and (b) Intimidation.**

Climate Change.

1. How does the false claim of a noble purpose in Viet Nam create the false presumption of a noble purpose in the later action?

With the presumption of a noble intent, some US leaders have claimed global warming is not a real problem, and some claim that capitalism will solve it.[290]

2. Without the false presumption of a noble purpose, what real purpose emerges, considering any common plan report, Signature Technique or other fact?

The real purpose emerges upon facts that demonstrate that the US government is failing to take appropriate emergency action. On April 10, 2024, United Nations Climate Secretary Simon Stiell stated: The next two years will decide whether or not humanity can "save the world" by getting the climate emergency under control, and that the bulk of the emission reductions will have to come from G20 countries.[291]

Therefore, "death" is in the wording of the U.N. Convention on the Rights of the Child treaty materials, Committee Comment 26:[292]

> Children are far more likely than adults to suffer serious harm, **including irreversible and lifelong consequences and death**, from environmental degradation… disproportionate and long-term effects. (Emphasis added.)

Children notice the cruelty. In the same Comment, children said:[293]

... "The environment is our life." "Adults [should] stop making decisions for the future they won't experience. [We] are the key means [of] solving climate change, as it is [our] lives at stake." "I would like to tell [adults] that we are the future generations and, if you destroy the planet, where will we live?!"

The 2015 Paris Climate Agreement and 2018 IPPC assessment warned of a failure by 2030 to curb global warming to a 1.5C degree increase. The UN states that goal must be achieved "to avert the worst impacts of climate change and preserve a livable planet." A 2025 International Court of Justice (ICJ) ruling says the world is failing to curb global warming to the amount. The two-year period in Climate Secretary Stiell's warning is shorter than the 12-year period in Paris Climate Agreement.[294]

Over 99 percent of climate scientists say climate change is real, presents an existential threat to human civilization, and that fossil fuel use needs to be greatly reduced to curb it.[295]

In January 2025, fires in Southern California—called a "Hellscape" by one climate scientist—have gained strength by climate change affecting both the winds and the dryness. Santa Ana winds whipping into those fires are worsened by high carbon emissions. Highlighting fossil fuel emissions, *Geophysical Research Letters,* a journal, cited in 2006 "the IPCC Special Report on Emission Scenarios (SRES) high (A2) and low (B1) emissions [Intergovernmental Panel on Climate Change, 2000]." The 2006 article said research suggests that Santa Ana Occurrences "are greater under a high-emission scenario."[296]

And, drought conditions from climate change are a cause of this Hellscape fire. California climate change scientists explain dryness and winds in the Southern California fires:[297]

The way to think about vapor pressure deficit is that it is the drying power of the air, said John Battles, a UC Berkeley forest ecology professor.

Readings from Jan. 8 show an extreme deficit across much of inland Southern California. Such conditions can draw much of the moisture from living plants, so **fires become almost unstoppable once they start**.

When it's that dry, wind has ultimate power, said UC Merced climatology professor John Abatzoglou. (Emphasis added.)

Climate change has accelerated since the 2018 IPCC warning. A 2021 video report by MSNBC, titled, "Extreme Weather Is 'New Normal' Thanks To Decades Of Climate Inaction," cites fires in the western US and Canada creating smoke in the eastern parts of the US. And, an Australian news report talks of climate change fingerprints.[298]

Acceleration fingerprints are real. Seas are warming faster than expected. Ocean heat records are broken. The US experienced severe heat, fires and storms in 2024. NASA reports that the past few years have seen:[299]

> a strong decrease in the Arctic sea ice cover and modeling results that indicate that global warming is amplified in the Arctic on account of ice-albedo feedback. This results from the high reflectivity (albedo) of the sea ice compared to ice-free waters.

Soon after Hurricane Helene left over 200 dead in the US, "Hurricane Milton exploded from a Category 1 storm into a Category 5 storm over the course of 12 hours," which stunned climate scientists and meteorologists, the Atlantic reported. Climate change was turbocharging Hurricane Milton, the DW channel in Germany reported in October 2024. And, CNN reported in October 2024:[300]

> The impact of two catastrophic hurricanes in the last two weeks has underlined that rapid climate change is a threat that can do far more damage to American lives than traditional antagonists such as terrorists and authoritarian states.
> The monster Hurricane Milton has left parts of Florida reeling and climate scientists are in no doubt that the strength of such storms is increased by rapidly warming oceans.
> This comes two weeks after Hurricane Helene significantly damaged communities like Asheville, North Carolina, hundreds of miles inland, that were seemingly immunized from the worst effects of climate change. Helene killed at least 232 people.

In early July 2024, the earliest Category 5 hurricane on record, Hurricane Beryl devastated some Caribbean islands. Prime Minister Ralph Gonsalves of St. Vincent and the Grenadines pointed out the US failure: **"The developed countries, the major emitters, are not taking this matter seriously."**[301]

As shown in (3) below, the US leaders fail to take appropriate action.

3. Do the facts show any Signature Techniques for business expansion and access to resources like used against Viet Nam?

Signature Techniques appear of: (a) pursuing short-term profits and advantages but passing the long-term disaster onto the young children of today; and of (b) maneuvering

to reduce other nations' power and gain an advantage for pursuing control.

The Signature Technique of passing the trouble forward to the future of today's young children appears in the recent Inflation Reduction Act (IRA) of the US government. The IRA was a "boon for [the] fossil-fuel sector," The *New York Times* reported. Fossil fuel climate scientist Bill Hare said the continued US expansion of fossil fuel production is **"hypocritical and not at all consistent with the global call to phase down fossil fuels."** (Bold print added.). Under the Act, Pres. Biden even disqualified electrical vehicle subsidies if even one supplier was from China. He snubbed the COP 28 summit, sending only his vice-president, even as global warming worsened.[302]

The IRA is only projected to spend, over a period of 10 years, about $800 billion on climate change and related energy projects, one-tenth of the yearly budget of about $800 billion for military spending. Yet in less than two weeks, the January 2025 Southern California fire damage is estimated at a value of $180 billion or more. That is penny wise and pound foolish.[303]

The IRA failure is pointed out by Prof. Chomsky:[304]

> the Act is a pale shadow of the legislation proposed. . . .
>
> It was cut down step-by-step by 100 percent Republican opposition to anything that might address the most severe crisis of human history—and infringe on their passionate service to extreme wealth and corporate power. Joined by a few right-wing Democrats, GOP radicalism succeeded in removing most of the substance of the original proposal.

A 2016 Atlantic Council study says climate change could "appeal to US national security interests. . ." bringing a "risk of overly nationalistic or militarized solutions. . . ." That means **the**

Signature Technique of pursuing control for business expansion and access to resources by force could be used when global warming disrupts worldwide economic matters. [305]

The US military is the world's biggest contributor of greenhouse gases. Yet the US continues extensive military activity to support its wrongful pursuit of control for business expansion and access to resources.[306]

The Signature Technique of ditching US voters from the facts has resulted in no candid national debate about what will happen to children in the future.

Adults who tell children not to worry about climate change are like the captain of the sinking Sewol Ferry. He told the students to stay below deck. He left the boat, then 250 students drowned in horror.[307]

(9) Creation of unpayable debts in Global South nations as plantation economies creates destabilization
Three-Step Analysis

1. How does the false claim of noble purpose against Viet Nam create the false presumption of noble purpose in a later action?

In the creation of Global South debt, the US has been presumed to have a noble purpose of leading the world to prosperity.

2. Without the false presumption of a noble purpose, what real purpose emerges, considering any common plan report, Signature Technique or other fact?

The real purpose in Global South sovereign debt is the Signature Technique of Destabilization that creates openings for US leaders to move for control for business and resources.

Sovereign debt is debt created by a colonial power as a price for decolonization and independence. It has often been imposed on nations in which colonial powers retained control of significant infrastructure and natural resources. That has hurt the ability of those nations to build their own economies and compete in international trade.

The need for an emerging nation to have a "clean slate" from sovereign debt was explained by the distinguished Mohammed Bedjaoui, President of the International Court of Justice 1994 to 1997. He was Algerian Foreign Minister, ambassador to United Nations, and Special Rapporteur to the International Law Commission. For real independence:[308]

> the free exercise by a people of its right to self-determination . . . was paramount: the exercise of this right was not—and could not be—encumbered by entailed financial obligations (flowing, for example, from the acquired rights of individuals and companies) in the form of debt.

Without a clean slate, a Global South nation cannot use its income to build infrastructure and to pay its citizens a fair wage so its society prospers. If the emerging citizens are forced to make concessions, that violates basic fairness.

For example, *Sovereign Debt Diplomacies* shows that the International Court of Justice held that, for independence for Mauritius, Britain could not require detachment of the Chagos Archipelago. That detachment violated the free will and genuine expression of the will of the people concerned.[309]

3. Do the facts show any Signature Techniques for business expansion and access to resources like used against Viet Nam?

Three-Step Analysis Deletes False Claim

In 1975, US leaders defeated efforts by the G77, a new Third World group, to gain an international agreement on reducing or canceling sovereign debt. Through 2024, US leaders have opposed sovereign debt relief. This was a use of the Signature Technique of Destabilization, which created opportunities for US leaders to move for control, often using force. The US effort in 1975 is exposed in *Sovereign Debt Diplomacies* (2021), a major study showing how debt relief has been denied:[310]

> The cables circulating between Washington DC, Geneva, and sometimes other Group B countries' capitals, show how this entangled problematization of debt was met with increasing hostile reactions from the US and Western countries between 1974 and 1978. During the negotiations, the cables—sometimes signed by Henry Kissinger himself—show a clear opposition to any mechanisms of debt restructuration.
>
> In another cable sent by Washington to delegates in Geneva, the US manifested its intention to oppose any debt relief motions put forward by the G77: 'We see no possibility that the US could participate in schemes for generalized rescheduling of Low and Developing Countries (LDC) debt. This includes funds to refinance commercial debt as well as moratorium type proposals.'

From then into 2024, much of the Global South has been crippled by sovereign debt.

- In Argentina, "public indebtedness increased by US $74 billion, jumping from 49 per cent of GDP to 94 per cent from 2015 to 2019," *Sovereign Debt Diplomacies* reports.[311]

- On Puerto Rico, *Sovereign Debt Diplomacies* shows that debt cancellation is not being considered. That book presents a chapter-long discussion of ways used to enforce repayment by Puerto Rico. (This chapter shows the US approach to debt in the Global South, though Puerto Rico is a "sub-sovereign."). Nowhere is debt relief in the picture.[312]
- Peru's long legal battle over the amounts of its debt is another example of a limited range of relief. No debt cancellation is discussed. Instead, Peru has faced a history of holdout creditors enforcing rights.[313]
- Indeed, the **1865–2024 system of US-French mutual security for control for business expansion and access to resources** produced similar results. For example, the US provided "security" for France, while it claimed economic rights in former colonies. Force was often used. In an extreme case into 2024, the French paid $1/250^{th}$ the value of Niger uranium while much of Niger was in poverty (Chapter 8).
- "In sub-Saharan Africa, 19 countries are unable to make debt payments or are at high risk of reaching that point," Mark Suzman, CEO of the Bill & Melinda Gates Foundation, reported that in 2024, in a *Foreign Affairs* article. That trouble was from the US-backed Congo coup (Chapter 8). Its goal was to prevent the 17 emerging nations—they gained independence that year—from having real independence.[314]

Godfrey Mwakikagile wrote (shown above) of how rich foreign nations have continued to profit from Africa, but postcolonial Africa remains poor:[315]

To a very large degree, their very prosperity depends on perpetuating the status of African countries and other underdeveloped regions of the world as plantation economies for the provision of cheap raw materials to the industrialised world, and as a source of cheap labour for the manufacture of consumer goods for the metropolitan countries.

As 2024 closed, the only relief from the West was whatever largesse the West might grant. Without showing any knowledge of the false nucleus of US foreign policy that falsely posited a noble intent, Suzman follows the US leaders' false reasoning. He posits the solution as:[316]

> Financial decision-makers have opportunities to do better at the upcoming meetings of the United Nations, the IMF, the World Bank, and the G-20. Any solutions they consider should prioritize making low-cost capital available to those countries that cannot access money in any other way. . . .
> If the leaders of global financial institutions and wealthy countries fail to do their part, there is a very real possibility that dozens of countries will languish for a decade or more. But with the right reforms and investments, these countries can provide for their people and outgrow their debt, perhaps for good.

But when the ignoble Signature Technique of seeking control is exposed, the hard-bitten pursuit of control appears. It is for US business expansion and access to resources. Moreover, in Africa, that pursuit has also been driven by virile US racism. The fact of extreme poverty in black nations in Africa is accepted in the US as a normal fact of life, rather than an indication of ongoing Western control for economic advantage.

If the boot of sovereign debt is lifted from the neck of the sub-Sahara and Sahel regions of Africa, they would prosper. Before the boot slammed down, Ghana sent professional and technical assistance to the Congo in 1960. In that mineral-rich nation, prosperity would have become a model for the other 17 emerging nations. But in the US NSC, people said Africans lived in trees and were incapable. The boot slammed down. The clean-slate theory requires the boot be lifted.

(10) Ukraine and Russia. Three-Step Analysis

1. How does the false claim of a noble purpose in Viet Nam create the false presumption of a noble purpose in the other action?

As a preliminary matter, Russia's Vladimir Putin has been doing a criminal invasion of Ukraine. Putin is a gangster, murderer, who has seized power. He has been gutting Russian culture and economics, so that some oligarchs supporting him have become billionaires.

However, the false claim of a noble US purpose on Viet Nam creates the false presumption of a noble US purpose on Ukraine-Russia-US relations.

2. Without the false presumption of a noble purpose, what real purpose emerges, considering any common plan report, Signature Technique or other fact?

The real purpose arises in that US leaders in the 1990s (1) overrode their own 1942 common plan report that said "tripartite cooperation" could lead to beneficial economic

Three-Step Analysis Deletes False Claim

development in Eastern Europe (Ukraine), Russia, and the US; and (2) denied **Russian concerns about invasions** from Eastern Europe. The 1942 report said: [317]

> . . . by the combined influence of Great Britain, the United States and Russia, the Soviet Union would be able to relax the strain of its armaments and to turn its efforts towards realizing the long-deferred promises of a higher standard of living for its own peoples. By controlling German armaments in cooperation with Britain and the United States, and by promoting the pacification and consolidation of East Central Europe through a similar policy of *tripartite cooperation, Russia would be able to devote a far larger share of its industrial effort to the production of goods for consumption.* (Italics added.)

Early cooperation had occurred as World War II ended. The US and Soviets entered the agreement on spheres of influence for each, with Russia gaining dominance over Eastern Europe. (*See, Corporate Tsunami*, Ch 19.)

In 1991, the door opened even wider for *"tripartite cooperation,"* as the USSR and the Warsaw Pact both ended. That removed the main reason for NATO to exist. Prof. Mary Sarotte points out in *Not One Inch* that, "The big play in Europe would have been to create a dynamic that established lasting cooperation, rather than confrontation."[318]

3. Do the facts show any Signature Techniques for business expansion and access to resources like used against Viet Nam?

By 1990, the US common plan worldwide had produced more than 30 coups, wars, and destabilizations advanced US control for business expansion and access to resources. Then,

the possibility of destabilizing Ukraine presented itself to US leaders.[319]

Similar to **ignoring Viet Nam's concern from centuries of shedding blood in defending against invasions**, US leaders **dismissed the Russian concern from shedding blood in defending against invasions from Eastern Europe. Russia's concern for security was known to all US diplomats.** In World War II, Germany invaded Russia through Ukraine and other Eastern European countries. Russia lost 28 million people. So, **US Secretary of State James Baker posed a hypothetical bargain, Professor Mary Sarotte says. In 1990, Baker asked, 'what if you let your part of Germany go, and we agree NATO will "not shift one inch eastward from its present position?"**[320]

But **after the USSR withdrew its troops and the US achieved access to East Germany, US leaders changed from Baker's statement about not extending NATO**, "[T]o hell with that," Pres George H. W. Bush said in 1990. Other US leaders followed suit. By 2009, **US leaders had gradually increased NATO** from 12 members to 28.[321]

The **2008 Bucharest Declaration declared that Ukraine and Georgia "will become members of NATO." This was the breaking point**, *Not One Inch* highlights.[322]

Sarotte points out that an expert on Russia, Stephen Sestanovich wrote in a prescient 1993 op-ed in the *New York Times*, that although doubts existed in "all the many" possibilities proposed for cooperating with Russia, "these doubts are nothing compared with the frustration and powerlessness we will feel once Russian democracy fails."[323]

Conclusion on Three-Step Analysis
on nations, regions, and topics worldwide

For the first time since 1945, US voters have the tools to analyze many foreign policy matters, new and old. The Three-Step Analysis removes the blinders. For, removing the false claim bares real facts.

These real facts show the actual circumstances, unclouded by the false presumption from the US-Viet Nam War, that has asserted that US foreign policy is noble. In many cases, the Three-Step Analysis illuminates facts that show the real reason that US policy causes many foreign people to anger.

Is this a world order in which all states have an equal stake, or is it an American empire that the United States imposes on others? In reality, the American project is and will remain an uneasy combination of the two.

—CFR Senior Fellow Mead (2004)[324]

CHAPTER 9

22 FACTS SHOW PURSUIT OF CONTROL NOT ANTI-COMMUNISM
(Some cites in earlier chapters)

Many facts show that the US activity in Viet Nam enabled by force during 1865–1975 was driven by the policy of pursuit of control for business expansion and access to resources, rather than an effort to fight communism.

The following 22 Facts each show that same policy continued through 1954 and became the real reason for the US-Viet Nam War: the pursuit of control to continue prior business by force. Together, these facts show a strong web of activity advancing that pursuit.

Much like robbing a bank keeps other potential robbers away, this pursuit kept communism at bay.

An overview of the 22 Facts shows that in 1619, American colonial reliance on force for economic advantage began with white colonists receiving black people as slaves, following attacks on Africa. Virtually the sole concern was to create successful farms, plantations, and businesses so the colonies could survive and prosper. That was long before communism became a real concern to US leaders. This system of force for economic advantage continued developing and growing as a policy and practice, despite communism becoming a concern in the US due to the 1848 publication of the *Communist Manifesto*, the October 1917 Revolution in Russia, the "first Red Scare of 1917–1920" (as Prof Colleen Woods describes), and beginning in the 1920s, communists training freedom fighters in Russia from various nations.[325]

1. The 1865–1954 early period of US business in Viet Nam enabled by violence used the Signature Technique of rejecting diplomacy, instead choosing to rely on control for business expansion and use of resources.

Commercial ships from the US had traveled in all the world's oceans since 1785. "Had we been dependent solely upon local business, we should have failed long since," John D. Rockefeller later said. "We were forced to extend our markets into every part of the world."

Between 1886 and 1889, annual profits of Rockefeller's Standard Oil tripled from $15 million to $45 million. A later study concluded that by 1885, an estimated 70 percent of Standard's business was being done abroad.[326]

That pre-1900 tripling of Standard Oil profits illustrates US economic growth based on investments, force, and war: While reaping those profits, Rockefeller invested in railroads, banks, insurance companies, copper, and steel. Later, copper prices rose sky-high due to military use in the US-Viet Nam War. In turn, copper availability from the Congo to US investors was dependent on military force, rather than on the fair trade that would have occurred if, instead of backing the 1960 coup, US leaders had joined Ghana's 1960 initiative in sending professional experts to the Congo upon its freedom from colonial control (Chapter 8).[327]

By the 1890s, the US pursuit of business by force was in competition with nine foreign consuls in Viet Nam (eight European consuls plus Thailand). The pursuit of US economic growth by force where needed—the real engine of US foreign policy—is shown by US consul reports and records on many activities. A sampling shows: US business activities, consular visits to the rubber plantation region north of Sai Gon, and French colonials fighting against some incidents of local, non-communist opposition.[328]

2. During 1945–2024, US leaders "ditched" the public from knowing about the common plan (as shown above), which shows it was for a wrongful purpose, not about a noble effort against communism.

If the common plan had been about opposing communism, US leaders would have trumpeted it to the public. So, not telling the public shows that US leaders knew the common plan was for wrongful control by force, including against Viet Nam.

Moreover, if the common plan had been laudable, it is less likely the leaders would have cut out the public role in foreign policy. Prior to 1940, the public role was to debate and give guidance to the general direction of foreign policy.

3. The common plan set up during 1939–45 was extensive. The goal was for business expansion and secured access to resources, disregarding sovereignty when needed. As this plan operated, the Signature Technique of destabilization created advantages against the Global South.

The 2024 article in the CFR journal admits: "For decades, American presidents have waged illegal wars. . . ." And, as shown above, US leaders waged not only wars but also destabilizations and coups.³²⁹

For those actions, Memo E-B19 called: "to secure the limitation of sovereignty by any foreign nations that constitutes a threat to the minimum world area essential for the *security and economic prosperity* of the United States." That pursuit was different than a purpose of fighting communism.³³⁰

The Three-Step Analysis (Chapter 8) applied to specific countries provides a clear look at facts that produce the same conclusion: The goal was control, not anti-communism.

A central example is: The plan for a world order in the CFR 1939–45 studies included US control in some of the Middle East. The CFR report, "Elements to be Considered in an Oil Policy for the United States" (1944), spoke of using a proxy military force in Israel for secured access to Middle East Oil.³³¹

The reason, Chomsky points out, is:³³²

> . . . in the unfolding new world order of that day. . . **control of the incomparable energy reserves of the Middle East would yield "substantial control of the world"**. . . Washington anticipated that it would end with the United States in a position of overwhelming power . . . **a "Grand Area" that the United States was to dominate.** . . . (Emphasis added.)

The goal of control of the Middle East for oil—rather than to save it from terrorism—thus explains why US leaders in 2023–24 fed arms to Israel during Israel's genocidal killing of 14,000 children.

As a discussion in Chapter 8 shows, the process of decolonization has left much of the Global South with massive debts. The "clean-slate theory" provides the common sense conclusion that self-determination of an emerging nation is not real, if shackled by debts and concessions to the former colonial powers as a price for decolonization. Such control has happened worldwide. Much of the Global South is treated as "plantation economies," as Mwakikagile shows. The false claim by US leaders cloaking the US attack on Viet Nam as noble, also cloaks as noble the ignoble pursuit of control of Global South economies. A noble effort would have recognized that fair trade could not occur if Global South nations were shackled to pay interest, rather than produce infrastructure and income for working citizens. But in 1975, US leaders defeated the G77 effort for debt relief.[333]

4. Gaining economic advantage for white people by using violence against colored people has been a Signature Technique since the beginning of US economics.

Chattel slavery in North America during 1619–1865 was exceptionally cruel. After slavery was abolished, the 1865–1950s period of at least 6,500 lynchings of black US citizens promoted economic advantages for whites. The violence included burnings at the stake. Although the 1964 Civil Rights Act specified equal rights for black citizens, in 1968 the Republican Party offered not to enforce that Act, if white backlash voters voted for presidential candidate Richard Nixon. This "Southern Strategy" has continued through 2024. In 2005 and 2010, former Republican chairpersons admitted that the Party still courted white backlash voters. The term includes overt racists and people with "racial fears," as *Dog Whistle Politics* explains. White racists were in a mob that attacked the US capitol after Republicans lost the 2020 presidential election.[334]

Some schools ban the teaching of the history of race discrimination. An argument for banning, ABC News reports, is: "Proponents say that some lessons blame children for actions of generations past or make them feel guilty for being white."

But that amounts to saying that crimes and wrongdoing cannot be exposed because the exposure makes later people feel bad. However, exposure of wrongs is needed so that society can learn from that history. For example, some US voters claim that on race, the playing field is level. But a 10-to-1 average asset ratio favoring white families over black families exists; it has been caused by long-term white racism. That cannot be understood without knowing the history of US race discrimination. Moreover, some whites have been filmed even as they committed high-profile murders against some black US citizens, such as the murders in 2020 of Ahmaud Arbery and of George Floyd. The thought processes of those murderers necessarily includes perceptions about race relations of prior decades.[335]

Virile US racism appeared early and long in Viet Nam. In 1873 and 1875 US leaders turned down Bui Vien's request for fair trade and no invasion. Those years, US leaders were allowing US black citizens to die in large numbers. Though freed from slavery, the blacks had no land and little food, as the US government gave the land back to the racists rebels who had enslaved the black people. The 1919 US delegation at Versailles denied petitions by Viet Nam and other nations of colored people; the US State Dept refused passports to black leaders to petition at Versailles. A 1924 report by Consul Smith said, "Annamites as a race are very lazy." During those years, white people in the US burned some black US citizens alive. Some of these burnings were in front of crowds. Some burnings were announced ahead of time in newspapers. But US leaders including Secretary of State John Foster Dulles retaliated against black leaders for their 1951 petition, *We Charge Genocide*, to the United Nations. Prof. Angela Davis has cited the "intersectionality" of racism in the US and Africa, and in "US military aggression in Viet Nam." In the 1960s, the US military used the term "gook," inferring that Viet people were subhuman.[336]

5. Viet Nam made numerous overtures for peace, some of which offered to follow US-style institutions and to give the US monopolies. Smaller than California, Viet Nam never posed a threat to US "security." Rather, by refusing Viet Nam's repeated offers of friendship, US leaders showed that they sought control for business expansion, not anti-communism.

With skillful diplomacy accepting these overtures, then working toward mutually beneficial trade, US leaders could have guided Viet Nam to be an ally of the US. The State Dept claimed to have skillful diplomats.

But rejecting the overtures, US leaders followed the common plan in the 682 reports and memos, to move for a world order of control for US business expansion and access to resources. Like Shakespeare's Macbeth, they wanted all the business, plus one more thing: control.[337]

US leaders never told the public about Viet Nam's overtures. US voters never had a chance to apply their traditional role and decide if Ho Chi Minh's childhood under colonial abuses meant he was a nationalist who sincerely wanted friendship with the US.

Viet Nam's overtures for peace included:

- The 1873 and 1875 trips by Bui Vien to Washington were early efforts to peace and mutual trade, rather than the West conducting invasion and war.
- In 1919 at Versailles, the petition that Viet Nam presented was, Duiker states, "fairly moderate in tone." It accepted French control, while calling for election of natives to the French Parliament, equal judicial

protection, and the abolishment of "special tribunals that were instruments of terrorizations."[338]
- In late 1944, Ho Chi Minh became Agent 19 of the US Office of Strategic Services (OSS). He sent intelligence reports to US forces in China, adding that Viet Nam "liked America best."[339]
- After World War II, a US Information Agency (USIA) report said:[340]

> They would like to see their economy geared to our own . . . Above all they want the good will of the American people and our government. From the top of the Annamite leadership to the bottom of the social scale in Tonkin, every person made a visible effort to please American officers and men. They offered courtesies and simple gestures of friendship at every opportunity. . . They inquired about our schools, our courts, our elections, about the workings of both houses of the Congress. They seemed to feel that every American contained within himself all the virtues and accomplishments of the nation they wanted most to emulate.

- 1945–46: Ho wrote eight letters to high US officials, asking for friendly relations. On November 1, 1945 (the day after the US-backed coup in Brazil), Ho's letter to the US secretary of state read:[341]

> [Could I send] to the United States of America a delegation of about 50 Vietnam youths with a view to establishing friendly cultural relations with the American youth on the one hand, and carrying

on further studies in Engineering, Agricultural as well as other lines of specialization. . . . They have been all these years keenly interested in things American and earnestly desirous to get in touch with the American people.

- In 1946, Ho signed an agreement with France. Viet Nam would temporarily be in the French Union. Buttinger says Viet Nam would be part of the French Union as a "free state with its own government, parliament, army, and finances." France agreed to withdraw its troops in five equal yearly amounts, ending in 1952. But the US backed France in continued attacks.[342]
- In 1947, Ho and diplomats tried for four months to convince US leaders to accept a monopoly on Viet Nam's rice exports, second in the world. The offer also included other monopolies and business matters.[343]
- In 1963, Diem floated the idea of a coalition government for unification following the Geneva Accords. The DRV responded favorably.[344]
- In 1966, Ho Chi Minh said, "If they want to make peace then we shall make peace and then invite them to tea afterwards."[345]

6. The US leaders broke the main, operative mechanism of the Geneva Accords—France's exclusive duty to administer the southern half of the single nation of Viet Nam.

They pressured France to leave. France departed. Without France there, the Accords could not function in the southern half of Viet Nam. For example, the Accords prohibited foreign soldiers (US) from entering. But US soldiers entered anyway. And, the Accords called for national elections, which the US canceled through its proxy, Diem.

7. The US claim of not being bound by the Accords is also wrong because the US was bound by the Nuremberg Ruling that prohibited aggressive invasions. It was independent of the Geneva Accords

8. During 1953–54, US leaders did the coup attempt in Viet Nam and three other coups against Brazil, Iran, and Guatemala. Each action was for control for business expansion and access to resources.

The US leaders railed about communism, but that was not the real reason for the illegal coups. On Viet Nam, they have long hidden their 1865–1954 rip-off, so they have never even discussed that real reason for the 1954 coup attempt in relation to the other three coups of 1953–54.

The 1953 overthrow of democracy in Iran was for oil and for the Allen Dulles business deal that Kinzer calls "the largest overseas development project in modern history." When Iran interfered by nationalizing oil and cancelling the Dulles business deal, US leaders joined with Britain in overthrowing Iran's democracy. That left no doubt that the US leaders' real intent was, like in Viet Nam, to pursue control for business expansion and access to resources by force..[346]

US leaders showed a faulty theory for such overthrows back in 1945 on Brazil. Brazil claimed that it, not Standard Oil, had a sovereign right to distribute Brazil's oil. Rejecting sovereignty, the State Dept said the **US did not accept "the theory of operations restricted only to the nationals of any given country."** A crack brigade of combat veterans that had fought under American command in Italy used US-supplied tanks, armored vehicles, and machine guns to oust Brazil's president. The coup gave Standard Oil control of oil distribution.[347]

In 1954 in Brazil, the US-backed military again struck. The

coup kept advantages for Standard Oil and other US companies. That was the driving force, rather than anti-communism.

In 1954 in Guatemala, the government of the poverty-stricken nation claimed a right to buy back unused land that United Fruit owned. The government paid United Fruit according to the land valuations United Fruit had filed for tax purposes. But the Dulles brothers instigated a US-backed coup that ended democracy in Guatemala. Decades of violence have followed.

Those coups show the hard-bitten character of US leaders for economic control of Viet Nam, Brazil (2 coups), Guatemala, and Iran, at the same time that they claimed that the problem in Viet Nam was communism. Claiming communism was the problem in Viet Nam, they never mentioned their hard-bitten, racist, decades long 1865–1954 rip-off of Viet Nam. They even ditched the US public from knowing about their 1943 report calling to keep Viet Nam in "Colonial Relationships."

9. The Nuremberg Ruling prohibited the dioxin spraying because it was done in furtherance of an aggressive invasion. But US leaders sprayed dioxin into the air anyway, causing serious physical injuries.

The use of dioxin was ineffective in the claimed goal of defeating communism: Instead, it angered many. Moreover, the spraying on between 2.1 million and 4.8 million people in 3,181 hamlets was a racial act, because the US never did that to white people.

10. Violation of the Golden Rule.

The aggressive attack by the US on Viet Nam violated the Golden Rule in the axiom on control by force. As the axiom shows, violations cause reasonable people to fight back. The 1946 statement of Isaiah Bowman explains why: forced territorial changes impact "*fairness* which is one of the essential elements of a stable peace" because they "touch the main nerve center of popular feeling" and if unfair, "tragic conflicts result."[348]

That principle of *fairness* is why, throughout history, wrongful attempts to control other people's property and lives has caused severe emotions. The axiom on control by force shows this in violations of the Golden Rule, in Shakespeare's *Macbeth*, Nguyen Du's *Tale of Kieu*, statements by Andre Malraux, Noam Chomsky, and colonial subjects; and by Viet Nam's long history of defeating all invasions.

11. Ho Chi Minh was motivated by his childhood experiences and TOHRAFA.

The French abuses during Ho's childhood, including the deaths of his infant brother from malnutrition and of his mother related to poverty and lack of medical care after hemorrhaging in childbirth, had a lifelong impact on him. Duiker points out that invasion abuses in Ho's childhood gave him a lifelong desire to expel the invaders.[349]

Motivated that way, he went abroad and applied the lesson from the great leader, Phan Boi Chau, that French firepower had isolated Viet Nam's fervent uprisings and defeated them piecemeal. Viet Nam would soon die, unless someone found a new way to overcome piecemeal defeats.

Searching for a way, Ho departed Viet Nam in 1911. In 1920 in France, he found a way. It combined (a) a communist method of secret cells spreading the leadership, and (b) the message that capitalists invade and murder for profit, which resounded in Viet Nam, where capitalists invaded and murdered for profit. Coupled with millions of people proud of the ancient Tradition Of Heroic Resistance Against Foreign Invasion (TOHRAFA), Ho had the key to creating a formidable force. (Chapter 2)

That force made an indelible impression on the US Joint Chiefs of Staff. They said in 1949 that the nationalism "cannot be reversed" and that it "could not be crushed by force."[350]

This confirmed the 1946 lesson from CFR founding director Isaiah Bowman, that violating a nation's territory touches the "main nerve center of popular feeling."[351]

12. In the late 1950s, US proxy Diem enacted the death penalty for a broader range of people than communists.

On August 21, 1956, the illegal Southern zone administration enacted Ordinance Number 47, providing the death penalty for anyone convicted of acting on behalf of any organization designated as communist. This included anyone formerly in the Viet Nam Independence League, whether a communist or not. In communist denunciation sessions, people who did not denounce Ho Chi Minh, the DRV flag, and the Communist Party were seen as acting on behalf of communists.[352]

The 70,000 murders during 1955–60 struck against a broader range of people than communists.

13. Throughout Viet Nam, the resistance fighters were a larger group than the Communist Party.

The overwhelming majority of civilians suffered under the French and US invasions, and they joined when Ho created a nationwide organization with the capability of avoiding piecemeal defeats.

Nguyen Khac Vien points out, "the main driving force" in the resistance war was the French taking over the land and giving it to a few collaborators. Likewise, the US leaders as much as admitted that by their 1943 report on "Colonial Relationships" describing "disaffections which were evident in Indo-China in the prewar decades."[353]

After 1945, Ho Chi Minh appealed for the disaffected people nationwide to work together. Buttinger points out that only Ho, not Diem or any other leader, spoke to the misery of the masses and thus none other than Ho held their allegiance. They participated in highly successful national programs to end malnutrition and illiteracy. Redistribution of land from the French and collaborators ended famine and added to popularity of the government.[354]

The JCS recognized the extensive popular will against the invasion, with the 1949 JCS statements that the nationalism "cannot be reversed" and that it "could not be crushed by force."[355]

In 1960, the National Liberation Front (NLF) formed in Viet Nam's southern half. It was composed of a wide range of groups, many of them not communist.

In 1965 in the South, the CIA agent in Hau Nghia Province northwest of Sai Gon reported, "98 percent of the insurgents in the province were local and that they neither got nor needed substantial aid from Hanoi." General William Westmoreland told a US senator, "The bulk of the Vietcong fighting us in South Vietnam were born and reared in South Vietnam." Indeed, not until May 1959 had work begun on a Ho Chi Minh Trail through the mountains, for support from the north. Substantial help had not arrived right away. Interviews of southerners by this author, for *Corporate Tsunami in Countryside Paradise*, confirm that they knew this was their country and that France and the US had no right to invade. The US State Dept later admitted that the north did not fight in the early years after 1954, but rather waited for the elections that Viet Nam (DRV) was sure to win.[356]

In the People's Army, a focused effort was made "to raise the leadership percentage of Party members in the army from 30 percent in 1966 to 40 percent in 1967," *Victory in Viet Nam*, a book by the People's Army of Vietnam reports. That shows that a high percentage of its soldiers were not communists.[357]

The People's Army applied Ho Chi Minh's understanding that educating the farmers about capitalist aggression was important. Soldiers not in the Communist Party received regular education. The People's Army later said, "Constant education to strengthen our resolve to defeat the American aggressors was a very basic method used to raise the fighting spirit, the determined to fight, determined to win spirit . . ." Indeed, US leaders provided real-time examples of capitalists invading and murdering for profit. The examples were not only in Viet Nam but also worldwide.[358]

By 1965, the US escalations in force had increased Viet Nam's resolve: "Nothing is doing more to lose the war for us than the indiscriminate use of air power," a US official was quoted in a *New York Times* report. The report said, "No one here seriously doubts that significant numbers of innocent civilians are dying every day in South Vietnam. . . ." Nick Turse documented "the indiscriminate killing of South Vietnamese noncombatants—the endless slaughter that wiped out civilians day after day, month after month, year after year. . ."[359]

14. Although advancing socialism was talked about by Ho and People's Army education officers, that was in the face of US leaders who had been at Viet Nam's throat since turning down offers of peace.

15. By the 1960s, business backed by war was still a main focus in US economic planning for Viet Nam.

In the 1960s, John D. Rockefeller III took part in planning a Mekong Basin Development Project. It envisioned a change from farming to create a new industrial heartland. Labor was planned to come from farmers displaced by the US-Viet

Nam War. Chase Manhattan Bank and other banks opened branches in Viet Nam. The president of Chase Far East operations said in 1965 that US troop increases and military actions "have considerably reassured both Asian and American investors."[360]

16. Viet Nam was not integrated into the USSR economy.

Viet Nam had been under control by France from the 1880s to World War II, then under invasion by Japan, then in 1954 under invasion by the US. So, Viet Nam was not integrated into the Soviet economy. The real reason for the war was to keep US business in Viet Nam, enabled by force.

17. In Viet Nam and worldwide, US leaders long claimed to oppose communism or terrorism, but have pursued control for business expansion and access to resources, often by force.

In *Freedom Incorporated* (2020), Prof Colleen Woods highlights that local struggles and progressive movements have often been mislabeled by US leaders as enemies in "a global war against communism." She says this "all too often ignored U.S. imperialist history."[361]

That encapsulates the powerful brothers, John Foster Dulles and Allen Dulles. Though they railed against communism, they knew since at least 1919 that Ho Chi Minh was a nationalist who pleaded for Viet Nam-US friendship. In 1919, they were delegates at Versailles, when the US rejected Ho's moderate petition for gradual freedoms and fair trade—before he found communism. Earlier as children, they had learned from their grandfather and "Uncle Bert" Lansing—their childhood fishing mentors—that colonial control added to US power. Their grandfather, John Foster, had received US consul reports from Viet Nam addressed personally to him as a US secretary of state in the 1890s.[362]

The Dulles brothers were key members of the CFR since the 1920s. The CFR was the "foreign policy establishment," *Newsweek* magazine later observed.

In March 1945, CFR member Nelson Rockefeller, undersecretary of state for Latin American affairs, said no kind of socialism would be tolerated, as it could open the door to communism. He signed, in Mexico, the Act of Chapultepec. It committed the US to train, supply, and indoctrinate the militaries of the rich elites of all "American hemisphere" nations except Argentina.[363]

The Dulles brothers joined the NSC in 1953, as President Eisenhower's secretary of state and CIA chief. All three were CFR members and kept their membership while in office. The CFR was the "foreign policy establishment," *Newsweek* later wrote. CFR member John J. McCloy was known as "chairman of the establishment." The Dulles brothers were on the NSC during the breaking of the 1954 Geneva Accords on Viet Nam and during the 1950s part in the 70,000 killings there. Also, they worked with the committee that had 15 CFR members, as it decided to do the 1954 coup in Guatemala.[364]

Of the 1954 coup in Guatemala, surviving workers later described the US-backed forces:[365]

> they started using that word 'communist.' Before, that word didn't exist. But they called all those who were poor 'communists.' All those who had to work to survive, or who took the land from some rich person, they called communists.

In Guatemala in the 1980s during US President Ronald Reagan's administration, a quota method of killing went beyond communists. The quota method involved killing 30 percent of the people, then offering food and safety to the remaining 70 percent. Reagan had little education about foreign history and cultures, but he followed his advisors. (*See* Chapter 7, above.)

Similarly, a US-backed Argentine general admitted in the mid-1970s: "First we kill all subversives, then we kill all of their collaborators, then those who sympathize with subversives, then we will kill all those that remain indifferent, and finally we will kill the timid."[366]

In Brazil's Amazon, killings of noncommunists included the extermination of the Cintas Largas tribe. They lived in a mineral-rich area of the Amazon. They numbered a few hundred. A Cessna bombed them, then a ground force hunted down and killed the survivors. A participant told this in a Catholic confessional.[367]

After Viet Nam defeated France in 1954, hawkish columnist Joseph Alsop traveled in southern Viet Nam. He then wrote in the 31 August 1954 issue of the *New York Herald Tribune*: "The Vietminh could not possibly have carried on the resistance for one year, let alone nine years, without the people's strong, united support."[368]

18. A 1945 US-Soviet agreement on areas to dominate lessened the chance that the Soviets would intervene in Viet Nam; a 1953 CIA estimate said there was little chance China would intervene.

(*See Corporate Tsunami,* Chapter 19, for extensive discussion and citations.) The 1945 US-Soviet agreement on spheres of influence left large areas of the world under US influence. On a Viet Nam request for help after 1945, a Soviet diplomat wrote, "to be left unanswered." Neither the USSR nor China intervened when US-supplied tanks and US-trained troops crushed democracy in Brazil in 1945, 1954, 1964, and 1968, for control of oil. The 1964 Brazil coup, *The Jakarta Method* observes, established a "violent dictatorship." On Brazil in 1964, Charles Maechling Jr., who led U.S. counterinsurgency and internal defense planning from 1961 to 1966, describes:[369]

> a major initiative in a military coup in Brazil, backed by Washington and implemented shortly after Kennedy's assassination, that instituted a murderous and brutal national security state there.

Reciprocating, the US did not intervene when, in 1948 in the Soviet area, Soviet tanks crushed democracy in Czechoslovakia.

The December 18, 1953 CIA assessment said that if US forces did not operate near Viet Nam's northern border with China, China would be less likely to intervene. Similarly in Korea, China had not intervened until US troops approached the border with China. So, US civilian leaders only put US soldiers into Viet Nam's southern half.

Neither the Soviets nor China intervened in Viet Nam. Like the Soviet non-intervention in Brazil in the face of US-backed violation of sovereignty, this is strong evidence of the existence of the 1945 non-interference agreement between the US and the Soviets.

19. From 1955 onward, many nations emerging from colonialism had a nonalignment policy, so the US could have chosen diplomacy for fair trade and mutual development with them not being in the communist camp. Instead, US leaders often chose the Signature Technique of pursuing control for business expansion and access to resources, often by force.

Upon becoming free in March 1957, Ghana led African nations toward nonalignment. *White Malice* describes:[370]

> This commitment had been a major theme of the Bandung Conference of African-Asian states in 1955 . . . to lay the foundations of a nonaligned 'third force', to resist the pressures from the West and from the East in the context of the Cold War.

In 1960, 17 African nations emerged from colonialism. Thus, when Ghana assisted the Congo in 1960, the US had a real opportunity to work for fair trade and economic development. Skilled diplomats of the US State Department could have worked with Ghana for those goals.

But US leaders backed the overthrow of Congo democracy. Some of the NSC said some Africans still lived in trees. They rejected Lumumba's statement that the Congo had a right to some profits from its minerals to be used for its people's standard of living. But the 1960 coup ended that: Its ripple effects have continued conflicts for control, not fair trade and mutual development, in much of sub-Saharan Africa and the Sahel. That is described by Mwakikagile, Gondola, de Witte and the UN Security Council Panel of Experts. (Chapter 8)

Likewise, US methods were a cause of the splintering and failure of a 2005 initiative to continue the 1955 Bandung Conference attempt at independence for emerging colonies. The 2005 effort was the New Asian African Strategic Partnership (NAASP). Its failure to have real impact, as explained by Dirk Kohnert, Institute of African Affairs (retired), is due to:[371]

> negative developments, including the polarization of Asian countries, the strengthening of political authoritarianism, and regional interventions. In addition,

most countries continued to grapple with economic and political challenges, including poverty, debt burdens, backwardness, ignorance, disease, and environmental degradation. Their access to the markets of the industrialized countries also remained limited.

That "polarization of Asian countries" features the US-backed coups in Thailand and the 1960s bloodbath in Indonesia. In Thailand since 1945, US leaders have backed anti-democratic coups by military-business groups (*khana*). This keeps prices down for exports to the US and Europe. (Chapter 8.)

Indonesia was hit in 1965 by US-backed "apocalyptic slaughter in Indonesia, a young nation littered with mutilated bodies." *The Jakarta Method* continues, describing:[372]

> What happened in Brazil in 1964 and Indonesia in 1965 may have been the most important victories of the Cold War for the side that ultimately won—that is, the United States and the global economic system now in operation. As such, they are among the most important events in a process that has fundamentally shaped life for almost everyone. Both countries had been independent, standing somewhere in between the world's capitalist and communist superpowers, but fell decisively into the US camp in the middle of the 1960s.

20. Despite the 1991 collapse of the Soviet Union and diminishment of communism, US pursuit of control for business expansion and access to resources has continued unabated. It is often unilateral, leading to "unprecedented loss of support throughout the rest of the world for the United States and its foreign policy objectives."[373]

From the 1991 end of the USSR through 2024, US leaders have continued pursuing control by force, hidden by the false claim. But without the existence of the USSR, their argument about the threat of communism made even less sense.

This development exposes the Signature Technique of creation of conflict worldwide, to seek advantage. Some unilateral actions turned into arrogant displays of US power. The effect, as John Lewis Gaddis explains the US since 1990:[374]

> It did, however, intensify unilateralism in several ways: through tactless diplomacy with respect to the Kyoto Protocol on global climate change, the International Criminal Court, and the Anti-Ballistic Missile Treaty... All of this led to an **unprecedented loss of support throughout the rest of the world for the United States** and its foreign policy objectives. The view seemed to be emerging that there could be nothing worse than American hegemony if it was to be used in this way. (Emphasis added.)

The "unilateralism" and "nothing worse than American hegemony" are driven by the nucleus of foreign policy in the false claim of a noble purpose on Viet Nam. That false claim, along with the US public being ditched from basic facts, has given an oligarchy control of US foreign policy. For example, "American hegemony" without public debate led to Niger exposing in 2024 that US "security" was actually for France to pay only $1/250^{th}$ of the market value of Niger uranium. So, Niger kicked the US out in 2024. So much for fault-ridden US power.

21. The cruelty of US leaders' refusals to join world efforts on climate change is a foreign policy choice wholly different than fighting communism or terrorism.

The US leaders' refusal to join the 1997 Kyoto Protocol is indefensible. At that time, a real chance existed to curb global warming. Now the situation is much more desperate. The 2018 warning by IPPC of a 12-year window to take extensive action has gone virtually ignored by the US. And, 99 percent of climate scientists say global warming is partly caused by human use of fossil fuels, and some of the warming could be curbed by human action.[375]

Such failures shrink US leadership in the world. The reactions against the US failure shows that the cruelty is obvious.

22. The pervasive false claim that omits the 1865–1954 US business enabled by force blinds much of the public. It appears in pervasively in society, in schools, books, and voter forums. It misleads many to ignore the business expansion by force. Instead, many unwittingly follow the false call by US leaders to save the world from communism and terrorism.

This information gulf violates the principle of the Pentagon Papers case and of Mead's observation. The public needs true facts on which to base foreign policy. The traditional role of the public was to provide general guidance for the direction of foreign policy.

To provide that general direction, Chapter 7 demonstrates nine sample areas in which the public now has the ability to remove the false claim on Viet Nam. In the new light, the public can see the real facts at play in foreign policy.

Therefore, the public, only now, has the ability to meet its traditional role to give guidance to the general direction of foreign policy.

Conclusion on 22 Facts

Each of the 22 Facts shows a purpose of US leaders for control for business advantage and access to resources. These facts, when combined with other methods such as Signature Techniques, show that no doubt exists as to the real reason for the US-Viet Nam War is as described above.

Leading these 22 Facts, the 1865–1954 period demonstrates that US leaders operated in Viet Nam, enabled by force, for business expansion and access to resources. This was different than anti-communism.

Because US leaders have simply rested on the false claim, they have failed to rebut the 22 Facts. No serious public-government debate about these facts has occurred. Instead, US leaders proceed based on keeping the public fooled by the false claim that says the US entered in 1954.

There are those who are Christians and support free enterprise and there are the others.

—John Foster Dulles (See Endnote 125)

CHAPTER 10

BUSINESS EXPANSION, NOT ANTI-COMMUNISM, HAS ALWAYS DRIVEN FOREIGN POLICY

During 1619–2024, America's economy pursued control for business expansion, often by force, largely independent of anti-communism. In foreign policy, a comparison of anti-communism with other institutional developments and with events, demonstrates that different and stronger forces drove business expansion by force than were found in anti-communism.

American business expansion, often by force, developed for more than two centuries prior to the beginning of US anti-communism in the 1840s. Business expansion was driven in large part by the growth of capital and, in the late 1800s, by corporations. This helped to power US business expansion overseas.

US anti-communism became a vocal and strong domestic political force, but it did not engage with many facts and events that were central to the foreign policy of business expansion by force. Anti-communism used a high level of rhetoric about communist ideology and excesses. But it ignored many facts about wrongs and abuses by the US foreign policy force.

Ignoring the wrongs and abuses in foreign policy confined anti-communism to a rhetoric that was inaccurate on Viet Nam and on much of the world. Prof. Larry Ceplair explains that anti-communism was like a strong religion. A central doctrine was that one camp was "monolithic and evil," while one was "good, motivated by a God-given, light-upon-a-hill moral responsibility for universal welfare." Applying that doctrine to the real reason for the US-Viet Nam War proves that anti-communism was stating the opposite of the reality. For, the proof in this volume of the US committing the Nuremberg violation and the US breaking of the 1954 Geneva Accords conclusively establishes that the US did an immoral and evil rip-off against Viet Nam's welfare, and that Viet Nam did a patriotic defense justified and motivated by the Golden Rule. Indeed, millions of Viet people knew the US was doing a violent, illegal invasion against what was right, good, and fair, the basis of the Golden Rule of religion and ethics.

Anti-communism was in complete error on that matter in this, the biggest US war since World War II.[376]

US anti-communism had far less content than the drive for overseas economic expansion

Anti-communism displayed much less content, structure, and power than did the foreign policy force.

The centuries-long system of US capital development worldwide by force included the 1865–1954 US period in Viet Nam as an important component. American business expansion, often by force, originated in 1619 in slavery for profit, in which anti-communism was not a factor. This motive has continued through 2024 as a force independent of anti-communism.

Business Expansion, not Anti-Communism, Has Always Driven Foreign Policy

In the late 1700s slavery increased in numbers and brutality—such as dismemberment on disobedient slaves. This alone shows a building block that endured through 2024: The use of force for economic gain.

By the end of the century, the American Revolution had nothing to do with anti-communism. Instead, it was in large part about unfair government doing taxation without representation. The emerging US governmentcontinued relying on economic growth using slavery. While anti-communism started in the 1840s and grew for a century and a half into the 1990s, the business expansion by force principle still drove the US economy. For example, the post-Civil War domination of black US citizens utilized at least 6,500 murders curing 1865–1950s without convictions. A main purpose of that domination was to keep economic advantages for whites. The work of Sherilyn Ifill, cited herein, conclusively demonstrates that. The simultaneous 1865–1954 US business rip-off of Viet Nam, enabled by the French colonial rip-off there, is no surprise. In those event, no historical record exists of a purpose of anti-communism.

Beginning in the 1840s, a debate erupted among US leaders, comparing capitalism with communism and socialism. In 1846, Horace Greeley of the *New-York Tribune* "feuded with fellow Whigs who viewed socialism as a dangerous threat to the traditional family, property, and social stability," a 2005 study by Adam-Max Tuchinsky describes. In 1848, the publication of the *Communist Manifesto* and the occurrence of the French Revolution sharpened this debate. Greeley provided a voice for communism, socialism, and varieties of social democracy, as alternatives to capitalism. Greeley's *Tribune* invited Karl Marx to take part. The *Tribune* published over 400 articles from Marx, as the debate raged for more than a decade.[377]

On the opposing side, as Tuchinsky describes, the *New York Courier* and *Enquirer* extensively criticized communism and socialism. The Enquirer said that socialism told workers "that society owed them employment, with ample wages; -and that they would never enjoy their rights until the present order of things should be overthrown."[378]

By the late 19th century, US leaders resolved that the US must follow capitalism. They poured great energy and investments into capitalist activity overseas. Worldwide, including in Viet Nam, US consuls sought out opportunities, large and small, for US businesses. Consuls filed regular and special reports on economic factors. The State Dept marked many of these reports for publication. Summaries and some details appeared in daily advance sheets. These were bound into weekly volumes and distributed in the business community. On Viet Nam, State also forwarded contents of rice reports to the Department of Agriculture and the Bureau of Statistics.[379]

Major US corporations entered Viet Nam early. Rockefeller banking interests entered Viet Nam by 1884, shown by Standard Oil's presence. U.S. Rubber, a Morgan Bank Company, had a presence in Viet Nam in 1917. He was David Figart, a buyer for General Rubber, which had formed in 1904 to provide rubber for U.S. Rubber.[380]

By the end of the 19th century, US businesses had expanded greatly, using investments and expertise. In 1901, for example, Morgan Bank financed the merger of 28 companies to form United States Steel (U.S. Steel), the first US corporation capitalized at over $1 billion. In 1903, U.S. Steel Export Company formed to handle its exports. By 1913, U.S. Steel annual exports increased from $100 million to $305 million. While these exports went mainly to Europe and South America, not Viet Nam, this illustrates capital, expertise, and corporations as a main driving force in the US economy; anti-communism was a factor in the thoughts of US leaders, but it was not a main driving force such as the drive for exports of steel and a large array of other commodities.[381]

Further illustrating the predominance of business expansion by force, rather than anti-communism, at the 1919 Versailles Peace Conference, the main two factors behind the US leaders rejecting the moderate petitions of Viet Nam and other colonies for gradual independence were (1) business expansion by force, and (2) virile racism. The corporate connections are extensively documented. On race, President Woodrow Wilson was very racist, even by the standards of the time. Other leaders displayed racism as well.

US and Western leaders rejected the petition by Ho Chi Minh for Viet Nam to gain gradual independence and fair trade. Their denial was on economic and racial grounds. One form of evidence of this is that Ho Chi Minh was not yet a communist. He simply presented what Duiker calls a moderate petition. It did not contain bombastic rhetoric. But the skin of Ho and his fellow citizens had a yellow color.

On coups in Central America and South America, business expansion by force—amid superficial anti-communist rhetoric—was by far the predominant purpose. Guatemala is illustrative. In 1906, the secret US mapping of Guatemala's interior, with notes on many factors on economic potential, was followed by the United Fruit Company gaining dominance over the economy by 1928. Poverty amid Western profits led Guatemala to reject the US method: Reacting against US dominance that created poverty, Guatemala established a democracy in the early 1940s. It began to reclaim some idle land of United Fruit. So US leaders brought a coup. Little influence of communism was present. But, even as the coup killed thousands of workers and United Fruit retained control of lands, US leaders falsely said they were saving the nation from communists.

Guatemala was part of a broad effort for US business expansion by the foreign policy force in Viet Nam, Central America, and the Pacific. This supports a conclusion that the ongoing policy of expansion would have occurred even if anti-communist rhetoric had not occurred. So, the expansion was an independent force.

US anti-communism during 1920s into 1950s

From the 1920s onward, US anti-communism developed as a strong domestic political force. In the 1920s, 32 states passed laws making it a felony to display a red flag in a public place. In 1934, Congress established a Special Committee on Un-American Activities. The head of the National Civic Federation urged it to "smash" communism in the US. A Gallup Poll showed that 74 percent of Americans wanted "to weed out those who want to overthrow the American system."[382]

In the late 1930s, Congress approved of committees to investigate communism. As the Chairman of a Special Committee on Un-American Activities (1939–45), Martin Dies explained, "exposure in a democracy of subversive activities is the most effective weapon we have in our possession." His Special Committee investigated Hollywood and labor, then he introduced three anti-subversive bills into Congress. Lacking much proof, they failed. Ceplair reports that Dies continued to expose some people by "pitiless publicity."[383]

In 1944, the National Association of Manufacturers appointed a committee to investigate "the menace of socialism in Europe." Into the 1950s, the House Un-American Activities Committee (HUAC) investigated virtually every profession. The FBI's J. Edgar Hoover warned the public that Communists were operating in most walks of life. A Soviet émigré, novelist

Ayn Rand, criticized communism as the "most urgent conflict of our times: the individual against the collective. . . .".[384]

A January 8, 1951 headline in The *New York Times* read: "Truman Warns Free World Must Arm to Meet Threat of Russian Conquest." Neither The *Times* nor the anti-communist movement mentioned Truman's reversal of FDR's policy of independence for Viet Nam.[385]

After World War II, the predominant force driving US policy overseas was still the pursuit of US business expansion by force

1. 1945 US-USSR agreement implemented mutual US-USSR respect for each other's power

The possibility of US-USSR conflict was greatly reduced by a 1945 agreement on areas for each to dominate, although anti-communists generally ignored this agreement. Anti-communists focused on things on which conflict did continue: ideology, some economic rivalries, and scientific achievements including nuclear abilities. On domination, anti-communists inaccurately styled the USSR as the bad guy and the US as the good guy, rather including the US as a bad guy in its pursuit of business expansion by force shown in this volume.

In 1945, the US and USSR agreed not to interfere with each other's "security interests." This agreement was made during the February 1945 Yalta Conference and the May 1945 UN formation conference. The lead US negotiator was the "chairman of the Establishment," international corporate lawyer John J. McCloy (CFR director 1953–72).

The agreement allowed the Soviets to dominate their border areas and the US to dominate areas the US saw as needed for security and economic health.

The Soviet part was seen as justified, as the Soviet Union had been invaded through Eastern Europe. The Soviets had lost about 28 million people in the war, while defeating two German invasions and wresting Eastern Europe from them. Neil Sheehan pointed out that rather than the US giving away the region, the Soviets held control of Eastern Europe by their wartime efforts, and the agreement recognized this. It was "a peace that permitted Soviet hegemony over Eastern Europe...." observed David Halberstam.[386]

The agreement allowed the US to dominate what the War and Peace Studies called a "Grand Area." It included the Western Hemisphere, the former British Empire including Middle East energy sources (with the British in a junior relationship), parts of Western Europe, southern Europe's sea lanes to the Middle East, and other parts of the Third World. Viet Nam was part of that Third World. Indeed, the USSR declined to intervene during 1945–1975, when the US attacked Viet Nam.[387]

On the US domination, silence from the anti-communist movement shows that it did not explain a major part of the US system. The US part has been called a "world order" by Senator John McCain, Henry Kissinger (Chapter 4) and others. The world order, the 2004 book by Mead pointed out, brought "inequality, instability. . . ." and condemnation by much of the world in a "majority verdict."[388]

Despite the US-USSR agreement, some points of friction with communism continued. In August 1946, the USSR demanded equal partnership with Turkey in managing the straits of the Dardanelles. US leaders sent an aircraft carrier through the Dardanelles. The USSR backed down.[389]

But in large part, US and USSR did not intervene in each other's areas under the agreement. In 1948, the Soviets crushed Czechoslovakia, but US leaders did not intervene. Over the years, the Soviet military quelled uprisings in Eastern Europe, such as in Hungary and East Germany, without US

Business Expansion, not Anti-Communism, Has Always Driven Foreign Policy

intervention. In the mid-1950s, Soviets dismantled CIA networks that the Dulles brothers had set up in Poland, Ukraine, and Albania, but the US avoided direct confrontation.[390]

In 1945, the US implemented the US-USSR agreement. An October 30, 1945 coup gave US corporations power in Brazil. Standard Oil controlled Brazil's oil distribution. Brazil claimed, as a sovereign nation, the right to control its oil distribution. The State Department said that the US did not accept "the theory of operations restricted only to the nationals of any given country." A Brazilian Army brigade that had fought in Italy under the US attacked, using US-supplied tanks, armored vehicles, and machine guns. They installed a dictatorship that favored US corporations.[391]

US leaders suppressed movements for democracy. A Greece democracy movement included people who had fought against the Nazis, but US leaders suppressed this movement, killing 160,000 people. This "defense of Greece against its own population," Chomsky illuminates, gave US investors and Nazi collaborators an advantage. In Italy, US leaders suppressed a democratic movement. In Venezuela in 1948, US leaders fomented a coup to benefit oil companies, among others, ousting the democratically elected president and using torture. In Germany, they spirited some Germans away by a "ratline" saving them from war crimes trials. Some arrived in the US to develop weapons such as dioxin (see below). Some arrived in South America and taught torture.[392]

Neither the Soviets nor China intervened in Viet Nam as the US unleashed tremendous destructive power in the invasion that violated Nuremberg. After 1945, Viet Nam sent numerous requests to the Soviet Union for help, which were ignored. About one such cable, a Soviet diplomat wrote, "to be left unanswered." Also, the CIA had predicted that if US troops did not venture near Viet Nam's border with China, Chine would be unlikely to intervene.³⁹³

2. US part is described in "blueprints" for a world order with US business expansion. Anti-communist silence on this exposes a major flaw in anti-communist rhetoric.

The US part of this world order recognized that the US had emerged from the war, as Prof Chomsky observes, "in a position of power that had no historical parallel." The US controlled 50 percent of the world's resources and had overwhelming military and industrial power, while other industrial nations had suffered serious war damage.³⁹⁴

The areas the US was to dominate largely matched areas covered in the 682 CFR War and Peace Studies reports and memos of 1939–45 (Chapter 4). These were "blueprints," Prof Laurence Shoup says. They set up a system to limit the sovereignty of other nations where needed for US "economic prosperity."³⁹⁵

Those CFR blueprints guided State Dept foreign policy. In 1971, *Newsweek* said, "The foreign policy establishment of the US was the CFR leadership."³⁹⁶

US business expansion, often by force, is a main thread in other War and Peace reports. Three reports spoke of controlling countries until US leaders deemed them to have developed sufficient economic and political institutions.³⁹⁷

Despite that goal, the foreign policy force instead told the US public that anti-communism was the purpose of the 1954 coup ousting democracy in Guatemala.

Interlocks of CFR and government were extensive. Key CFR members on the coup were John Foster Dulles and John J. McCloy. "Chairman of the Establishment," McCloy sat on the CFR and United Fruit boards. The CFR had 15 members, including the Dulles brothers, on a committee that decided on the coup for United Fruit's benefit. The Committee Chair was Frank Altschul of the CFR and of Lazard Freres bank. Lazard was connected with French financier Gustave Homburg, who had major rubber plantation investments in Viet Nam. About 15 days of war ensued in Guatemala. It ended on June 27, 1954, after having killed 9,000 Guatemalans. About 7,000 were jailed, and the coup led to over 18,000 workers being fired.[398]

Detailing more CFR interlocks on Guatemala, Prof Shoup says, "Also serving on the United Fruit board were three other Council members."[399]

3. Targeting Viet Nam for business expansion by force was part of the common plan, but this was never discussed in public by the anti-communist movement.

In the common plan, five reports in the early 1940s show business expansion by force in Viet Nam. Also, in the late 1940s, State planning documents show that Viet Nam was to provide resources for Marshall Plan reconstruction of Europe. Early 1940s reports:[400]

1. 1941 report said Viet Nam posed "no great problems" to being in a US trading system along with Japan;
2. 1942 report recommended using a Viet Nam port to control the South China Sea;
3. A Sept 14, 1943 report, called "to *secure access* to the trade and raw materials of the region." (Italics added.);
4. A Nov. 16, 1943 report called to seize Viet Nam to continue "Colonial Relationships." But the report said it would require "a long and disastrous period of repression";

5. A year-end review by the CFR Steering Committee said that the Nov. 16, 1943 report meant "there should be a continuance of the French Colonial Regime in Indo-China."

Following those five reports, the targeting by bombing and by dioxin chemicals shows ongoing planning. It was by a corporate-military-scientific structure. This is illuminated in a direct connection between the NSC, DARPA, and the US Army Chemical Corps poison program of the CIA. (See Chapter 7.)

Evidence that those reports were part of a plan to target Viet Nam to support business expansion was that during 1960–75, US leaders used on Indochina, mostly on Viet Nam, the **heaviest bombing and use of explosives in history**. This matched the requirement for "a long and disastrous period of repression." It included more than three times, by weight, of the bombs and explosives used by the US in all of World War II. In Indochina, the US used explosives equal to 640 times the power of the Hiroshima atomic bomb. Most of it was dropped on the southern half of Viet Nam.[401]

The dioxin spraying during 1961–71 occurred during this targeting Viet Nam. It was sprayed on people in such quantities that during 2024, Viet Nam had an estimated more than 100,000 child victims living with birth defects caused by Agent Orange/dioxin/toxins sprayed by the US.

Business Expansion, not Anti-Communism, Has Always Driven Foreign Policy

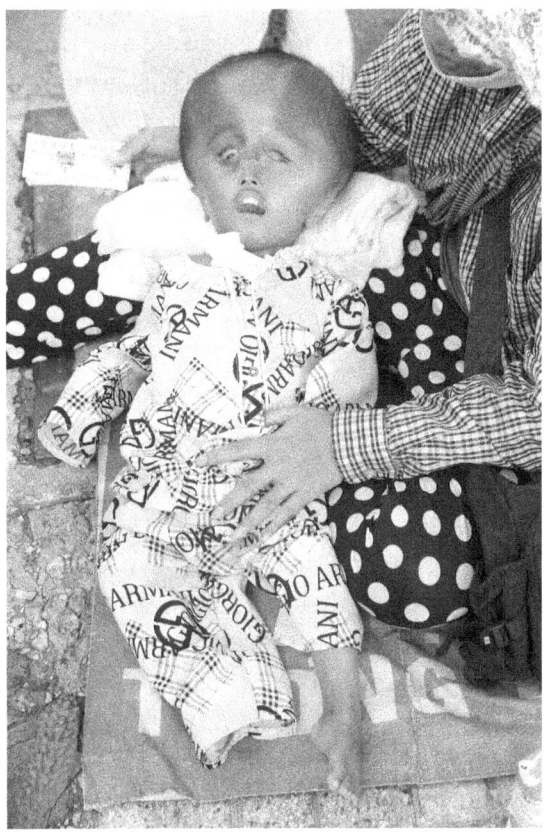

This dioxin victim in Viet Nam in 2021 rests in his mother's lap as she sells tickets by the roadside. He exhibits hydrocephalus, which is on the US government list of conditions presumed caused by dioxin. Where such conditions are found in descendants of US soldiers, the US government pays them, but it does not pay children in Viet Nam who have the same conditions.

Photo 2021 by Daniel Sebold.

In addition to the damage to the children, Viet Nam estimated that in 2020, about 3 million people had some effect from Agent Orange/dioxin/toxins sprayed by the US during the war. (See VAVA cites in this volume and in *Corporate Tsunami in Countryside Paradise*.)

4. Many more facts about the Grand Area are not even stated by anti-communists.

The extensive study by Professor Ceplair says of anti-communists: Their belief is based on "shaky assumptions".[402]

They simply omit most of the **22 Facts** in Chapter 9. The 1865–1954 US business in Viet Nam is conspicuously absent. So is the 1943 report calling for disastrous repression to keep Viet Nam in "Colonial Relationships." Among the 22 Facts, a 2024 article in *Foreign Affairs* admits: "For decades, American presidents have waged illegal wars. . . ." US leaders waged wars and over 100 destabilizations and coups. During 1946–2000, "the United States undertook more than eighty election interferences around the world," Prof Chomsky reports. Those include the 1956 elections in Viet Nam that the US canceled. But anti-communists simply fail to explain those.[403]

Anti-communists regularly failed to talk about the **Sequence and Logic in the Life of Ho Chi Minh.** No doubt exists that childhood events made him an impassioned patriot, as Duiker points out.

The weakness of anti-communist rhetoric is underscored by its failure to discuss the clear fact that the 1954 Geneva Accords kept Viet Nam as one nation, north and south, in which the overwhelming majority opposed the colonial invasions by France and the US.

The **Axiom on Control by Force** applies to Viet Nam's resistance war. Viet Nam was an independent nation with a harmony-based ancient religion connected to harmony in nature that guided most villagers to be downright nice people. Many courageous Viet soldiers resisting the US invasion were patriots not in the Communist Party. The ten young women martyrs of Dong Loc were not members of the Party (Chapter 6).

Like them, millions of Viet Nam villagers in the southern half took part in defeating France in the 1945–1954 war. After

Business Expansion, not Anti-Communism, Has Always Driven Foreign Policy

the 1954 Geneva Conference, they did not disappear. When US soldiers attacked in the 1960s, those millions fought back. US soldiers on the ground found out the hard way. General Maxwell Taylor puzzled in 1964: [Their] "amazing ability to maintain morale . . . continuously to rebuild their units and to make good their losses . . . one of the mysteries of this guerrilla war [for which] we still find no plausible explanation." However, the obvious explanation is that Viet Nam being one nation, when resistance fighters died in the south, more southern villagers replaced them.[404]

In Viet Nam's northern half, many young people not members of the Communist Party joined the Peoples Army, motivated by the wrongful US invasion. Some later joined the Party. Each military unit had a party chapter. For example, in his northern village area, Tran Ngoc Tho was known since age 14 as a courageous and strong youth. At age 17 in 1965, he was elected as Militia Platoon Leader in his village. He joined the Peoples Army in 1966. After many battles, he was a highly decorated soldier. In 1967, the Peoples Army worked to increase the percentage of Party members in leadership roles from 30 percent to 40 percent. Thus in 1968, Tho, a recognized leader in combat, was invited to become a Party member.[405]

After graduating from a medical university in Ha Noi, Doctor Dang Thuy Tram volunteered in December 1966 to join the army and serve in the south. During three years of courage in a clinic in a free fire zone, she wished to join the Party. But she was not initially accepted. Finally, she was invited to join. On June 22, 1970, she was killed by rifle fire by a US platoon.[406]

A conclusion is that the foreign policy force had strong, wide-ranging structure independent of anti-communism, while anti-communism, though it grew as a strong domestic political force, used woefully inaccurate rhetoric that omitted many events and facts. It had some influence on the foreign policy, but far less than the influence and operation of the many component parts of the foreign policy force. In contrast to anti-communism, the many structural forces in the foreign policy force established significant positions and took strong steps in foreign policy. This included strong development of foreign economic policy in the pursuit of profits through business expansion, often by force. Anti-communism did not change the character of the foreign policy force for business expansion, often by force, that developed from 1619 onward.

5. Southeast Asia and East Asia nations were subjected to the same foreign policy force pursuit of business expansion by force, while US anti-communism continued to fail to mention key facts.

In addition to Viet Nam and Thailand (Chapter 8), Korea, and China-Taiwan were subjected to US business expansion by force.

Korea. The US and USSR came face to face as World War Two ended in 1945. Their armies occupied the southern and northern parts, respectively. At the same time, many Koreans clamored for independence from foreigners, after having been a colony of Japan.

Anti-colonial sentiment in Korea had developed after Japan seized Korea as a protectorate in 1905 and annexed it in 1910. A nationalist movement grew. That movement remained strong after the 1945 defeat of Japan in World War II. By 1946, popular unrest grew at still being subjected to foreign control. Many Koreans wanted Korea for Koreans. The unrest against foreign control was aggravated by inflation, government collection of rice, and the failure of land reform.

Allan R. Millett points out: "One cannot deny the existence of a popular Korean rage in 1946."[407]

Millett shows that US leaders acted to crush that movement's wish for independence. A Korean civil war broke out in the 1940s. US-backed forces killed 30,000 to 100,000 people. They mislabeled many independence-minded Koreans in the South as leftists. This paralleled the US leaders' illegal denial, in violation of the Nuremberg Ruling, of Viet Nam's legitimate wish for independence.[408]

Leading the mislabeling was John Foster Dulles. In 1950, as an Ambassador at Large to the State Department, he visited Korea. Dulles did not show support for the Korean independence movement, instead he backed a US proxy, Syngman Rhee, a Christian graduate of three US universities. The view of Dulles—to oppose "the others," who were not Christians for free enterprise—harmed the possibility of Koreans gaining independence. Instead, other US power backed Rhee. He fit the Dulles mold.[409]

China and Taiwan Without the presumption of noble action in Viet Nam, facts show that the US conflict over China and Taiwan developed as a result of US colonialism, but US anti-communists ignore or excuse these facts. After the US gained independence from Britain in 1783, a US merchant ship, *Empress of China*, entered China in 1784 and announced US business by firing a 13-gun salvo. The 1844 US-China Treaty of Wanghia and the 1842 Treaty of Nanking opened China to the West. In 1854, the US Yangtze River Patrol was founded. In 1866, five US gunboats operated on the Yangtze. In contrast, no Chinese gunboats were on the Mississippi River in the US.[410]

In 1895, John Foster, grandfather and colonial teacher of the young Dulles brothers, traveled to Shimonoseki, Japan, where he became involved in the Shimonoseki plot to overthrow China's dynasty. The effort failed. But he continued trying to increase US influence in China. In 1903, John Foster wrote of the region including Viet Nam that "recently acquired territorial possessions in the Pacific Ocean, have given new interest and importance to the international relations of the United States with the Far East."[411]

A US Congress report on US soldiers in China says:[412]

1912–1941 China. The disorders which began with the overthrow of the dynasty during the Kuomintang rebellion in 1912, which were redirected by the invasion of China by Japan, led to demonstrations and landing parties for the protection of U.S. interests in China that continued from 1912 on to 1941. The guard at Peking (Beijing) and along the route to the sea was maintained until 1941. In 1927, the United States had 5,670 troops ashore in China and 44 naval vessels in its waters. In 1933 the United States had 3,027 armed men ashore. The protective action was generally based on treaties with China concluded from 1858 to 1901.

Of 1927 in China, U.S. Marine Corps Major General Smedley Darlington Butler, the most decorated Marine in U.S. history at that time, wrote, "I was a racketeer, a gangster for capitalism . . . In China in 1927, I helped see to it that Standard Oil went on its way unmolested. . ."[413]

China's reaction under Axiom on Control by Force
At the 1919 Versailles Conference, China and many colonies learned that nonwhite nations could not expect independence. John Paton Davies pointed out that China in 1924–25 had small, organized opposition to imperialism, as well as against warlord control. Most opposition was among some groups of

Business Expansion, not Anti-Communism, Has Always Driven Foreign Policy

students and workers, and a few communists. Chiang Kai-shek came to head a nationalist Kuomintang. Mao Tse-Tung realized that millions of farmers, rather than city workers, would be a major force in a revolution. In 1924, Mao started organizing farmers. Large numbers were ready and willing to revolt.[414]

In June 1926, Chiang led his army to some victories against warlords. But, Davies points out, Chiang went further and smashed many of the communist-nationalists of Mao.[415]

By the time of China's 1945–49 civil war, Davies explained, China's nationalists and communist-nationalists had organized more extensively. But US leaders used the Signature Technique of failure to engage in diplomacy with those elements. This eliminated a chance of the US helping China to become a developing nation free of imperialism. Thus, as Ceplair concluded: "It is not factually correct to say that the United States "lost" or "surrendered" China to the Communists." Instead, the US failed to connect with people in China who, under the Axiom on Control by Force, were in a normal human reaction to imperialism (and warlordism).[416]

Davies noted that rather than being controlled by Russia, Mao and China's communist movements "were intensely Nationalistic." In contrast, Chiang Kai-Shek was "selfish and corrupt, incapable, and obstructive," as reported by John S. Service, a longtime foreign service office in China. Backing the corrupt Chiang, Truman created what Davies called "self-inflicted wounds." Showing himself a novice on foreign policy, Truman said in early 1946, "We should rehabilitate China and create a strong central government there." That showed no insight and no ability, Davies pointed out, writing in 1972 about the US disaster in Viet Nam. He observed that China had 10 times the population and 30 times the area. Truman's comment showed that a US president lacked education in history and foreign affairs.[417]

Upon becoming Secretary of State in 1953, John Foster Dulles cleaned house of diplomats who criticized Western colonialism in Asia. Dulles fired John Paton Davies for "bad judgment" and "security" concerns though Davies had explained China with accuracy. Dulles also criticized John S. Service, who had argued that the Communist leader Mao Tse-Tung was well-liked, and that Nationalist leader Chiang Kai-Shek was "selfish and corrupt, incapable and obstructive." Davies and Service had tried to find ways for the US to work with Mao. So, US leaders continued backing the corrupt Chiang. Chiang lost China's civil war. His Kuomintang fled to the island of Taiwan. And, Dulles used the Signature Technique of Ditching the public from facts.[418]

After the Viet Nam War ended, US anti-communists, though having big holes in their factual knowledge, strained to criticize the Left.

In the 1980s, despite the lack of knowledge about the real reason for the war, many people defended anti-communism and criticized opponents of that war. Ceplair says one book "described and analyzed every component of the 'radical left'" in the United States." Another described 1,200 participants in a conference titled, "Anti-communism and the US" as "idiotically happy" and having "just crept out of the woodwork." "They [the participants] fluttered back to their nesting places in academia, the alternative press, college campuses, the Rainbow Coalition, senior centers, progressive unions, and Communist Party headquarters, dedicating to wiping out that nasty word [anti-communism]." Similarly, the Tiananmen Square Massacre in China convinced some new anti-communists that in the US, "New Left Revisionists" were wrong. In the 1990s, Guenter Lewy wrote that although the Communist Party was no longer a threat to US national security, the "New Left" made "exculpatory explanations" that "served to conceal the harsh essence of the Communist ideology." He claimed to see, as Ceplair describes it, a "'profound lack of moral integrity' in the intellectuals who were or are sympathetic to Communists, and labeled anti-communism 'a moral imperative.'"[419]

Anti-communists used simplistic logic on both the US and overseas: They said communism is bad, therefore where anyone reacts against the US system, it must be because of bad communism, rather than against US business by force.

Conclusion on business expansion by force predominant, rather than anti-communism.

Though many forces and developments were behind US business expansion by force in Viet Nam and worldwide, US anti-communists failed to even mention many. The wide-ranging proof of the forces and events includes the 1619–2024 US business expansion by force, with blueprints from the intensive studies of 1939–45 preparing the world order. And, the 1945 US-Soviet agreement on areas to dominate were key.

The false claim hiding the real reason for the US-Viet Nam War has long been the predominant driver of US foreign policy, but anti-communists generally omit this topic.

More proof arises in the point of view of Viet Nam, which was a natural reaction under Golden Rule analysis. This point of view coincides with growth of opposition to US foreign policy. This opposition is in the form of blocs of nations, and of opposition in individual nations. But anti-communists take pains not to mention the justification of Viet Nam and other nations.

Ceplair is correct in saying of anti-communists: Their belief is based on "shaky assumptions".[420]

PART III

US PUBLIC REDEMPTION?

All of this led to an unprecedented loss of support throughout the rest of the world for the United States and its foreign policy objectives.

—John Lewis Gaddis (2005)[421]

First to fight for right and freedom
And to keep our honor clean

—US Marine Corps Hymn

CHAPTER 11

US CIVILIANS FALL SHORT ON SOLDIERS' PLEA

MANY US soldiers returned from the US-Viet Nam War, agonizing, motivated to find out why the US had been in a war that required killing millions of villagers. Viet Nam Veterans Against the War formed in 1967. It pointed out that "the American people had not been told the truth concerning the nature of U.S. involvement." Surely, civilians would join soldiers in searching for the real reason for that war.

After all, the war had killed and wounded plenty of US soldiers, too. Woody Rumbaugh (see Preface) would have lived on, if the US had not attacked Viet Nam. So would the rest of the 58,281 who died. Their families would not have been hurt by their deaths. The same would be true for the approximately 3.5 million citizens of Viet Nam who died, and of the hurt to their families.

Some veterans told the public they had realized the US government had lied. The lie had pitted them against millions of villagers who had fought back against the US invasion. Soldiers testified about atrocities they had committed, trying to stop the villagers. Edward Sowders testified in a Congressional Hearing:[422]

> We'd been taught to believe that they were all fanatical, and that they were all VC or VC sympathizers, even the children. Many of us, however, began to understand through our personal experiences in Viet Nam the depth of the lies and deceptions practiced upon us and the American people by our country's leaders.

Many veterans tried to convince the public that the government had lied. About 2,000 veterans gathered in Washington and hurled their war medals at the Capitol steps. They hurled epithets, too. Surely the public would respond. Indeed, the veterans had been drafted from the public.[423]

But the false claim prevailed: Even these veterans did not know of the 1865–1954 US business activity in Viet Nam, enabled by force. That was the hidden explanation for the otherwise unexplainable, 1955 US attack. So, most of the public accepted the government's false assertion that the US had entered with a noble intent in 1954. They returned to their jobs and personal lives. The soldiers' attempt failed to lead the nation to find and live by the truth. Many veterans dropped out of society. Searching for an explanation, a former US pilot, Randy Floyd said in a filmed interview, "I think Americans have tried, we've all tried very hard, to escape what we've learned in Viet Nam, to not come to the logical conclusions of what's happened there."[424]

Escaping blame for the real reason for that war, US leaders continued elsewhere to pursue business expansion by force without telling the public. For example, four US soldiers died in combat in 2017 in the West African nation of Niger. But

US Civilians Fall Short on Soldiers' Plea

most of the US public did not even know US soldiers were there, much less in combat.[425]

On the combat in Viet Nam, the proof shows that Viet Nam was correct in defending and winning victory. It was "a humiliating defeat," a real US hero said. The US commander at the Battle of Ia Drang Valley, Lt Col Hal Moore, a Korean War veteran, refused personal evacuation and stayed on the ground with his soldiers in this close-quarter battle.[426]

One of 235 US soldiers killed in the three days and nights of battle at Ia Drang was Thomas Metsker. His wife, Catherine Metsker McCray, said years later, "I can only hope that we learned something from Vietnam and that all was not for nothing."[427]

They tell me the fault line runs right through here.

> —John Hartford lyrics
> sung by Cass Elliott[428]

Tomorrow is the most important thing in life
Comes into us at midnight very clean
It's perfect when it arrives and it puts itself in our hands
It hopes we've learned something from yesterday.

> —Epitaph, John Wayne
> (*see* Endnote 12)

Observe good faith and justice towards all nations. . . .
—George Washington Farewell Address
(*See* Chapter 1)

CHAPTER 12

IMPERATIVE FOR VOTERS TO TRANSFORM FOREIGN POLICY FAULT LINE
(Citations to facts appear earlier in this volume or in *Corporate Tsunami in Countryside Paradise*.)

During 1619–2024, US foreign policy of business expansion, often by force, created conflicts worldwide. At its core, that policy included the 1865–1954 US business operations in Viet Nam, enabled by force. The false claim of a 1954 US entry has misled virtually 100 percent of US voters. Though many of those voters have long realized that US leaders have been running an imperial system, many more falsely think the 1954 entry was for a noble purpose. So, they think that US foreign policy since then has had a similar noble intent.

But the US leaders' system of business expansion, often by force, harmed Viet Nam, and it still causes many foreigners to die or live in poverty. This has long broken the Golden Rule, a universally understood principle of morality. So, much of the world understandably reacts against the US.

The traditional role of US voters was to debate and guide the general direction of foreign policy. But in the 1940s, architects of US business expansion by force decided to ditch the public from facts needed for that role. Thus it is that only now, knowing the truth on the real reason for the US-Viet Nam War—the biggest US war since World War II—that US voters can reclaim that role.

US soldiers who fight overseas deserve voters acting on truth. Moreover, without voters acting on truth, the international character of the US is flawed and foreigners are wrongfully damaged. The US dooms itself to fight endless wars.

MAIN CONCLUSION

The real reason for the US-Viet Nam War, and the real reason behind US foreign policy through 2024, has been business expansion by force rather than anti-communism and/or anti-terrorism. The false claim that the US entered Viet Nam in 1954, presented as a noble effort, misleads many voters to believe falsely that a noble effort has continued driving foreign policy through 2024.

MIDDLE-LEVEL CONCLUSION

Together, the varied fact patterns leave no doubt that business expansion by force, not anti-communism, was the real reason for the US-Viet Nam War, and that business expansion often by force, not anti-terrorism, has continued as the main reason behind US foreign policy. The 22 Facts, Three-Step Analysis, Signature Techniques, and other fact patterns leave no room for serious doubt.

SUPPORTING CONCLUSIONS

1. During 1619–2024, the American economy developed in part by the pursuit of business expansion enabled by force.

2. North American business expansion by force originated in 1619 in slavery for profit, in which anti-communism was not a factor at all. This kind of expansion has continued as a prime force for more than four centuries.
3. In this system, US leaders pursued business expansion in Viet Nam during 1865–1954, enabled by force.
4. Virile racism has backed that 1619–2024 policy.
5. In Viet Nam and other countries, trading opportunities, large and small, were important to the US economy.
6. Around 1900, pre-teen Ho Chi Minh learned a lifelong lesson: By the 1890s, French firepower had allowed it to surround any uprising and defeat it piecemeal. Viet Nam was near death as a nation. It would die, unless someone found a new way for an uprising to avoid piecemeal defeats. Ho devoted his life to searching for a way and implementing it.
7. The culture of Viet Nam was based on a religion of harmony that required people to search for harmony with other people. Most of Viet Nam's people reacted against the disharmony of France and the US invading and murdering for profit.
8. Viet Nam's century, 1858–1975, of resistance war was a reaction against the French and US violating the Golden Rule by invading. And, it gained fuel from the Tradition Of Heroic Resistance Against Foreign Invasion (TOHRAFA).
9. From around 1900 onward, an informal foreign policy force has conducted most of US foreign policy. This force consists of corporations, government institutions, the NSC, associations, the CFR, officials, international lawyers, experiences overseas, experts, reports, military power, and other components. It built up a foreign policy of business expansion, often by force. Presidents

inherited this policy, rather than inventing it. They put their personal stamp on some of its actions, but did not fundamentally change it.

10. US anti-communism, while vocally strident, did not engage, either in rhetoric or in structure, with the business expansion by force that the foreign policy force was doing. Anti-communism failed to speak against the wrongs and abuses of US foreign policy detailed in this volume, such as the pre-1954 US business decades in Viet Nam enabled by force. Moreover, anti-communism displayed much less content, structure, and power than did the foreign policy force. The latter was composed of corporations, government and many other parts that did extensive planning. Anti-communism was not connected, other than superficially by rhetoric, to those structural drivers of the important system of business expansion by force. Voicing anti-communism while pursuing business expansion by force, US leaders were like bank robbers robbing banks, while trying to keep other robbers at bay.

11. In 1919 at Versailles, US leaders rejected colonial petitions by many nations of people of color, who asked for gradual independence. Viet Nam was among the nations turned away. The denials were based on colonial business expansion by force and by racism. These nations learned that independence was for white nations only (see *Corporate Tsunami*).

12. A component part of the foreign policy force, the Council on Foreign Relations (CFR) was founded in 1921 by a group of corporation leaders, international lawyers, and a few academics. Its leaders became known as the "foreign policy establishment." Its founding consensus, Michael Wala describes, was: "Access to raw

materials and markets of the whole world should be *secured* for the United States."

13. In their 1939–1945 War and Peace Studies, 100 CFR people drafted 682 reports and memos as "blueprints" for a "grand area" for US economic dominance in the "world order". Some areas, including Viet Nam, would require military force. US leaders decided not to tell the public, or the project would be "ditched." The project was donated to the State Department, which was occupied with World War II.

14. In the 1939–1945 "blueprint" reports, US leaders targeted Viet Nam for colonial control. The 1943 report calling to keep Viet Nam in "Colonial Relationships" by "a long and disastrous period of repression" shows targeting. That intent shows in US leaders ignoring Viet Nam's 1945 declaration of independence and overtures for fair trade and friendly exchanges. Showing intent for control, US leaders regularly escalated force during 1945–72. The virulent US racism, reflected in labeling Viet Nam citizens as "gooks," showed no respect for Viet Nam. This was an imperial targeting.

15. For imperial securing of resources, a National Securing Council was established in 1947. It was misnamed the National *Security* Council, For, it pursued business by force. This implemented the 1921 CFR consensus for "secured access" to resources and markets.

16. After France fell in defeat in 1954, the plain words of the Geneva Accords, Article 14(a), kept Viet Nam as one country and gave France alone the duty to temporarily administer the southern half until 1956 elections. A temporary line between the north and south was only for separating the armies. The Accords explicitly stated

that this line "should not in any way be interpreted as constituting a political or territorial boundary."

17. Despite that clear provision of the 1954 Geneva Accords, US leaders kicked France out (by applying superpower pressure on issues in Europe and on funding France). So, France departed from Viet Nam. This broke the main operative provision of the Accords.
18. Having broken the Accords so the Accords could not function in the southern half, US leaders then misled the US public to believe the Accords divided Viet Nam into two countries. In 1955, they set up a mock "South Viet Nam." But that did not undo the overwhelming numbers of people of Viet who lived in the southern half. They had fought the French invasion. Then they fought the US invasion
19. US leaders attacked after 1954, trying to continue their early business by force. That was the real reason for the US-Viet Nam War. Anti-communism, though supporting the US attack, was not the real reason for the war.
20. Unwitting US soldiers found out the hard way that the vast majority of people in the southern half were fighting against the US, not for it.
21. The US attack violated the Nuremberg Ruling that prohibited aggressive invasions.
22. In furtherance of this Nuremberg violation, US leaders sprayed Agent Orange/dioxin. In 2021, an estimated 150,000 children in Viet Nam were living with birth defects from this poison that violated Nuremberg.
23. Inaccurately portraying the Cold War against communism, US leaders omitted to tell the public about the 1865–1954 US business by force, the five War and Peace reports calling to attack Viet Nam to control it, and the

682 War and Peace reports and memos as "blueprints" for worldwide areas of US domination.
24. After the 1975 US defeat, US leaders escaped blame by the US public for the real reason for the war. They have continued misleading much of the public to believe they have had a noble purpose in foreign policy after that war, though, they continued to pursue business expansion worldwide, often by force.
25. The false claim is pervasive in the US in books, high schools, colleges, universities, adult forums, and websites.
26. In 2025, Viet Nam, in a speech to a wide audience that included world dignitaries, told of its strategic partnership with the US, and also said that the US had done an imperial invasion. The US public, not knowing of the 1865–1954 US period in Viet Nam, has failed to respond and has failed to cure the US government fault through 2024.
27. The business expansion by force caused worldwide anger against the US, by violating the Golden Rule. Ironically, Isaiah Bowman, an architect of that system, wrote that territorial matters "touch the main nerve center of popular feeling" and if unfair, "tragic conflicts result."
28. The business expansion by force has caused cruelty to generations of children: The 64,000 children recently killed and maimed in Gaza; over 100,000 children of dioxin birth defects today in Viet Nam; and today's young children facing a future higher death rate from global warming.
Some people say 'one dead US child killed by an undocumented immigrant is one too many,' which shows that 64,000 dead and maimed children of Gaza are 64,000 too many.

29. The US leaders' cruelty, seen as a model, explains why some children in conflict do school shootings.
30. The US public has the ability to regain its traditional role of debating and guiding the general direction of foreign policy, if it asserts its traditional role of receiving true facts from its elected officials.

COMBINED FACTS AND FACT PATTERNS PROVING THE CONCLUSIONS

A strong fabric of proof that business expansion by force was the real reason for the US in Viet Nam, and for foreign policy through 2024, is established by many facts and fact patterns. The fact patterns include: **Business Expansion in Viet Nam during 1865–1954 Enabled by Foce; Business Expansion far more than Anti-communism**; **22 Facts; Signature Techniques Worldwide; Ditching the Public From Facts**; **Targeting Viet Nam; Breaking the Golden Rule; an Axiom on Control by Force**; **Three-Step Analysis; Creation of Cruelty to Children; Sequence and Logic of the Life of Ho Chi Minh; Alternative Plan to take over the war if France lost; and the Foreign Policy Force**.

Readers and researchers are likely to find additional fact patterns among the myriad facts bearing on the US purpose in Viet Nam, and its role in driving foreign policy through 2024.

Each of the following discussions of facts and patterns supports one or more of the Main Conclusions:

I. US Business Expansion by Force backed by racism, was by far the predominant cause of the US-Viet Nam War, rather than anti-communism being the cause.

    A. Business Expansion by Force was important in the origin of the America's economy. Americans started chattel slavery in 1619, driven by profit. Slavery was a form of business expansion by force. Tobacco and cotton farming expanded, as by 1775, 500,000 slaves labored in the 13 colonies. Cotton produced by slave labor was a main force in the US becoming an industrial power.

The works of Sherilyn Ifill demonstrate that economic domination was a key purpose of the force used in the racial brutality in the US. Following the Civil War, US cotton produced with low-wage labor from black US citizens under violent domination became an important US export to Viet Nam. This exemplified US business expansion by force: Force existed in the US production, and force existed in the Viet Nam colony receiving it for small manufacture by the dominated population. (See Chapters 1 & 3.)

The simultaneous periods of US business expansion by racial domination in the US and Viet Nam during 1865–1950s are no surprise.

B. **The main goal of expansion in Viet Nam, enabled by force, was to find business opportunities, large and small**. In 1858, the year that France invaded Viet Nam, The *New York Times* reported to the US business community:

> The bayonets of allied commerce and Christianity will open Annam [Viet Nam] to the world. The missionary and the merchant will press in. And the history of an extinct people will be written by the historian of two or three generations in the future.

Following that report, and breaking the virtually universal Golden Rule that George Washington stated in his farewell address ("good faith and justice towards all nations"), US merchant ships entered Viet Nam in

1865. After 1865, "as American economic production grew, domestic markets became glutted, leading to new American economic interest in burgeoning markets in East Asia, Latin America, and Africa," Professor Harold Hongju Koh observes in 2024.

That interest in 1865 saw some US ships loading cargoes of rice for sale overseas. Large-scale exports of Viet Nam's rice stolen by the French invaders created widespread malnutrition. This trouble started in the 1880s and lasted the entire colonial period, a French colonial report stated at a 1945 conference in the US. The malnutrition was a main cause of the later war. Thus, the US was directly involved in this early cause of the later US-Viet Nam War.

This 1865 activity illustrates some of the **22 Facts** in Chapter 9 weaving a fabric of strong proof of what really happened—in contrast to the contention that the US entered Viet Nam in 1954 to fight communism. Many of these facts are omitted by US leaders, when they purport to inform the public.

During 1889–1950s, US consuls in Viet Nam and worldwide sought business opportunities, large and small. That helped the US economy grow. In Viet Nam in the 1920s, small items included sales of tire repair kits, sardines, and canned fruits from California. On tire repair kit sales, nine consuls around Asia contributed to the 1921 composite article the State Dept distributed in the weekly reports to US business community. This reflected US business growth based on small items as well as large.

Large items that found "great favor" in sales in the 1890s included Oregon pine, Standard Oil kerosene for lamps, and wheat flour. From 1920 onward, US imports of Viet Nam rubber increased. Viet Nam rubber production was far higher per acre than in Singapore and Indonesia, though total exports were less. In the 1930s, Viet Nam rubber helped meet an almost vertical curve in US demand for rubber.

In 1939, the US received 12 percent of Viet Nam's exports.

The imports of US wood, fruits, flour, and fish in this land of vast forests, prolific rice fields, abundant fruits, and plentiful fish is evidence that the colony pursued Western profits while causing native malnutrition.

C. **Pre-World War II US Business Expansion by Force using Structure of Corporations.** In the late 19th and early 20th centuries, US foreign policy gained strength by the growth in foreign trade utilizing corporate structures, physical infrastructures, experience with foreign nations, investments, planning, expertise, skilled workers, assertions of military power, and reports from State Dept consuls worldwide. As the 20th century unfolded, this system operated as a colossus. It pursued business expansion, often by force.

1. Leading the way, the 1901 merger of 28 companies into U.S. Steel, the first US corporation capitalized at over $1 billion, created new power driving economic growth overseas. In 1903, U.S. Steel Export Company formed to handle its exports. By 1913, U.S. Steel annual exports increased from $100 million to $305 million. While these exports went mainly to Europe and South America, not Viet Nam, they were important to the US economy. (See Chapter 11.)
2. Around 1900 Standard Oil found about 70 percent of its markets overseas. 'Our overseas operations

saved us from failing,' John D Rockefeller wrote in his memoirs. (See Chapter 1.)
3. In 1919, US corporation figures at the Versailles Peace Conference kept colonial control over Viet Nam and many colonies worldwide.
4. In 1921, major corporation figures and Wall Street corporate lawyers formed the Council on Foreign Relations (CFR). Its founding consensus was, as Professor Michael Wala describes: "Access to raw materials and markets of the whole world should be *secured* for the United States." *Newsweek* magazine said later, in 1971, "The foreign policy establishment of the US was the CFR leadership."

D. **Racism supported business by force more than it supported anti-communism**. The start of chattel slavery in 1619 was driven by profit, not by anti-communism. Chattel slaves were treated as having no rights, so they could be whipped to work, sold, and moved from their families. Slavery was a form of business expansion by force. It continued for more than two centuries. When US anti-communism began in the 1840s, slavery was already an independent force that ran at a high level.

After slavery ended in 1865, white racists continued to use force to protect economic advantages for whites. Sherilyn Ifill's works establish this economic purpose of the violence. During 1865–1950s, that economic purpose was behind the 6,500 lynchings of black US citizens. Domination and terror kept large numbers of black citizens in low wage work, often picking cotton for white farm owners. Cotton was a main commodity in the US becoming an industrial power. This built wealth for white people. Cotton became an important US export to Viet Nam. (See Chapters 1 & 3.)

While US racists generally opposed communism, they derived significant power directly from their economic stranglehold for decades over black people. For example, white farm ownership remained intact during the 6,500 murders of black US citizens that kept black citizens in low paying farm labor supporting the white farmers. White farm ownership even increased greatly. Under the Homestead Act, during 1868–1934, lands in the Midwest and West were given free to millions of whites but generally not to blacks.

The simultaneous violence on colored people for profit in Viet Nam and the US during 1865–1950s is no surprise.

In 1968, the US Republican Party called for white backlash voters. In 2005 and 2010 former Republican chairpersons said the Party continued to call for white backlash voters. From then through 2024, white racists and whites worried about race have formed a significant voting bloc. (See Chapter 9.)

E. **The failure of anti-communism to mention many key facts shows that it did not enter into the real decision-making arena of the foreign policy force. So, anti-communism was much less a factor**. The foreign policy force had strong, wide-ranging structure independent of anti-communism, while anti-communism used woefully inaccurate rhetoric that omitted many events and facts. Many structural parts of the foreign policy force powered it to establish significant positions and take strong steps overseas. An example is the 1960 overthrow of democracy in the Congo. This denied real development in much of Africa through 2024. By such steps, the foreign policy force implemented strong development of foreign economic policy, albeit in the pursuit of the destructive business expansion, often by force, like the US attack on Viet Nam.

The weakness of anti-communism is reflected in that its rhetoric failed to even mention, much less rebut, key facts and events. A sampling of its omissions includes: (1) the 1865–1954 century of US business by force in Viet Nam; (2) the War and Peace Studies targeting Viet Nam; (3) the 1945 US-Soviet agreement on areas for domination; and (4) the continued existence of Viet Nam as one nation, north and south, in which the overwhelming majority opposed the colonial invasions by France and the US.

Prof. Larry Ceplair pinpoints a reason for the shallow inaccuracy of anti-communism (Chapter 10). He says a central doctrine in it was that, like in a strong religion, one camp was "good, motivated by a God-given, light-upon-a-hill moral responsibility for universal welfare," while the other camp was "monolithic and evil." But the real reason for the US-Viet Nam War shows that this tenet of anti-communism was in error. The US did an immoral, evil rip-off against Viet Nam's welfare. This is established by US violation of the Nuremberg Ruling against invasions. Applying Ceplair's terms, Viet Nam did a moral defense, justified and motivated by the Golden Rule: Millions of Viet people knew the US was doing an evil, violent invasion against what was right, good, and fair. Anti-communism was in complete error on this, the biggest US war since 1945.

F. Ho Chi Minh was a patriot from age five, who as an adult made major efforts for peace with the US that the foreign policy force rejected.

Imperative for Voters to Transform Foreign Policy Fault Line

The violence and abuses that Ho Chi Minh knew of and experienced from age five onward started a lifelong desire in him to rid his nation of foreign invaders. When about 10 years old, learned that by the 1890s, France was able to surround all resistance forces and defeat them piecemeal. Viet Nam would die as a nation, and Ho would die too if he fought back, unless someone found a new way for an uprising to avoid being defeated piecemeal. These lessons undergird the Sequence and Logic in the Life of Ho Chi Minh:

- In 1911, at age 21, Ho Chi Minh sailed overseas, looking for a way to build such a resistance.
- It would not be easy. In 1919, when the US had been in Viet Nam more than 50 years, Ho wrote, "Frenchmen and *other foreigners* go around in freedom, reserving all the resources, usurping all the exports and imports." At the same time, "Our people must sweat boiling tears in the hardest kinds of work . . ." (Italics added, see *Corporate Tsunami*.)
- Visiting the US, he learned of virulent racism. In 1919, he wrote of whites in the US burning black people alive. And, he wrote of the Ku Klux Klan, a violent racist organization in the US. Racism has been a significant part of the US through 2024 (see below, & see Chapters 1 & 3, and see *Corporate Tsunami*).
- In 1919 at Versailles, Ho presented to the US delegation a petition that William Duiker calls "moderate." It asked for gradual progress toward independence. US leaders acknowledged receiving it. By silence, they rejected it.
- In 1920, Ho found a way to build an uprising to avoid piecemeal defeats. A communist revolt would (1)

spread leadership by secret cells, reducing the danger of it being destroyed; and (2) say that capitalists invade and kill for profit, a message that came to resound in Viet Nam, where capitalists were invading and killing for profit.

- In 1941, as the War and Peace Studies were underway, Ho Chi Minh returned to Viet Nam and set up his organization, designed to avoid piecemeal defeats. The name for Ho's organization was "Viet Nam Independence League." (Viet Nam Doc Lap Dong Minh Hoi) [Việt Nam Độc Lập Đồng Minh Hội]. "Doc Lap" meant "independence."
- In 1946, Ho made a major offer to the US, to grant a monopoly on Viet Nam's lucrative rice trade. Other capitalist-style overtures, such as for a Ford auto plant in Ha Noi, showed that Ho was more interested in trade and independence than in communism. Harley Davidson Company, US insurance companies, and four US oil companies came to Ha Noi after World War II seeking business.

If the capitalist leaders would stop killing, these capitalist US businesses were welcome.

Skilled US diplomats could have worked with those overtures as a good opportunity to develop capitalist relations with the patriotic Ho. Rejecting this chance, US leaders showed their real goal in Viet Nam was business expansion by force.

By painting a false picture that Ho was a bitter agent of international communism, US leaders misled the public not to look at the three centuries of US fault in business expansion by force, including the long period in Viet Nam.

II. In a key part of the 1619–2024 system, US leaders tried to continue the decades of US business in Viet Nam by specific actions during 1939–72.

   A. In the **1939–45 War and Peace Studies, the CFR prepared 682 reports and memos** for the State Department, setting up a common plan for a post-World War II world order of US economic dominance. Some of the papers spoke of controlling nations until US leaders deemed them to have developed enough to justify independence.

   Among them, Preliminary Memorandum E-B19 (see Chapter 9) called for:

   > coordination and cooperation of the United States with other countries *to secure the limitation of any exercise of sovereignty* by foreign nations that constitutes a threat to the minimum world area essential for the security and economic prosperity of the United States and the Western Hemisphere.

   B. **Targeting Viet Nam for continued business expansion by force.** The War and Peace Studies targeted Viet Nam (a) for US continued business expansion, and (b) to intimidate smaller nations into bowing to the US world order. Four of the reports stated reasons to control Viet Nam. They did not mention communism. A fifth report reviewed and confirmed the intent to attack Viet Nam.

   - A June 20, 1941 report. "The Economic Organization of Peace in the Far East," said Indochina presented "no great problems" to being included in a regional economy with Japan and Thailand. Japan needed "important political and social changes." The changes happened fast in 1945, after the massive violence of two atomic bombs. On Indochina, mostly on the southern half of Viet Nam, US leaders used 640 times the explosive power of the Hiroshima atomic bomb. (See Chapter 8)

- A Sept. 11, 1942 report, "Postwar Security Arrangements in the Pacific Area," said the US should hold a port, preferably in central Viet Nam, to control the South China Sea (Viet Nam's Eastern Sea). Southeast Asia was a "cheap source of vital materials." US national interest required "placing political and economic control in hands likely to be friendly to the United States."
- A Sept 14, 1943 report, "Regionalism in Southeast Asia," said it was important "to *secure access* to the trade and raw materials of the region." (italics added)
- A Nov. 16, 1943 report mainly on Viet Nam was titled "The Future Status of Indo-China as an Example of Postwar Colonial Relationships." That title alone showed the US colonial intent.

Contravening the 1940 report, this 1943 report said that "a long and disastrous period of repression" would be required if a new United Nations wanted to keep control of the peoples of the East any longer. For, "disaffections which were evident in Indo-China" showed the "failure of France" to do anything that "won the confidence and respect of the "Indo-Chinese. . . ." and thus "It is impossible" that the people would accept a return to colonial control.

This report called for supporting France in a re-invasion.

Imperative for Voters to Transform Foreign Policy Fault Line

- A year-end review by the CFR Steering Committee said that the Nov. 16, 1943 report meant "there should be a continuance of the French Colonial Regime in Indo-China."

C. **Targeting Viet Nam in 1945 by supporting France, in 1950 by an Alternative Plan to take over the war if France lost, and during 1954–72 following Viet Nam battlefield victories.** Continual targeting despite setbacks shows the importance of the 1943 goal of "The Future Status of Indo-China) as an Example of Postwar Colonial Relationships." By 1945, France needed US approval and aid to re-invade Viet Nam. For, during World War II, France's infrastructure had been devastated by Germany. In contrast, the US had emerged as a relatively undamaged superpower. In 1945 US leaders gave their superpower approval for France to re-invade. And, they supplied most of France's invasion costs. (see *Corporate Tsunami*).

- Viet Nam victory. During 1950, the US-backed re-invasion ran into serious defeats in battles.
  - US escalation: US leaders pursued a 1950–54 Alternative Plan to take over the war if the French lost. This is extensively covered in *Corporate Tsunami in Countryside Paradise*. It included commitments to provide "security," by cutting out the real Viet Nam from Colombo Plan economic development in Viet Nam. Some US soldiers traveled in the country gaining knowledge and contacts.
- Viet Nam victory. In 1954, Viet Nam defeated France. The plain words of the Geneva Accords,

Article 14(a), kept Viet Nam as one country and gave France alone the duty to temporarily administer the southern half until 1956 elections. A temporary line between the north and south was only for separating the armies. The Accords said the line "should not in any way be interpreted as constituting a political or territorial boundary."

- <u>US escalation</u>. US leaders bullied France to leave, by applying superpower pressure. This broke the main operative provision of the Accords for France to temporarily administer the southern half until elections.
- US leaders then misled the public to believe that the Accords divided Viet Nam into two countries—despite the plain words of Article 14(a), and despite the express statement that the temporary line "should not in any way be interpreted as constituting a political or territorial boundary."
- Building on that clear falsity, US leaders falsely said the US was fighting a North Viet Nam. No such country ever existed. And, US leaders attempted to superimpose a new "South Viet Nam" on part of the existing nation of Viet Nam. But the overwhelming majority in the southern half still supported the single nation of Viet Nam, north and south. They had fought the French invasion. Then they fought the US invasion. The US attempt was as if a nation invaded the US at New Orleans and said that created a "South United States." That would not be accepted by the overwhelming majority in the US.

The 1954 Geneva Accords "recognized Viet-Nam as one state," Prof. Quincy Wright, on the editorial board of the American Association of International Law, explained in 1965. Joseph Buttinger wrote in 1972 that claiming the 1954 Accords created "two separate nations was not only an absurd concept for anyone familiar with the history of Vietnam but also a legally untenable proposition. . . ." (See Introduction, Chapter 7, and Endnote 146.)

- US escalation: In late 1954 and early 1955, US leaders ordered "pacification," though no one was fighting back. The US State Dept later admitted that during this early period, no one was fighting back. By Feb 1, 1955, a US proxy force had killed large numbers of villagers. During 1955–60, this proxy force killed about 70,000.

  The killings were savage, and Viet Nam saw the US as completely wrong.

- Viet Nam victory. In 1960, Viet Nam villagers took control of about 90 percent of villages in the southern half.
  - US escalation: The 1960 "deteriorating situation" worried US civilian leaders, a USAF report said (see Chapter 5). Despite the Army Chemical Corps in 1959 proving dioxin caused death in some cases, and the Corps halting work on dioxin due to its "insidious" nature, the Corps had soon resumed work on it. The US began spraying dioxin in 1961.
  - US leaders escalated the number of soldiers and began using explosives.

- <u>Viet Nam victory</u>. During 1964, Viet Nam scored significant victories.
  - <u>US escalation</u>: US leaders tripled the dioxin spray per acre to three gallons and nearly quadrupled the number of acres sprayed. One gallon per acre was enough, some army scientists believed. They were overruled by the Department of Defense (DOD). DOD was controlled by the civilian government. (See Chapter 5.)
- <u>Viet Nam victory</u>. At the start of 1965, the DRV controlled most of the southern countryside and scored a resounding victory in a six-day battle east of Sai Gon, at Binh Gia. Five US advisors died—the most yet in one battle. A proxy force report said the guerrillas and main forces showed the ability to work together, a significant development. (See Chapter 5.)
  - <u>US escalation</u>. In September 1965, The *New York Times* reported: "No one here seriously doubts that significant numbers of innocent civilians are dying every day in South Vietnam. . . . US air raids . . . have resulted in widespread destruction of hamlets and mounting civilian casualties." (See Chapter 5.)
  - <u>US escalation</u>: During 1960–75, US leaders used on Indochina more than three times, by weight, of the bombs and explosives used by the US in World War II. In Indochina, the US used explosives equal to 640 times the power of the Hiroshima atomic bomb. Most of it was dropped on the southern half of Viet Nam.

    Despite newspaper photographs in 1967 showing a child born with a duck-like face, the spraying of dioxin continued into 1971. "Monster" births also occurred by 1967. Mothers were left in shock. (See Chapter 5.)

During 1961–71, the US sprayed dioxin and "at least 2.1 million people but perhaps as many as 4.8 million people in 3181 hamlets were sprayed." (Stellman study, see Chapter 7.)

The wrongful US attack on Viet Nam for years killed about 3 million people, compared with the one-day attacks in the US on Sept 11, 2001, which killed 2,977 people. For the latter, US leaders claimed the right to go to war for years. But on the former, the US leaders claimed Viet Nam was not justified in fighting back.

III. The pervasive false claim has misled much of the public to support wrongful foreign policy through 2024 and to deny child victims of Agent Orange/dioxin some remarkable quality of life compensation.

The pervasive false claim of a 1954 entry into Viet Nam, which sounds noble, conceals the 1865 entry and the 1865–1954 US activity enabled by force. This misleads the public into thing that ongoing foreign policy has been noble. The nine areas discussed in Chapter 8 show it has not been noble.

The false claim permeates US society in high schools, colleges, books, websites, and public forums. A leading high school history website, National Endowment for the Humanities, completely omits the 1865–1954 US period of business enabled by force. With millions of high school and college students graduating each year, having been taught the false claim, much of the US public has little or no chance to see what US foreign policy really is.

Some more key facts falsely presented or withheld from public debate include:

- Mistranslation of the simple term, "South Region" into the erroneous term "South Viet Nam," in National Front for the Liberation of South Region (Mien Nam) of Viet Nam. Use of the name, "South Region," shows the real fight in the 1960s was about keeping the South Region in the single nation of Viet Nam.
- US leaders rejected Viet Nam's requests from 1873 into the 1960s for peace and fair trade. US leaders wanted all the trade and raw materials, plus one more thing: control. That was like in Shakespeare's *Macbeth*.
- US histories generally omit that Ho Chi Minh's childhood was marked by severe Western abuses that led him to search for a way to force the foreigners out, and he discovered the method of a communist revolution.
- In 1959, the US Army Chemical Corps ceased developmental work on dioxin due to its insidious nature. Then, without explanation to the public, the Corps resumed work on it. In 1960, Viet Nam's southern uprising took control of 90 percent of the villages and hamlets. US leaders responded by starting to spray dioxin in 1961. No explanation was made to the US public or to Viet Nam about its insidious nature. Viet Nam quickly protested. But US leaders kept spraying it. At times when Viet Nam was gaining battlefield victories, US leaders increased quantities and dosages per acre of the sprays.
- Monster births were reported in 1967. One child was born with a duck-like face. A photo of it appeared in newspapers. But US leaders continued spraying.
- After the war, US leaders have not informed the public of the facts and issues on Agent Orange/dioxin damage

Imperative for Voters to Transform Foreign Policy Fault Line

to the people of Viet Nam, including (1) the large number of child victims of birth defects living today, (2) the duty to compensate victims for the 1955–75 US attack that violated the Nuremberg Ruling, (3) the duty to compensate victims for the US breaking of the 1954 Geneva Accords to pursue the 1955–75 US attack, (4) the large amount of good that would come from paying an amount equal to even one month (about $70 billion) of the US military budget, into a quality of life compensation fund for the children living with birth defects from Agent Orange/dioxin.

- Denying the public an inquiry into JFK's discovery about Viet Nam fighting against colonialism. He was taking some steps to withdraw. This ran deep: It threatened the 1619–2024 system of business expansion by force. After his murder, the Warren Commission failed to investigate many facts. Among them, the missing back of JFK's head came from a frontal shot, meaning a crossfire. That missing part of his head was clearly observed in the Dallas emergency room. The Warren Commission denied it was missing.

IV. Violating basic moral principles, US foreign policy causes reactions, isolating the US as a wrongdoer. History and literature on the Golden Rule form the Axiom on Control by Force. The Golden Rule is virtually universal. Most people in the world understand it. The Axiom shows that throughout history, when a it is violated by theft or murder, reasonable people often fight back.

Announcing the opposite of the Golden Rule, US leader John Foster Dulles declared that the world had two kinds of people: Christians who supported free enterprise, and "the others."

Against "the others," he conducted destructive business expansion, often by force. This violated the Golden Rule. But, Jesus had confirmed the importance of the Golden Rule by including it in the Sermon on the Mount. So, Dulles showed that he did not believe in Jesus. Thus, he violated Christian doctrine on how to get to Heaven.

US leaders have pursued through 2024 more than 100 coups, invasions, and destabilizations worldwide, including Viet Nam.

The revelation of the real reason for the US-Viet Nam War removes any mystery as to why much of the world angers at the US. That anger, for decades through 2024, has caused the US a lack of respect and a decrease in world leadership.

Many reactions have arisen to US business by force. In Africa, Nick Turse wrote in 2015 of "American operations serving as a catalyst for blowback." In West Africa, the US was kicked out of Niger in 2024. US military had provided "security" as France took Niger uranium but paid 1/250th of market value. Many citizens of Niger lived in poverty.

Seeking to reduce or end trade with the US due to US leaders' violations of the simple Golden Rule, BRICS+, OPEC+, and the Community of Latin American and Caribbean States (CELAC) cover much of the world. CELAC is a reaction to the heavily-documented US business by force in Central America and South America.

In Guatemala in 1906, Lt. Joe Stilwell did a secret mapping tour. By 1928, United Fruit gained control of Guatemala's economy. In 1932, US warships waited offshore of El Salvado, while the US State Dept demanded no wage increases for coffee workers. This led to strongman Martinez killing at least 10,000. In the 1950s, as *The Devil's Chessboard* highlights, the US used 13 dictators in Central and South America, who "allowed U.S. corporations to exploit their nations' people and resources, and they cracked down on labor agitation and social unrest as Communist-inspired." These US-backed dictators used savage tortures and pocketed millions of dollars from the US. During 1945–76 US leaders backed 23 coups, most of them in this region.

As of 2024, CELAC is working with the EU in a concerted effort to overcome the poverty of its region. Much of the poverty is caused by the US-backed coups and repression. From this region, many refugees stream to the US southern border. But US leaders ignore a lesson that grade school children are taught: Clean up the messes you cause.

On many nations and topics, the Three-step Analysis removes the false presumption of noble policy, thus shedding light on other facts of US expansion by force that cause reasonable people to react. Chapter 8 has examined: (1) Thailand, Viet Nam, & Japan; (2) Gaza, Palestine, & Israel in Middle East; (3) Viet Nam and Africa under US-France mutual "security" 1865–2024; (4) Afghanistan; (5) Syria; (6) American hemisphere; (7) Children of Dioxin, Gaza, & Climate Change; (8) Creation of unpayable debts by force on nations as plantation economies; and (9) Ukraine and Russia.

On Gaza in Palestine, removal of the false presumption of a noble purpose shines new light on a 1943 War and Peace report. It says a one-state solution would inject "racial opposition" and "hatreds" that would take "statesmanlike guidance" to diminish. Despite that prediction, US leaders have backed a one-state solution. That was despite most nations on earth supporting a two-state solution. US "statesmanlike guidance" would have had fertile ground to work with. But US leaders backed a one-state solution by providing weapons to Israel as Israel attacked and killed 14,000 children in Gaza in 2024.

V. Cruelty to children through 2024 from the US leaders' system of business expansion by force

Children have suffered harm by this system: In Central America, it has caused poverty, climate change, and emigration; in Africa, it has derailed economic development; in Gaza, it supported bombing that killed and maimed 64,000 children in 2024 and 2025; in Viet Nam, it caused about 150,000 children to be living in 2021 with birth defects from dioxin sprayed in furtherance of the wrongful US invasion; in the US, it provided a model of using violence, even as some school children consider using gun violence; and, this system refused to take appropriate action to help curb global warming despite the increasing risk of a higher future death rate for today's young children.

Climate change threatens horror to children, and some of them realize it. UN Committee Comment 26 to the UN Convention of Rights of the Child, Paragraph 73. says young children of today face an increased risk of death from future climate change. Indeed, worsening weather conditions are now striking the US and the world every year. The 2018 Paris Climate Agreement and 2018 IPPC assessment warned of catastrophe if the world fails by 2030 to curb global warming to a 1.5C degree average increase over pre-industrial levels. A 2025 ICJ ruling says the world is failing to curb global warming to that amount. In 2025, the ICJ says that goal is not being met, and that climate change "imperils all forms of life." US government efforts have fallen way short (See Chapter 8.)

That is a prediction of future horror for many of today's young children. By keeping the US public ditched from the ignoble facts on Viet Nam, the foreign policy force has prevented many voters from seeing the capability of US foreign policy to cause harm ignobly to many children.

Imperative for Voters to Transform Foreign Policy Fault Line

Facts Warrant Voters to Surmount the False Claim On Viet Nam that Harms the US & the World

Very strong proof in the revealed facts and the variety of fact patterns show beyond reasonable doubt what happened: No North Viet Nam existed, rather US leaders attacked the single nation of Viet Nam including its southern half, and the predominant reason for the attack was to continue the 1865–1954 business enabled by force. This was part of the 1619–2024 business expansion, often by force. Duped on all that, much of the public thinks the US has made noble efforts in 1954 to fight communism and into today to fight terrorism.

This new showing moves the US public to a crossroads. The public can choose to take the road of the US regaining stature as a moral and respected world leader. Or, the US public can follow like sheep focusing on their personal feed bags while the leaders of the flock pursue business expansion, often by force that overrides the Golden Rule and creates conflicts and wars. Because this volume has destroyed the concept of American Exceptionalism, the quality now exposed is American Sheepiness.

What will the crossroads decision be? As Juan Gonzalez observes in *Harvest of Empire*, "the American people still cling to a basic sense of fairness, that once they understand the facts, they rarely permit injustice to stand." (See Introduction.)

Fairness was invoked when Viet Nam's head of government pointed out, at the April 30, 2025 celebration, that the US had done an imperial invasion. The US public failed to respond, not having true facts.

The public has the ability to learn the facts on Viet Nam. Indeed, the public and television Now, many voters networks devote countless hours analyzing sports and other matters.

Likewise, voters have the time and ability to understand basic facts on Viet Nam and ongoing foreign policy. The government has no right to mislead the people. Learning the facts and analysis in this volume, enough voters could join progressives to guide the nation to dump the business expansion by force.

Now, many voters—from high school age through adulthood—can apply the real facts to overcome the pervasive false belief. Millions of voters can help the US public resurrect the public role. As Mead wrote, in US democracy, the public role is to guide the general direction of foreign policy. That is in the premise of the *Pentagon Papers* case: The public must be told the truth on foreign policy.

This is especially true where members of the US public are sent to die. What greater insult is there to a US soldier, than to send him or her to die or be maimed, based on the false claim that has long formed the nucleus of US foreign policy?

When US voters realize that approximately 3.5 million citizens of Viet Nam died in the illegal US invasion, these voters can see that the principle of fairness shows those were wrongful killings by the US. The world has not forgotten.

With such truths displayed in this volume, if five percent of US voters would shift to wanting a moral foreign policy, that could shift national politics. For, the nation is already fairly evenly split.

A foreign policy change would honor the people of Viet Nam, the fallen US soldiers of Viet Nam and later conflicts, and members of the US public who assert that the US public is not a flock of sheep to be led by false claims. Such a change would rekindle relations with nations injured by US pursuit of control for business expansion. The US could finally operate in harmony with foreigners based on fairness. This would help heal this complex world. Through its complexity, the simple, real lesson of the US-Viet Nam War is based on the elementary Golden Rule and the Axiom on Control by Force: The human heart, treated unfairly, will fight forever.

The End

ACKNOWLEDGMENTS

Giving great thanks to all who have contributed to my knowledge during these 50 years of digging and writing on the real reason for the US-Viet Nam War, and its connection to the real foreign policy since then, this book incorporates the Acknowledgments section from this author's companion volume, *Corporate Tsunami in Countryside Paradise.*

For this volume, Kelvin Prince has read and commented from his lifetime in sub-Saharan Africa, confirming the accuracy of the US-France-Viet Nam-Africa links revealed in this book. Peter MacGregor has edited parts of this book and made helpful comments. As on my first book, John J. Fitzpatrick has added his valuable views on this work.

To my wife, Nguyen Thi Ngoc Hanh, I give immeasurable thanks. Her harmony-minded ways and life of hard work capture the ancient spirit of Viet Nam in its peaceful welcome to all foreigners who arrive in peace. Insights from her have helped me to see across our two different cultures. This is a window into common human values.

As during the writing of my first book, two Viet Nam Era veterans have continued to deepen my understanding of human values, US society, and the US-Viet Nam War. They are Tomas Heikkala, who served in Viet Nam, and Gregory Laxer, who refused to go, was court-martialed, and wrote an illuminating book, *Take This War and Shove It! : A Most Unwilling Soldier 1967– 1971.*[429]

ENDNOTES

PREFACE

1. Laxer, G. (2021). *Take This War and Shove It! : A Most Unwilling Soldier 1967– 1971*, Unbearable Truth Publications.
2. Viet Nam as two words. Huu Ngoc, with Lady Borton (ed) (2016). *Viet Nam: Tradition and Change*. Ha Noi: The Gioi, and Athens, Ohio: Ohio University Press, pp. 29, Kindle location 916.

INTRODUCTION

3. Bayonet slaughters, decapitated notables. Lanessan, Jean Marie Antoine de (1895). *La colonization francaise en Indo-Chine*. Paris: F. Alcan, p. 30; Roesch, B. (2020) *Corporate Tsunami in Countryside Paradise : 1875– 1900 Origin of US War in Viet Nam*. US: Voter Knowledge Press, p. 32.
4. Long and disastrous repression. CFR, *War and Peace Studies, 1939–45*, CFR Territorial Group, (November 16, 1943). "The Future Status of Indo-China As An Example Of Postwar Colonial Relationships, T-B69," NY: Council on Foreign Relations, pp. 1–2, 4.
5. National Endowment for the Humanities (NEH), an independent federal agency, leading website for high schools. NEH Vietnam War. https://edsitement.neh.gov/vietnam-war-lesson-guide
6. Absurd to say Geneva create two states. Buttinger, J. (1972). *A dragon defiant : a short history of Vietnam*. (Praeger University Series U-742). New York: Praeger, p. 116. Geneva left Viet Nam one nation, did not mention North or South Viet Nam, absurd. Geneva Agreements 20–21 July, 1954. *Agreement on the Cessation of Hostilities in Viet-Nam 20 July, 1954*, (espec Articles 1, 14), and Final Decl. The Avalon Project, Yale Law School, https://avalon.law.yale.edu/20th_century/inch001.asp

7   Gaza "statesmanlike guidance," "racial opposition". Council on Foreign Relations, *War and Peace Studies of the Council on Foreign Relations, 1939– 1945,* T-B68 "The New Zionism and a Policy for the United, States," October 19, 1943, Territorial Group, pp. 1, 3 ("racial opposition," "statesmanlike guidance"), 4–5 (US position), 6–8; Post-WW II policy on foreign oil.

8   Diminishing capacity and foreign policy change is needed. Chivvis, C. & Stephen Wertheim (October 14, 2024). "America's Foreign Policy Inertia: How the Next President Can Make Change in a System Built to Resist It." *Foreign Affairs,* September/October 2024, Volume 103, Number 5, NY: Council on Foreign Relations.
Last chance with Global South. Vinjamuri, Leslie, and Max Yoeli (November 15, 2024). America's Last Chance With the Global South: In an Age of Great-Power Competition, Washington Needs the G-20. *Foreign Affairs,* November/December 2024, Volume 103, Number 6, NY: Council on Foreign Relations.
On Middle East, Washington less influence credibility in region. Indyk, Martin (*February 20,* 2024) The Strange Resurrection of the Two-State Solution: How an Unimaginable War Could Bring About the Only Imaginable Peace. March/April 2024. *Foreign Affairs,* NY: Council on Foreign Relations.

9   Americans when understand facts. Gonzalez, *Harvest of Empire.* Penguin, p. xxxii, Kindle location 501.

10   Voters ultimately decide. Mead, *Power, Terror, Peace, and War,* p. 6, Kindle location 129. Case of The Pentagon Papers, Justices Black and Douglas on "inform the people." *New York Times Co. v. United States,* 403 U.S. 713 (1971), 717 (Black, J., concurring).

11   Chomsky & Davis, public need see US connections domestic and foreign. Chomsky, N. (2022). *The withdrawal : Iraq, Libya, Afghanistan, and the fragility of U.S. power.* (Interview by Vijay Prashad), The New Press, p. ix, Kindle location 35. Viet Nam April 30, 2025. Parade celebration and speech, video Viet language. VTV Shows May 6, 2025 "Xem lại Lễ diễu binh, diễu hành kỷ niệm 50 năm Giải Phóng Miền Nam, thống nhất Đất nước đầy tự hào," https://www.youtube.com/watch?v=IV-E_mdO1mg Statements at 47:53–48:28 (After defeating France, VN had peace, but the US invaded in the footsteps of France in a plan to seize half the country, an imperial US invasion.) 50:17 of 2:18:50 "Resistance war against America to save the country." 56:07–56:12 (friendly relations with US)

PART 1

12   Lyrics to California Earthquake. https://genius.com/John-hartford-californiaearthquake-lyrics. Fault line, in California Earthquake.

https://genius.com/Cass-elliot-california-earthquake-lyrics Cass Elliott singing fault line. https://www.youtube.com watch?v=uqAJaNwBlyY.

13. Inscription on John Wayne grave. Grave of John Wayne, Pacific View Memorial Park, Newport Beach, California, author visit.

CHAPTER 1

14. French attack. *New York Times* (1859, Nov. 29). Additional from Europe. Arrival of the Africa. State of the War Question–CochinChina. *New York Times,* p. 8. Retrieved from ProQuest Historical Newspapers. *New York Times* (1851–2009). US about 10 ships a year for 3 years before 1868 HK to Saigon US 30 ships a year by early 1870s, regional ports, 1884 oil US direct Sai Gon; by 1888 large, US ships load rice cargoes late 1860s. Denis Freres initiated. Miller, R. (1990). *The United States and Vietnam, 1787–1941.* Washington, DC: National Defense University Press, pp. 70–79 (3 yrs before 1868 p. 70), 141–42 (rice cargoes late 1860s).

15. US post-Civil War expansion overseas. Koh, Harold Hongju (2024). *The National Security Constitution in the Twenty-First Century.* Yale University Press, p. 51, Kindle Location 654.

16. Total 900 French killed. Foreign News, *Michigan Farmer* (1843–1908) 1.18 (Apr 30, 1859):141, ProQuest Historical Newspapers.

17. Tradition Of Heroic Resistance Against Foreign Invasion (TOHRAFA), by Prof Christoph Giebel. Giebel, C. (Summer 2010). Lectures on the Vietnam Wars, HSTAS 265, Seattle: University of Washington; Roesch, *Corporate Tsunami in Countryside Paradise,* pp. 16–27.

18. Viet Nam's spiritual culture Tran Ngoc Them, close to nature, enjoyable way of life, ancestors. Roesch, *Corporate Tsunami in Countryside Paradise,* Chapter 4.

19. Administrator said undernourished, every Governor General. De la Roche, J. A Program of Social and Cultural Activity in Indo-China. Ninth Conference of the Institute of Pacific Relations. Hot Springs, Virginia, January 1945, French Paper No. 3, pp. 5–6. US ships load rice cargoes late 1860s. Denis Freres initiated. Miller, *The United States and Vietnam, 1787–1941*, p. 141.

20. Bui Vien to US 1873. Trịnh Vân Thanh (1966). *Thành ngữ Điển tích danh nhân từ Điển*. Sài Gòn : Hỗn Thiêng, v. 1, p. 77; Huu Ngoc, *Wandering through Vietnamese culture,* pp. 902–03. Bui Vien two trips US. Huu Ngoc, *Wandering through Vietnamese culture,* pp. 902–03.

21. US oil Viet Nam direct 1884, 1888 large, Denis Freres initiated. Miller, *The United States and Vietnam, 1787–1941*, pp. 141–42. Standard buy Vacuum, agents, China, SEA. Anderson, *The Standard-Vacuum Oil Company and United States East Asian policy, 1933–1941,* pp. 15–19, 203–04, 206. Standard Oil facilities in China and Southeast Asia 1930s. An-

derson, *The Standard-Vacuum Oil Company and United States East Asian policy, 1933–1941*, pp. 3–5, 206.

22 Oil discovery US 1859. Spence, H. (1962). *Portrait in Oil : How the Ohio Oil Company Grew to Become Marathon.* NY: McGraw-Hill, p. 52. Rockefeller 1859 vision, by 1865 export refined oil. Tarbell, I., Chalmers, David M., ed. (1969). *The History of the Standard Oil Company Briefer Version*, NY: Norton, pp. 28, 118–21; Hawke, D. F. (1980). *John D.: the founding father of the Rockefellers.* NY: Harper & Row, p. 95. Standard Oil Lamps, kerosene Asia early 1860s. Anderson, I. (1975). *The Standard-Vacuum Oil Company and United States East Asian policy, 1933–1941.* Princeton, N.J.: Princeton University Press, p. 19, see pp. 15–16. Standard 90 percent US oil refining. Smith, R. (2014). *On His Own Terms : A Life of Nelson Rockefeller*, NY: Random House, p. 11, Kindle location 714.

23 US oil Viet Nam direct 1884, 1888 large, Denis Freres initiated. Miller, *The United States and Vietnam, 1787–1941*, pp. 141–42. Standard buy Vacuum, agents, China, SEA. I. Anderson, I. I. (1975). *The Standard-Vacuum Oil Company and United States East Asian policy, 1933–1941.* Princeton, N.J.: Princeton University Press, pp. 15–19, 203–04, 206.

24 Standard Oil 1885, 70 percent abroad. Smith, *On His Own Terms*, p. 11, Kindle location 719. Foreign markets. Rockefeller, J., *Random Reminiscences of men and events*, pp. 10, 121.

25 New York oil men want State to appoint an American consul. Miller, *The United States and Vietnam 1787-1941*, pp.141-42. Tonsales contact with New York oil men. Miller, *The United States and Vietnam 1787-1941*, p.142.

March 10, 1889 appointing US consul. Miller, The United States and Vietnam, pp. 141–44. Name of Tonsales. Tonsales, A. to Department of State, February 25, 1893. United States Consulate (1957). Despatches from United States consuls in Saigon, 1886–1906. Washington: National Archives and Records Service, Central Service Administration, Reel 1, No. 38, pp. 1–4.

Denis Freres stature, on Banque de l' Indochine. BelleIndochine (1922). *Annuaire des enterprises coloniales, 1922*, No.651. Paris. Compagnie Franco-Indochinoise, importers of rice to Dunkirk, France, No. 656 Denis Freres general commerce, imports, exports, representation, armaments, guarantors; many products imported and exported. Imports include rice, rubber, copra, jute, sugar, and minerals. Exports include wine and spirits, cotton, and tobacco. French Indochina, Direction Des Affaires Économiques. (1925). *Annuaire Économique De L'Indochine, Hanoi:* Impr. d'Extrême-Orient, p. 39, Denis Freres imports, exports, and metallurgy. p. 46 Sales of matches and cements in Viet Nam; p. 47 irons and metals, p.48 machinery, pumps

Denis Freres, handled main rice exporter. Challamel, *Annuaire De La Marine De Commerce Francaise Guide Du Commerce D'Importation Et D'Exportation*, p. 950.

[26] Address of Denis Freres. www.entreprises-coloniales.fr (mise en ligne 20 mai 2014; Derniere modification Octobre 2015). *Denis Freres en Indochine (1862–1922)*, location in document: **Denis Freres d'Indochine Societe Anonyme au Capital de 2,000,000 de piastres** (no page numbers in document). Oil imports. Schneegans, Edouard. to Department of State (Feb. 10, 1894). "Kerosene oil." Despatches from United States consuls in Saigon, 1886–1906, Reel 1, No. 49 pp. 1–4, Chronological, no frame numbers.

[27] Foreign consulates 1890s in Sai Gon. Challamel, A. (Editeur) (1898). *Annuaire de la Marine de Commerce Francaise Guide du Commerce d'Importation et d'Exportation*. Paris, Havre Ministere de la Marine, *pp. 949–50*.

US consuls in Viet Nam 1889–1939. Roesch, *Corporate Tsunami in Countryside Paradise*, pp. 437–39, *Appendix I: List of Consuls and Vice Consuls*.

[28] US exports to Viet Nam great favor. Business consul letter to Secretary of State Elihu Root (1905, Sept. 29). *Despatches from United States consuls in Sai Gon, 1889-1906*, Washington: National Archives and Records Service, General Services Administration, Reel 1, No. 13, p. 2, format one microfilm reel.

[29] Recession 1920–21. Krugman, P. (2011, April 1). "1921 and All That." https://krugman.blogs.nytimes.com/2011/04/01/1921-and-all-that. Petroleum oil and cotton rank in US exports to Viet Nam. Wright, P., Holland, W. L., & Institute of Pacific Relations. International Research Committee. (1935). *Trade and trade barriers in the Pacific*. London: P.S. King & Son, Table 155, pp. 413–415. US produced about 3/5 world's cotton, export half of that. United States. *Foreign Commerce Yearbook: Trade with the United States by Principal Commodities, 1929* U.S.G.P.O, pp. 227–28. Cotton imports by IndoChina 1934, 1935, 1936, manufactures. United States. *Foreign commerce yearbook* / U.S. Department of Commerce, Bureau of Foreign and Domestic Commerce 1937, USGPO, pp. 307–08.

[30] Quote on slavery transform cotton industry most important, colonial-like. Baptist, E. (2014). *The Half has Never Been Told: Slavery and the Making of American Capitalism*. NY: Basic Books, Perseus Book Group, Introduction, Kindle location 256.

[31] US slavery dates, cotton industry most important, colonial-like. Baptist, E. (2014). *The Half has Never Been Told: Slavery and the Making of American Capitalism*. NY: Basic Books, Perseus Book Group, Introduction, quote at Kindle location 256, facts at Kindle locations 94–288;

Chapter 9, Kindle location 6564–6587; Chapter 11, Kindle location 8367–8425. Agricultural exports, expansion from 1830. Williams, W. (2009). *The tragedy of American diplomacy* (50th anniversary ed.). NY: WW Norton & Company.

[32] Favored nation over Royal Dutch. Smith, Leland, consul to State Department (1921, December 1). "Monthly Report on Commerce and Industries, for November, 1921," Records of the Department of State relating to internal affairs of France, 1910–1929, Reel 150, frames 0015–22. US autos gas. Smith, Leland (1922). Statistics concerning the number of automobiles in Indo-China. Records of the Department of State relating to internal affairs of France, 1910–1929, Report, February 2, 1922, 85.1g/797, Reel 152, frame 0633. Tire repair kits. K. de G. MacVitty, consul, Sai Gon, Indochina, and 10 other US consuls, composite article by Rubber Division, Dept Commerce. Weekly Commerce Reports, Washington, D.C.: U.S. G.P.O., January 9, 1922, pp. 68–69, 294. San Francisco Chamber visit. Briggs, Lawrence P. consul to State Department (1921, December 1). Monthly Report on Commerce and Industries, for November, 1921. Records of the Department of State relating to internal affairs of France, 1910–1929, Reel 150, 85/g.00/7, p. 7. San Francisco misc tons Indo-China increasing. United States. Maritime Commission. Division of Research (1923–1935). *Report on Volume of Water Borne Commerce of the United States by Ports of Origin and Destination*, Part 1. Commerce of US ports with foreign ports; Part 2. Commerce of foreign ports with U.S. ports. (CIS US Executive Branch Documents, 1910–1932 ; no. SB7.2-2.12). Washington: U.S.G.P.O. California canned fruits. Waterman, Henry S., Voluntary Report (1930, May 3). Analysis of the Causes of the Great Depression. Records of the Department of State relating to internal affairs of France, 1910–1929, Reel 83, 851g.50/1, frames 1365, 1370. US commerce activity in 1920s Viet Nam; number of consuls. Roesch, *Corporate Tsunami in Countryside Paradise*, Ch 10, Appendix 1. Petroleum oil and cotton rank in imports. Wright, P., Holland, W. L., & Institute of Pacific Relations. International Research Committee. (1935). *Trade and trade barriers in the Pacific*. London: P.S. King & Son, Table 155, pp. 413–415. US exports canned sardines decrease. United States. *Foreign commerce yearbook* / U.S. Department of Commerce, Bureau of Foreign and Domestic Commerce 1930, USGPO, 536.

[33] IndoChina exports to US 1934–36. United States. Foreign commerce yearbook / U.S. Department of Commerce, Bureau of Foreign and Domestic Commerce 1937, USGPO, p. 310

[34] Remington typewriter 1930 imports Denis Freres. www.entreprises-coloniales.fr (mise en ligne 20 mai 2014; Derniere modification Octo-

bre 2015). *Denis Freres en Indochine (1862–1922)*, location in document: Denis Freres d'hampionnat de dactylographie (no page numbers in document).

35 Rice exports Indochina to US 1930. United States. *Foreign Commerce Yearbook: Trade with the United States by Principal Commodities, 1928* U.S.G.P.O., p. 350. Rice exports from Viet Nam 1923–1929, tons, ranking. Robequain, Charles (1935). *L'Indochine Francaise*. Paris: Libraire Armand Colin p. 192. Rice exports. Gottmann, Jean, Raw Materials in the Western Pacific. Institute of Pacific Relations. Conference. (1945). *[Papers presented to the Ninth Conference of the Institute of Pacific Relations, Hot Springs, Virginia*, January 1945]. New York, French Paper No. 1.

Per acre rubber production, factors. Smith, Leland L. (May 2, 1922) "Transmitting translation of a report upon the rubber Plantation of Xatrach," *Records of the Department of State relating to internal affairs of France, 1910–1929*, 851g.6176/3, Reel 152, frames 0303–0304. Almost vertical curve demand increase natural rubber. Gottmann, Raw Materials in the Western Pacific, pp. 6–7. U.S. Rubber consumption 1921–30, 64.5% of world total. Barker, P., & United States. Bureau of Foreign Domestic Commerce. (1939). Rubber industry of the United States, 1839–1939 (Trade promotion series ; no. 197). Washington: U.S. G.P.O., p. 11.

36 In 1930s, US led Europe nations except France, in value from Viet Nam. Leading 1931– 35. *Foreign commerce yearbook / U.S. Department of Commerce, Bureau of Foreign and Domestic Commerce : 1935. (1935)*. .S. G.P.O. : *For sale by the Supt. of Docs., 1934-1953*, p. 285. Leading during 1935–38. *Foreign commerce yearbook / U.S. Department of Commerce, Bureau of Foreign and Domestic Commerce : 1938.* (1938). U.S. G.P.O. : For sale by the Supt. of Docs., 1934-1953, p. 325. Lucrative colony. Buttinger, J. (1967). *Vietnam : A Dragon Embattled,* New York: Praeger, p. 7. In 1939, 12 percent of exports to US and imports from US. Fall, B. (1967). *The Two Viet-Nams: A political and military analysis* (2nd rev. ed.). New York: Frederick A. Praeger, p. 29.

CHAPTER 2

37 Effect of childhood trauma. Duiker, W. (2012). *Ho Chi Minh : A Life,* US: Hyperion, Epilogue, Kindle location 11934–11942.

38 Mother, brother die. Văn Thị Thanh Mai, *Hồ Chí Minh : Hành Trình từ Làng Sen Đến Ba Đình (1890–1969),* pp. 31; Mai Luận, Đắc Xuân, and Trần Dân Tiên (2015). *Hồ Chí Minh from childhood to president of Việt Nam.* Viet Nam, Thế Giới Publishers; Đảng Cộng sản Việt Nam. Tiểu ban nghiên cứu lịch sử Đảng. Tỉnh ủy Nghệ An. Bùi Ngọc Tam, chủ biên (2011). Hồ Chí Minh thời niên thiếu. Nghệ An: NXB Văn

Hóa Thông Tin, pp. 17–19; Duiker, *Ho Chi Minh : A Life*, Chapter 1, Kindle location 634. Mother Đisadvantaged woman, died, engraved in HCM heart. Trần, M. (2001). *Những người thân trong gia Đình Bác Hồ (Tái Bản.ed.)*. Vinh: NXB Nghệ An, pp. 72–73.

39 Nghe An heroes against invaders. Nguyễn Văn Dương, sưu tầm & biên soạn (2012). *Nguyễn Sinh Cung– Nguyễn Tất Thành : Giai Đoạn 1890–1911*, Pleiku, Gia Lai, Viet Nam: NXB Hồng Bàng, pp. 25–28; Văn Thị Thanh Mai (2010). *Hồ Chí Minh : Hành Trình từ Làng Sen Đến Ba Đình (1890–1969)*. Hà Nội: NXB Chính Trị Quốc Gia, p. 18.

40 French attack province 1875, 1885 Chau experiences. Chương Thâu, *Phan Bội Châu (1867–1940) Nhà Yêu Nước Nhà Văn Hóa Lớn*, pp. 25–28. Phan Boi Chau village four km from Lang Sen of young HCM. Văn Thị Thanh Mai (2010). *Hồ Chí Minh : Hành Trình từ Làng Sen*. Chau beside Phan Dinh Phung, death, De Tham. Buttinger, *Vietnam : a Dragon Embattled,* pp. 129–30, 145, 151. Chau mandarin, contempt. Buttinger, *Vietnam : a Dragon Embattled*, pp. 145, 151. Resistance movements collapse; lesson lack nationwide; piecemeal destruction, may cease as nation. *Buttinger, Vietnam: a Dragon Embattled*, pp. vii, 129–30, 139–40, 160 (piecemeal), 432 (piecemeal). Grip unbreakable. *Ham, Vietnam: the Australian War,* Chapter 2, Kindle location 446. PBC, leaders, 1904 national organization. NXB Nghệ An (2017). *Phan Bội Châu, Con Người và sự Nghiệp Cứu Nước*. Vinh: NXB Nghệ An, pp. 54–57. Poor family, Save King. Nguyen Khac Vien (2015). *Vietnam: A Long History (Tenth edition)*. Ha Noi: The Gioi Publishers House, pp. 161, 389.

41 Giving a name. Huu Ngoc (2004). *Wandering through Vietnamese culture*. Ha Noi: The Gioi, pp. 393– 96. Nguyen Tat Thanh depart Viet Nam 1911, activities, return to Viet Nam 1941. Ho Chi Minh Museum (2016). *Ho Chi Minh Biography*. Viet Nam: The Gioi Publishers, pp. 21–90.

42 Name Nguyen Ai Quoc 1918; Paris photography shop. Ho Chi Minh Museum (2018). *Exhibit. After World War II I made my living in Paris. ..."* Ha Noi. Ho Chi Minh Museum.

43 Petition points. Viet Nam National Museum of History (April 2018). Revendications du Peuple Annamite. *Colonial Exhibits*, Room 3. Moderate tone, delivers in Paris and Peace Conference; petition turned down. Duiker, *Ho Chi Minh*, Chapter 2, Kindle location 1281–1407.

44 Quoted passage on lynchings reprinted. Roesch, *Corporate Tsunami in Countryside Paradise*, Chapter 11, p. 116. Ho writings in 1924. Bảo Tàng Hồ Chí Minh. Hồ Chí Minh Tiểu Sử, pp. 54–55, 66. Lynching, announcements 1917–1924. Hồ Chí Minh, Hồ Chí Minh Toàn Tập,

v. 1912–1924, pp. 330–36, 361–66. Nearly 5,000 lynchings of black people US 1885–1960. Averaged more than 5 lynchings each month, 75 years. Ifill, On the courthouse lawn, Introduction, Kindle location 147–160.

45 Nguyen Ai Quoc 1920 reading Lenin, strategy. Quinn-Judge, S. (2002). *Ho Chi Minh : The Missing Years, 1919–1941*. Berkely, CA: University of California Free Press., p. 33; Duiker, W. (1995). *Sacred War : Nationalism and revolution in a divided Vietnam*. NY: McGraw-Hill, p. 23. Believing farmers would support resistance, Ho redoubled efforts. Đinh Xuân Lý & Trần Minh Trường, Đồng chủ biên (2013). *Hồ Chí Minh với Cách Mạng Việt Nam : Cuộc Đời, sự nghiệp, và Đạo Đức*. Hà Nội, NXB Đại Học Quốc Gia, pp. 12–25, 38–39. Lenin's view. Lenin, V. (1967). *Lenin on the National and Colonial Questions : Three articles*. Peking: Red Star Publishers, www.redstarpublishers.org/leninnatcolq.doc, p. 22. Lenin's guidelines uniting groups including farmers. Duiker, W. (1996). *The communist road to power in Vietnam* (2nd ed.). Boulder, CO: Westview Press, Chapter 2, Kindle locations 714–717, 951.

46 HCM later described 1920 reading Lenin. Viet Nam National Museum of History (2018). Trích: Con Đường dẫn tôi Đến chủ nghĩa Lênin (1960). *Colonial Exhibits*, Room 3.

47 Pham Van Dong quote, Ho laws of history, spark of truth. Pham, V. (1990). *Ho Chi Minh : a Man, a Nation, an Age, and a Cause*. Ha Noi: Foreign Languages Publishing House, pp. 13–16. Pham Van Dong prominence. Buttinger, *Vietnam : a Dragon Embattled*, p. 224.

48 Parisian socialists on revolutions. Duiker, Ho Chi Minh : A Life, Chapter II, Kindle location 1703–1715. Writings for Le Paria. Bảo Tàng Hồ Chí Minh (2017). Hồ Chí Minh Tiểu Sử. Hà Nội: NXB Chính trị quốc gia-Sự thật, pp. 54–55. Theory workers, not farmers, important, Ho reputation spokesperson colonies; 1923, invited to Russia study Marx. Duiker, Sacred War, pp. 23–26. Arrival date. Ho Chi Minh Museum (2017). Displays. Ha Noi: Ho Chi Minh Museum. Ho Moscow 1923–24. Duiker, W. (1991). Ho Chi Minh's Duong Kach Menh, monograph, Pennsylvania State University, pp. 26–27.

49 Theory Moscow, revolution in industrial society, farmers unimportant. Still, Lenin thought Asian farmers allies. Duiker, *Sacred War*, p. 24. Lenin on intelligentsia, city revolution, farmers unimportant, central state power. Chomsky, N. (1989), Youtube (Nov 30, 2008). Chomsky on Lenin, Trotsky, Socialism & the Soviet Union, film excerpt, mr1001nights, https://www.youtube.com/watch?v=yQsceZ9skQI, 2:01–7:49.

50 Ho advocated role of farmers; independent thinker. Duiker, Ho Chi Minh's Duong Kach Menh, p. 2. In Moscow, June 23, 1924 speech,

Fifth Congress Comintern, Ho criticizes Party on colonial question. Duiker, *Ho Chi Minh : A Life,* Chapter III, Kindle location 2207–2278. Ho criticizes party in 1924. https://www.marxists.org/reference/archive/ho-chi-minh/works/1924/07/08.htm, citing, Ho Chi Minh (July 8th, 1924). "Report On The National And Colonial Questions, at The Fifth Congress Of The Communist International," in Toàn Tập (collected Works), vol. 1 (1981).

51 Ho request paid position in southern China, arrive Quang Chau November 11, 1924. Duiker, *Ho Chi Minh : A Life,* Chapter III, Kindle location 2272–2336. Arrival date southern China. Đỗ, B., & Lê, Ngọc Nhi. (2009). Từ bến Nhà Rồng Đến quảng trường Ba Đình. Hà Nội: NXB Hà Nội. p. 20. Nguyen Ai Quoc to Russia, study, charge, to China, sending people into Viet Nam. Roesch, *Corporate Tsunami in Countryside Paradise,* pp. 113–20. Ho establish VCP, then into ICP. Phan Xuân Thành, Giám Đốc Bảo Tàng, Lệ Thị Thu Hằng, biên tập (March 1996), Kỷ Yếu Hội Thảo Khoa Học: 65 Năm Xô Viết Nghệ Tĩnh, Sở Văn Hóa Thông Tin, Bảo Tàng Xô Viết Nghệ Tĩnh.

52 Ho request paid position in southern China, arrive Quang Chau November 11, 1924. Duiker, *Ho Chi Minh : A Life,* Chapter III, Kindle location 2272–2336. Arrival date southern China. Đỗ, B., & Lê, Ngọc Nhi. (2009). Từ bến Nhà Rồng Đến quảng trường Ba Đình. Hà Nội: NXB Hà Nội. p. 20. Nguyen Ai Quoc to Russia, study, charge, to China, sending people into Viet Nam. Roesch, *Corporate Tsunami in Countryside Paradise,* pp. 113–20.

53 September 1940 Japan invade at Lang Son. Viet Nam National Museum of History (April 2018). "Quân Đội phát xít Nhật tiến vào tỉnh Lạng Sơn tháng 9, 1940," *Colonial exhibits,* Room 6. September 1940, Japan and French agreement. Brocheux, P. (1995). *The Mekong Delta: Ecology, Economy, and Revolution, 1860–1960* (Monograph (University of Wisconsin-Madison. Center for Southeast Asian Studies) ; 12). Madison, WI, USA: Center for Southeast Asian Studies), University of Wisconsin-Madison, p. 182.

November 1940, uprising eight provinces southern delta; internal betrayal. Bombings, thousands arrested, executed, large numbers to Con Son prison. Nguyễn, T., & Trần, Hương Nam (1968). *Không còn Đường nào khác : Hồi ký* (Tái bản. ed.). Hà nội: Phụ nữ, p. 3. Executed over 100 leaders, imprisoned thousands on Con Son island prison. Bradley, M. (2000). *Imagining Vietnam and America : The Making of postcolonial Vietnam,* 1919–1950 (New Cold War history). Chapel Hill: University of North Carolina Press, p. 231 n.7, Kindle location 3494–3502 n. 7. 1940 French attack, prisoners. Sheehan, *A bright shining lie,* pp. 208–09, Kindle location 3814–3833.

Endnotes

54 Date Ho return. Viet Nam National Museum of History (April 2018). Painting, *Nguyen Ai Quoc returned to homeland on January 28, 1941.* Colonial exhibits, Room 6. Founding Viet Minh Front May 1941 by Ho. Viet Nam National Museum of History (April 2018). Khuổi Nậm shack in Pac Bo . . . establishment of Việt Minh Front in May, 1941. *Colonial exhibits*, Room 6. Founding Viet Minh, Viet Nam Independence League. Buttinger, *Vietnam : A Dragon Embattled*, p. 265.

Viet Nam Independence League (Việt Nam Độc Lập Đồng Minh Hội), "Độc Lập" means "independence" and "Đồng Minh Hội" means "League" or "Association." Nguyễn Lân (2006). *Từ Điển từ và Ngữ Việt Nam*. TP. Hồ Chí Minh: NXB Tổng Hợp TP. Hồ Chí Minh, pp. 661, 674, 874. Viet Minh means "League of Independence for Viet Nam." Chomsky, N. & Ngo Vinh Long (April 30, 2005). Remembering Vietnam. Massachusetts Institute of Technology, recorded by Roger Leisner of 'Radio Free Maine.' Uploaded by itcanbepictures.com, Boulder, CO to YouTube on October 13, 2015, video location 0:13:34–0:13:42, https://www.youtube.com/watch?v=guPlS0_ww&t=3888s

55 By late 1943, League controlled areas. Buttinger, *Vietnam : A Dragon Embattled, v.1,* p. 275. Flying Tiger flights Red River Delta. Scott, R. (1943). *God is my copilot.* New York: Scribner. Rescue US pilot Shaw, walks one month to US forces China. Duiker, *Ho Chi Minh : A Life,* Chapter 9, Kindle location 5880–5893. Ho and US pilots. Bradley, *Imagining Vietnam and America*, Chapter 4, Kindle location 1792–1797.

56 Borderline famine and misery, Gourou said. Buttinger, *Vietnam : A Dragon Embattled*, p. 56. Two meals a day. Gourou, P. (1945). The Standard of Living in the Delta of the Tonkin (French Indo-China). Ninth Conference of the Institute of Pacific Relations, Hot Springs, Virginia, January, 1945, v.5, French, French Paper No. 4, p. 12, 14.

57 About 2 million North starved to death 1944–45, French and Japan leaders seized rice crop, effects continued. Hội Đồng chỉ Đạo biên soạn công trình lịch sử kháng chiến chống Pháp khu tả ngạn sông Hồng. (2001). *Lịch sử kháng chiến chống Pháp khu tả ngạn sông Hồng, 1945–1955*. Hà Nội: Chính trị quốc gia, pp. 22–23 and footnote 1, 47–48. Granaries, Ngo, "*Vietnam: The real enemy*," p. 14.

58 August Viet Nam seizing power. Nguyen Khac Vien, *Vietnam: A Long History*, pp. 214–22.

59 September 2, 1945, day Japan surrender, Ho read declaration to 500,000 in Ha Noi. Sheehan, *A bright shining lie*, p. 147, Kindle location 2700. August Viet Nam seizing power, and Sept. 2 DRV into existence. Nguyen Khac Vien, *Vietnam: A Long History*, pp. 214–22. More than 1 million listened in Sai Gon. Historical Marker established 23.9.1978 in park at intersection of Đường Lê Duẩn and Đường Phạm

Ngọc Thạch, city center, Ho Chi Minh City, Viet Nam, author visit March 2016. Ho Chi Minh provisional president; form DRV August September 1945. Marr, D. (2013). *Vietnam State, War, and Revolution (1945–1946)*. Berkeley, University of California Press, pp. xiv, 4, 19. During 1886–87 Ba Dinh three-village resistance. Nguyen Khac Vien, *Vietnam : A Long History*, pp. 144–45; Buttinger, *Vietnam : a Dragon Embattled*, p. 128; Burke, J.(2001). *Origines: the Streets of Viet Nam, a Historical*. Hà Nội: NXB Thế Giới, p. 15.

[60] DRV written offers of monopolies including rice. Bradley, *Imagining Vietnam and America*, Chapter 5, Kindle location 2141–2203. Logevall, *Embers of war*, Chapter 8, Kindle location 3562–3574.

Report to President and Dept of State. Shoup, *Imperial brain trust*, p. 225. Viet Nam and Japan in postwar regional trade, textiles. CFR, *War and Peace Studies of the Council on Foreign Relations, 1939–1945*, "The Economic Organization of Peace in the Far East" June 20, 1941, War and Peace Studies, E-B33, pp. 2–4, 15–20.

Report, hold port Da Nang or Cam Ranh Bay. CFR, *The War and Peace Studies of the Council on Foreign Relations, 1939–1945*, "Postwar Security Arrangements in the Pacific Area," September 11, 1942, A-B69, pp. 3–4. 429.

Report, secure access raw materials. September 14, 1943, CFR report SEA cheap raw materials, control by friendlies. Territorial Group (1943, September 14). "Regionalism in Southeast Asia, T-B67." *CFR Studies of American Interests in the War and the Peace*. NY: Council on Foreign Relations, Inc., pp. 1, 5–6, especially 6.

Viet Nam would require long repression. CFR, *War and Peace Studies, 1939–45*, CFR Territorial Group, (November 16, 1943). "The Future Status of Indo-China As An Example Of Postwar Colonial Relationships, T-B69," NY: Council on Foreign Relations, pp. 1–2, 4.

CFR, *War and Peace Studies*, 1939–45, Steering Committee (December 31, 1943). "List of Memoranda Issued in 1943 with Recommendations or Conclusions, No. SC-B4," NY: Council on Foreign Relations, p. 14 (to continue French colony.)

[61] Official view of Cold War in 1947. Koh, *The National Security Constitution in the Twenty-First Century*, p. 71, Kindle Location 952.

PART II
CHAPTER 3

[62] Robeson and others petition. Civil Rights Congress (1951). *We Charge Genocide: The Historic Petition to the United Nations for Relief from a Crime of the United States Government Against the Negro People (PDF)*. Civil Rights Congress, 1952, pp. xvi–xviii,173–74. Robeson and wife, Eslanda

Endnotes

Goode Robeson, wife of Paul. Robeson, P. (1988). *Here I stand*. Boston: Beacon Press, Kindle location 3. Violence in Viet Nam1865–1954. This volume Chapter 1; Roesch, *Corporate Tsunami in Countryside Paradise*, Chapters 1, 3, 5–20.

[63] Georgia 1946 lynchings in *NYT*. Ginzburg, R. (1962). *100 years of lynchings*. Baltimore, MD: Black Classic Press, pp. 255–56, Kindle locations 3553–3564. Destroyer, tanks, planes, and artillery fire on Hai Phong, places fleeing civilians seen, killed close to 20,000 civilians, say Viet Nam people, up to 6,000 civilians killed by naval fire admitted Suffren commander, Devillers report. Buttinger, *Vietnam: A Dragon Embattled*, pp. 427–29.

[64] Naval artillery residential, casualties thousands. Nguyen, *A Long History*, p. 233. Attack on Hai Phong. Hội Đồng chỉ Đạo biên soạn (2001). *Lịch sử kháng chiến chống Pháp khu tả ngạn sông Hồng, 1945–1955*. Chính trị quốc gia, p. 26. Killing 6,000 or more. Congressional Research Services, Library of Congress (1984), *The US Government and the Vietnam War: Executive and Legislative Roles and Relationships, Part I 1945–1961*, US Govt Printing Office, Washington (prepared for the Committee on Foreign Relations United States Senate), p. 26.

[65] Georgia 1946 lynchings in *NYT*. Ginzburg, *100 years of lynchings*, pp. 255–56, Kindle locations 3553–3564. Devillers report "horrible." Buttinger, *Vietnam: A Dragon Embattled*, pp. 428.

[66] Lansing refuse passports 1919. Fox, Stephen (1970). *The Guardian of Boston: William Monroe Trotter*. New York: Atheneum Press. Uncle Bert and others guide young Dulles brothers. Roesch, *Corporate Tsunami in Countryside Paradise*, pp. 77, 90.

[67] Wilson racism. Eisgruber, C. (2020, June 27). "President Eisgruber's message to community on removal of Woodrow Wilson name from public policy school and Wilson College." https://www.princeton.edu/news/2020/06/27/president-eisgrubers-message-community-removal-woodrow-wilson-name-public-policy. Wilson favorite prof, influence at Versailles. Kinzer, S. (2013). *The Brothers: John Foster Dulles, Allen Dulles, and their secret world war*, (First ed.), NY: Time Books/Henry Holt and Company, Chapter 1, Kindle locations 327, 525–533.

[68] Robeson and others petition. Civil Rights Congress (1951). *We Charge Genocide: The Historic Petition to the United Nations for Relief from a Crime of the United States Government Against the Negro People (PDF)*. Civil Rights Congress, 1952, pp. xvi–xviii,173–74. Eslanda Goode Robeson, wife of Paul. Robeson, P. (1988). *Here I stand*. Boston: Beacon Press, Kindle location 3.

69 Robeson overseas opera star, passport canceled, Dulles. Horne, G. (2016). *Paul Robeson : The Artist as Revolutionary*. London: Pluto Press, pp. 10, 104, 127, Kindle locations 247, 2012, 2407–2423.

70 Robeson passport revocation, Dulles, testimony. Zinn, H., & Arnove, Anthony (2004, 2014). *Voices of a people's history of the United States* (10th Anniversary edition). NY, Oakland: Seven Stories Press, Chapter 16, Kindle locations 7551–7607. Robeson passport. Performer, petition. Horne, *Paul Robeson : The Artist as Revolutionary*, p. 105, 126–28, Kindle location 2025, 2392–2436.

CHAPTER 4

71 Einstein quote. Benjamin, M., & Evans, Jodie (2005). *Stop the next war now : Effective responses to violence and terrorism*. Maui, Hawaii: Inner Ocean Pub., p. xii, Kindle location 291.

72 CFR founding, consensus 1921 access to raw materials quote, praise; part of internationalism. Wala, *The Council on Foreign Relations and American foreign policy in the early Cold War,*, pp. 9, 21, back cover.

73 Grand area, limitation of sovereignty. CFR memo E-B19, The War and United States Foreign Policy: Needs of Future United States Foreign Policy (October 9, 1940).

74 Blueprints. Shoup, L. & Minter, William (1977). *Imperial brain trust : The Council on Foreign Relations and United States foreign policy*. New York: Monthly Review Press, p. 119. Secure a larger area, grand area from CFR Preliminary Memorandum E-B19, The War and United States Foreign Policy: Needs of Future United States Foreign Policy (October 9, 1940). Shoup, *Imperial brain trust*, pp. 130–31, 175–76, 187. World order. McCain, J. (2017, February 19). 'I Worry About the President's Understanding' Some Issues. NBC News, Meet the Press, Youtube video, 00:33–01:07. Theodore "Roosevelt Corollary." US key role post-war system, unfairness. Kissinger, H. (2014). *World Order*. New York: Penguin Press, pp. 251, 278–79, Kindle locations 3537, 3906–3918. World order defending freedom. Isaacson, W., & Thomas, Evan (1986). *The wise men: Six friends and the world they made: Acheson, Bohlen, Harriman, Kennan, Lovett, McCloy*. New York: Simon and Schuster, p. 19, Kindle location 102. CFR book refers to world order. Mead, *Power, Terror, Peace, and War*, p. 157, pp. 15, 52 (majority), 54, 69, Kindle locations 230, 729 (majority), 730, 901.

75 An unfolding new world order. Chomsky, N. (2016). *Who Rules the World?* (First U.S. ed.). New York: Metropolitan Books, Henry Holt and Company, p. 44, Kindle location 784.

76 Ditched, Bowman says. Grose, *Continuing the Inquiry*, p. 23; Wala, *The Council on Foreign Relations and American foreign policy in the early Cold War*, p. 31. Others agree not share. Schulzinger, *The wise men of foreign affairs*, pp. 61–62. Not shared with public. Shoup, *Imperial brain trust*, p. 119.

77 Kennan on 50 percent; that is freedom to rob, exploit. Chomsky, N., & Peck, James. (1987). *The Chomsky reader* (1st ed.). New York: Pantheon Books, pp. 306–07, Kindle location 6464–6489.

78 Public debate on imperialism is on nature of democracy. Kinzer S. (2017). *The true flag : Theodore Roosevelt, Mark Twain, and the birth of American empire* (First ed.). NY: Henry Holt and Company, p. 5–11, Kindle locations 63–167.

79 Report on "Colonial Relationships." Council on Foreign Relations (1946). The Future Status of Indo-China as an Example of Postwar Colonial Relationships, War and Peace Studies, T-B69. Council on Foreign Relations, *The war and peace studies of the Council on Foreign Relations, 1939-1945*.

80 Report on "Colonial Relationships." Council on Foreign Relations (1946). The Future Status of Indo-China as an Example of Postwar Colonial Relationships, War and Peace Studies, T-B69. Council on Foreign Relations, *The war and peace studies of the Council on Foreign Relations, 1939-1945*, pp.1–2 of 4.

81 Voters ultimately decide. Mead, *Power, Terror, Peace, and War*, p. 6, Kindle location 129.

82 The Pentagon Papers, Justices Black and Douglas on "inform the people." New York Times Co. v. United States, 403 U.S. 713 (1971), espec. 717 (Black, J., concurring). Ellsberg, D. (2002). *Secrets: A memoir of Vietnam and the Pentagon papers*. New York: Viking., pp. 256–257, 289, 383, Kindle locations 4928–4935, 5515, 7192.

83 Citizen-critic, Pentagon Papers lower court, citizens' need to know. First Amendment, Powell. Chomsky, N., & Herman, Edward S. (2002). *Manufacturing Consent : The Political Economy of the Mass Media*. NY: Pantheon Books, p. 496, Kindle location 7018.

84 Changes needed on use of force. Koh, *The National Security Constitution in the Twenty-First Century*, pp. 407–416, Kindle locations 5842–5970.

85 Foreign policy posts CFR during Truman 42 percent, Eisenhower 40 percent, Kennedy 51 percent, Johnson 57 percent. Shoup, *Imperial brain trust*, pp. 62–64.

86 *Newsweek* says CFR "foreign policy establishment." Shoup, *Imperial brain trust*, pp. 4, 7, citing *Newsweek* issue of Sept 6, 1971.

87 Foreign policy by officials, not public. Jacobs, Lawrence R., and Benjamin I. Page. Who Influences U.S. Foreign Policy? *The American Political Science Review*, vol. 99, no. 1, 2005, pp. 107–23. Cited in Chomsky, N. & Nathan J. Robinson (2024). *The Myth of American Idealism : How U.S. Foreign Policy Endangers the World.* NY: Penguin Publishing Group, p. 239, Kindle location 4170.

88 CFR hundreds in govt, 2011 example. Shoup, *Wall Street's Think Tank*, p. 95, Kindle Location 2028.

89 CFR world's most powerful private organization, think tank; CFR 1998 connection in foreign matters; composition of CFR leadership. Shoup, L. (2015). *Wall Street's think tank: the Council on Foreign Relations and the empire of neoliberal geopolitics, 1976–2014.* New York: Monthly Review Press, Amazon Digital Services LLC, pp. 92–95, 299–318, Kindle locations 1971–2030, 6632–7050. NSC influence and power, 70 years. Gans, J. (2019). *White House Warriors : how the National Security Council transformed the American way of war* (First edition). Liveright Publishing Corporation, a division of W. W. Norton & Company, pp. 3, 209–13, Kindle Locations 62. 4059–4072, 4110–4174.

90 Foreign policy ecosystem. Chivvis, C. & Stephen Wertheim (October 14, 2024). America's Foreign Policy Inertia: How the Next President Can Make Change in a System Built to Resist It. *Foreign Affairs*, September/October 2024**,** Volume 103, Number 5, NY: Council on Foreign Relations. Leading forum is journal Foreign Affairs. Shoup, *Wall Street Think Tank*, p. 70, Kindle location 1447.

91 World Bank and IMF linchpins of postwar order. Talbot, *The Devil's Chessboard*, p. 177, Kindle location 3383. Heavy social and economic costs imposed by IMF. Penet, Pierre & Flores Zendejas, Juan. (ed.) (2021). *Sovereign Debt Diplomacy: Rethinking Sovereign Debt from Colonial Empires to Hegemony.* UK: Oxford University Press, Kindle location 1026.

92 Presidents have waged illegal wars for decades. Hathaway, O. (July 16, 2024). For the Rest of the World, the U.S. President Has Always Been Above the Law: Americans Will Now Know What A Lack Of Accountability Means. *Foreign Affairs.* NY: Council on Foreign Relations. NSC and others direct illegal coups, destabilizations, and wars. Roesch, *Corporate Tsunami in Countryside Paradise,* Chapters 17–20, 22–23, 29–30, and Appendix III.

93 At least 118 actions 1947–89. O'Rourke, Lindsey A. (2018). Covert Regime Change: America's Secret Cold War, US and London: Cornell University Press, p. 97, Kindle location 2385. Partial list of coups. Roesch, *Corporate Tsunami in Countryside Paradise,* Appendix III. Over 80 election interferences. Chomsky, *The Myth of American Idealism*, p. 27, Kindle location 534. Kissinger in CFR. Shoup, *Imperial brain trust,*

pp. 5, 41–42, 65, 89, 200–01. Former NSA advisor, former secy state, Kissinger not trust Chilean voters. Chomsky, *The Myth of American Idealism*, p. 24, Kindle location 488.

CHAPTER 5

94 System regarded as source. Russell, B. (1967). *War Crimes in Vietnam*. London: Allen & Unwin, p. 120.

95 Report on "Colonial Relationships." Council on Foreign Relations (1946). The Future Status of Indo-China as an Example of Postwar Colonial Relationships, War and Peace Studies, T-B69. Council on Foreign Relations, *The war and peace studies of the Council on Foreign Relations, 1939-1945*.

96 Quote JCS nationalism cannot be crushed or reversed; Army planners estimate 80 percent. Chomsky, N. (2015). *Rethinking Camelot : JFK, the Vietnam War, and U.S. Political Culture*. NY: Haymarket Books, Chapter 1, Kindle location 1946–1959. Paul Mus stature, on Ho support. Logevall, Embers of war, Chapters 8 and 9, Kindle locations 3513–3520, 3948. Resentment, 80 percent 1949; stoppage of rice to sea-ports. Hailey, Indo-China Has Become Vital Cold War Front. *New York Times*, February 12, 1950, p. 131.

In 1951, JFK colonial trip, in Viet Nam. Logevall, *Embers of war*, Preface, pp. xii–xiii, Kindle location 66–95. JFK newsreel. *Film segment, first floor display*. JFK Presidential Museum, Boston, Mass, 2008 author visit. JFK 1951 realization, ensuing efforts to get out, *Stars and Stripes & NYT* headlines. Douglass, James W. (2008) *JFK and the Unspeakable: Why he Died and Why it Matters*, Maryknoll, NY: Orbis Books, pp. 218–85, KL 4404–5540 (news reports pp. 219, 285, Kindle locations 4420, 5549).

97 Colombo press release. United States. Department of State. (1951, July 3). Statement on the Official Beginning of the Colombo Plan, No. 586. State Dept: Wash., D.C.

98 Changes in Japan, defeat. Council on Foreign Relations, *War and Peace Studies of the Council on Foreign Relations, 1939–1945*, The Economic Organization of Peace in the Far East, June 20, 1941. *War and Peace Studies*, E-B33, pp. 4, 20.

99 Explosives on IndoChina about 100 times combined impact Hiroshima and Nagasaki atomic bombs. Miguela, Edward, Gérard Roland (2011). Bombs and explosives Viet Nam three times over World War II. Miguel, E. & Gerard Roland. (October 2005). "The Long Run Impact of Bombing Vietnam," US: Department of Economics, University of California, Berkeley, p. 2. The long-run impact of bombing Viet-

nam. *Journal of Development Economics* 96 (2011) 1–15, espec p. 2. //efaidnbmnnnibpcajpcglclefindmkaj/http://emiguel.econ.berkeley.edu/wordpress/wp-content/uploads/2021/03/Paper__The_Long-Run_Impact_of_Bombing_Vietnam.pdf

[100] End WW II, French economy weak, status military forces. Christofferson, T., & Christofferson, Michael Scott. (2006). *France during World War II : From defeat to liberation* (1st ed., World War II–the global, human, and ethical dimension; 10). New York: Fordham University Press, pp. 31–32, 34–35, 172–177, 180. Re-invasion killed 500,000 Viet people. Logevall, *Embers of war,* p. 1056 fn. 5, Kindle location 14189.

[101] Bernard Fall says about 66,000 killed 1957–1961 citing Kolko's 12,000 by end 1957. Chomsky, *Rethinking Camelot,* Chapter 1, Kindle location 1008–1013. During 1955–1959 killed 70,000 southern delta, more in Central; Hue-Thua Thien 23,400 Party cadre, 160 alive. Ngô, V. (May 2009), From Polarization to Integration in Vietnam. *Journal of Contemporary Asia*, Vol. 39, No. 2, pp. 295–304, especially 297–300. End 1959, 60 to 90 percent party members south killed. Ho, S.K., & Ha M.H., & Vo, V.S (1996). *Lịch Sử Việt Nam 1954–1975*, TP. HCM: Từ Sách Đại Học Tổng Hợp TP. HCM, p. 169. Killed tens of thousands. Ban Chấp Hành Đảng Bộ Tỉnh Bà Rịa-Vũng Tàu, (1993). *Đường Hồ Chí Minh Trên Biển Bà Rịa-Vũng Tàu*, NXB Chính Trị Quốc Gia, p. 16. From about 60,000 in 1954, to 5,000 five years later, more than 90 percent, some purges. Miller, *Misalliaddnce*, p. 197.

State White Paper 1961 said communist activity after Geneva mainly "political action. . . ." Herman, E., (1972). *Atrocities in Vietnam: Myths and Realities.* Boston: Pilgrim Press, p. 20. Pike on NLF political only. Chomsky, *Manufacturing Consent*, Chapter 5, Kindle location 4944. Force first by Southern regrouping zone. Buttinger, *Vietnam : A Dragon Embattled*, p. 982.

August 9 Diem cancel elections, October 26, 1955, "Republic of Vietnam." Futrell, *The United States Air Force in Southeast Asia*, p. 39, Kindle location 671–676. Believed killed 10,000 to 15,000 in north, Buttinger, Vietnam : *A Dragon Embattled*, pp. 913–15. August 17, 1956, Ho started "Campaign of Rectification of Errors." Stopped the killings. About 10,000-15,000 had been executed, some wrongly. (estimates as high as 75,000 but cannot be regarded as reliable) Herman, *Atrocities in Vietnam: Myths and realities*, p. 23.

[102] USAF study "deteriorating situation" high civilians directed USAF in spraying in Viet Nam. Buckingham, W., & United States. Air Force. Office of Air Force History. (1982). *Operation Ranch Hand : The Air Force and herbicides in Southeast Asia, 1961–1971.* Washington, D.C.: Office of Air Force History, U.S. Air Force, pp. iv, 7–8.

[103] Vision in 1957, helicopters like cavalry, from the Chief of R and D US Army, Lt Gen James M.Gavin; helicopters bring soldiers for lightning fast ground assaults. Harold G Moore, Lt. Gen., USA (Ret.), Joseph L Galloway, *We Were Soldiers Once-and Young: Ia Drang, the Battle that Changed the War in Vietnam*, p. 10. Random House, NY (1992). GE defense contractor 1896, jet engines. Woodmansee, J. (1975). *The World of a Giant Corporation: a report from the GE project*. Seattle: North Country Press. GE growth in WWII. Miller, J. (1947). *Men and volts at war; the story of General Electric in World War II*. New York, London: Whittlesey House, McGraw-Hill Book Company, pp. 106-109, 115-117, 147.

[104] NSC Dioxin decision from Taylor-Rostow October 1961 trip, report. Martini, E. (2012). *Agent Orange: History, Science, and the politics of uncertainty* (Culture, politics, and the Cold War). Amherst, MA: University of Massachusetts Press, Chapter One, Kindle location 550–558. On the trip, James W. Brown of Army Chemical center helped make the case. Martini, *Agent Orange*, Chapters 1, 3, Kindle locations 549–556 and n. 41, 838 (J. W. Brown). Civilian government controlled dioxin use decision. Gilpatric, Roswell; Dept of Defense; National Security Council (Nov. 21, 1961). *National Security Action Memorandum No. 115 Defoliant Operations in Vietnam*, 30 November 1961. (NSAM 115). United States Government https://www.jfklibrary.org/asset-viewer/archives/jfknsf-332-017#?image_identifier=JFKNSF-332-017-p0002.

[105] NSAM 115 includes some conditions for spraying dioxin in areas inhabited by humans; inhabitants will be advised the spray is not harmful. Gilpatric, *NSAM 115*, pp. 3, (Zone D) 4 (Zone D; inhabitants will be told not harmful), and 5 (mil exploitation). Chief scientist, USAF on sprayings of people. Sills, *Toxic war*, Chapter 8, Kindle location 1746–1753.

[106] NSC in NSAM 15 authorizes first spraying; starts late 1961. Frey, "Agent Orange and America at war in Vietnam and Southeast Asia," *Human Ecology Review*, Vol. 20, No. 1 (Summer 2013), p. 3. August 5, 1961, chemical defoliants research CDTC, August tested. Futrell, *The United States Air Force in Southeast Asia*, Part Three, Kindle locations 1313, 2057–2129. August 10, 1961 drop chemical mixture containing dioxin. Trần Đinh Đích (2016). *Nhiều Hoạt Động Kỷ Niệm 55 Năm Thảm Họa Da Cam*, Tạp Chí Da Cam, Số 4/2016. Hội Nạn Nhân Chất Độc Da Cam/Dioxin Việt Nam, The Vietnam Association of Victims of Agent Orange/Dioxin, p. 8. August 10, first spray mission, helicopter, Viet crew. Tilles, *The History of Chloracne and dioxin*, Section 3.4.2, Kindle location 2406–2414. In August 1961, US-supplied chemicals, Southern regrouping zone aircrews spray "herbicides." Buckingham, *Operation Ranch Hand*, p. iii.

[107] Nov. 6, 1961, NSAM 115 says charge "poison gas." NSAM 115, pp. 2–3. November 6, 1961 Radio Ha Noi said "poison gas" making people sick. Buckingham, *Operation Ranch Hand*, pp. 17–21.

[108] Dioxin mist, 97 percent on ground less than minute. Sills, *Toxic war*, Chapter 10, Kindle location 2188, 2500. Fog, sensations. Tilles, *The History of Chloracne and Dioxin*, Section 3.4.4, Kindle location 2575–2582. Spray drifted down, Recorded interview of Nguyen Van Can by author with interpreter, June 20, 2017.

TCDD dioxin is a solid, toxicity. Tilles, G. (2018). *The History of Chloracne and Dioxin: A Skin Disease at the Crossroads of Occupational, Environmental and Political Concerns. A Paradigm of Endocrine Disruption.* Amazon Digital Services LLC, 4.4 Appendix IV, Kindle location 4225. Video on dioxin showing solid powder being poured into container; helicopters spraying. DocsOnline (Mar 31, 2014). *Vietnam 40 years after: Children of Agent Orange.* https://www.youtube.com/watch?v=at2AcXii-YQ (00–3:41 free video).

Cites on dioxin in Sills, *Toxic war*: 2,4,5-T a crystal, mixed with alcohol or other chemicals, becomes a liquid called an ester. Chapter 1, Kindle location 401; 2,4,5-trichlorophenol (2,4,5-T) known as TCP, Chapter 2, Kindle location 741; most potent is TCDD, Chapter 2, Kindle location 758; inhalation danger, p. 99, Kindle location 2500.

[109] Hoffmann report October 5, 1959 to Pentagon, library, others links dioxin TCDD with 2,4,5-T and deaths. Sills, *Toxic war*, Chapter 5, Kindle locations 1216–1277, 5980 n. 16 (date of report). Mid-1950s, German discover TCDD in 2,4,5-T cause chloracne, communicate to US. Sills, *Toxic war*, Chapter 2, Kindle location 763–774. Kassel on stopping research 1959; but research continued. Sills, *Toxic war*, pp. 48–50, Kindle location 1257–1270. Chief scientist, USAF on sprayings of people. Sills, *Toxic war*, Chapter 8, Kindle location 1746–1753. 829. Agent Orange on base camps. Sills, *Toxic war*, Chapter 13, Kindle location 2974. Dioxin increase1965. Roesch, *Corporate Tsunami in Countryside Paradise*, p. 347.

[110] Chloracne 1937 meeting, three deaths; Monsanto, US Public Health, Harvard, General Electric and others. Chloracne symptoms, preventive recommendations, but still chloracne, some leading to death; Tilles, *The History of Chloracne and Dioxin*, 3.1.9, Kindle location 854–961. Chloracne World War Two. Tilles, *The History of Chloracne and Dioxin*, 3.1.9, Kindle location 1014–1065.

[111] Situation 1964. Willbanks, *Vietnam War Almanac*, items: April desertions and low enlistment, draft, p. 61, Kindle location 1515–20; April Southern regrouping zone forces seen as ineffective, p. 66, Kindle location 1550; May 2 USNS Card escort aircraft carrier sunk, p. 67, Kindle location 1576. May 3, Southern regrouping zone Rangers 100

wiped out, p. 67, Kindle location 1582; May 14, Southern regrouping zone force wiped out, 54 dead, 50 wounded, p. 68, Kindle location 1608. TNT on Card, aircraft lost, US casualties. Mã Thiện Đồng (2011). *Người Đánh chìm Tàu chiến Mỹ USNS Card*. TP. Hồ Chí Minh. NXB Tổng Hợp TP. Hồ Chí Minh, Foreword, pp. 17–20, 95–100. Dioxin increase 1965. Corporate

[112] Intelligence. Sills, P. (2014). *Toxic war : The story of Agent Orange*. Nashville: Vanderbilt University Press, p. 52, Kindle location 1278. Feb 600 DRV stood off 3,000, p. 60, Kindle location 1424–29; Southern regrouping zone sentiment for neutrality, p. 61, Kindle location 1445. Battlefield losses, views, first half 1964. Willbanks, J. (2013). *Vietnam War Almanac: An in-depth guide to the most controversial war in American history*. NY: Skyhorse Publishing, items: March 16 McNamara reports unquestionably worse, p. 62, Kindle location 1470; April, DRV regular troops North Zone to Southern regrouping zone, p. 64, Kindle location 1507.

[113] Views and battlefield losses, June and July 1964. Willbanks, Vietnam War Almanac, items: June 17 Top advisor reported Viet Cong greatly improved, p. 73, Kindle location 1725; two outposts Sai Gon area overwhelmed, p. 75, Kindle location 1756; July 3, 4 and 6 guerrilla attacks, casualties, pp. 75–76, Kindle location 1770–76; July 11–12, largest battle, 1,000 guerrillas killing 200, seizing 100 weapons, p. 76, Kindle location 1787; July 13, guerrillas ambush, killing 16 Southern regrouping zone, 3 US soldiers, p. 76, Kindle location 1787; July 15–16, 16 clashes stepped-up activity, indicate soldiers from HCM Trail, p. 77, Kindle location 1798.

[114] Increased dioxin from one to three gallons per acre. Sills, Toxic war, pp. 52–53, Kindle location 1288–1311. Dioxin acres sprayed 1963–65. Buckingham, *Operation Ranch Hand*, p. 200, Table 4. Scientists believe lower concentration, DOD overrule; scientists testify much too high. Sills, *Toxic war*, Chapter 6 Ranch Hand, Kindle location 1290.

[115] By 1965 NLF controlled most of countryside. Ham, P. (2007). *Vietnam : the Australian War*. NY, Australia: HarperCollins Publishers Australia Pty Ltd., Chapter 6, Kindle location 1359. NLF control of areas. Ngo, "Vietnam: The real enemy," pp. 6–34, especially 23. DRV victory at Binh Giã; Ho Chi Minh Trail on the Sea weapons. Ban Chấp Hành Đảng Bộ Tỉnh Bà Rịa-Vũng Tàu, *Đường Hồ Chí Minh Trên Biển Bà Rịa-Vũng Tàu*, pp. 7, 83. Southern regrouping zone losses at Binh Gia, resistance capability. Hieu Dinh Vu, "THE BATTLE OF BINH GIA (12/28/1964)" REPUBLIC of VIETNAM ARMY RANGER, http://www.bietdongquan.com/article1/armyranger.htm Six-day battle at Binh Gia. Willbanks, *Vietnam War Almanac*, p. 101, Kindle location 2357–2373; Sheehan, *Bright shining lie*, p. 382, Kindle location 7127–7133.

[116] Commentators on no mass support in south. Chomsky, *The Myth of American Idealism*, p. 69, Kindle location 1270.
[117] July 1965 meetings with LBJ. Bird, K. (1992) (Kindle ed. 2017). *The chairman : John J. McCloy, the making of the American establishment.* New York ; London ; Toronto ; Sydney ; Tokyo ; Singapore: Simon & Schuster, Kindle locations 12101, 12154, 12169 (July 1965 meetings); Kindle loca-tions 12193, 12200 (July 1965 LBJ decision to escalate). Senior Advisory Group. Shoup, *Imperial brain trust*, p. 240. Kill more VC. McMaster, Dereliction of duty, Chapters 12, 13, Kindle locations 5074, 5464.
[118] Quote on civilian deaths widespread; Turse research methods. Turse, N. (2013). *Kill anything that moves : The real American war in Vietnam* (1st ed., American empire project). New York: Metropolitan Books/Henry Holt and Company, pp. 14–22, Kindle location 241–375 (Quote at 365).
[119] Civilians dying every day, indiscriminate aerial bombing villages, napalming village, interview pilot. By CHARLES MOHR Special to The New York Times, "Air Strikes hit Vietcong–and South Vietnam Civilians," New York Times (1923–Current file) 05 Sep 1965: E4.
[120] Huge bombs, shells; in a bind, unload, usually kill more. Turse, *Kill anything that moves*, pp. 22, 86, Kindle location 369, 1479–1484 and n.43. Attacks on village. Truong Thi Bon. Recorded interview of Truong Thi Bon by author with Trần Thị Phương Thủy, May 8, 2019.
[121] News reports, photos deformities, late 1967, face like duck. Wilcox, F. (2011). *Scorched Earth : Legacies of chemical warfare in Vietnam* (A Seven Stories Press 1st ed.). New York: Seven Stories Press, pp. 156–157, Kindle location 1959–1965. In 1967 new birth defects Sai Gon, coincide increased Agent Orange. Schuck, P. (1986). *Agent Orange on Trial : Mass toxic disasters in the courts.* Cambridge, Mass.: Belknap Press of Harvard University Press, p. 22.
[122] Number of people sprayed estimate; other hamlets numbers not available. Stellman, Jeanne Mager and Steven D. Stellman (Published online: May 09, 2018). "Agent Orange During the Vietnam War: The Lingering Issue of its Civilian and Military Health Impact." https://ajph.aphapublications.org/doi/full/10.2105/AJPH.2018.304426.
[123] Sept. 11, 2001 attacks. https://en.wikipedia.org/wiki/September_11_attacks

CHAPTER 6

[124] Blessed righteous. Jesus, *Bible, New International Version*, Matthew 5:6.
[125] One standard to Europe and another for everyone else. Spektor, Matias (January 2025). "Rise of the Nonaligned: Who Wins in a

Multipolar World?" Foreign Affairs: Vol. 104, Number 1, January/February2025,p.41.https://www.foreignaffairs.com/united-states/rise-nonaligned-multipolar-world-matias-spektor. Dulles on Christians for free enterprise. Blum, W. (2003). *Killing hope: U.S. military and CIA interventions since World War II.* London: Zed, Introduction. 10, Kindle location 242.

[126] Golden Rule: Hinduism Golden Rule: "This is the sum of duty; do naught onto others what you would not have them do unto you." — Mahabharata 5,1517 https://americanhumanist.org/paths/hinduism/Right actions, Buddha. Dhammananda, K. S. (1987). *What Buddhists believe* (Expanded and rev. ed.; 4th ed.). Buddhist Missionary Society, *Vol. 1*, pp. 282–90. Islam and Golden Rule. http://islam.ru/en/con- tent/story/golden-rule-islam. Do to others. *Bible*, New International Version, Matthew 7:12. Hindu rule. Mahabharata; Judaism on Golden Rule. Sussman, Lance J. Rabbi. "What Judaism Says About the Golden Rule." https://reformjudaism.org/learning/torah-study/acharei-mot-kdoshim/what-judaism-says-about-golden-rule. Golden Rule virtually all religions, ethics. http.en.wikipedia/golden_rule. To some, no ideals stretch across time, cultures. Kloppenberg, James. T. (2012). *The education of Barack Obama* (Princeton Shorts ed.). Princeton University Press, Kindle location 912.

[127] Malraux newspaper, colonization against elementary principle of justice. Nguyen, M. "Who has the Right to colonize?" *L'Indochine Enchainee*, (1925–1926), ed. 19, Sai Gon, pp. 1–2. Annamite children dying. Malraux, A. (1925). "Question Annamite: La Mortalite Infantile et la Repartition des Impots," *L' Indochine Enchainee*, edition 7, 1925, Sai Gon.

[128] Kieu, love endures, false debt and separation 15 years, universal value on destiny under foreign domination. Nguyen, D., translated by Counsell, Michael (2017). *Kieu: The Tale of a Beautiful and Talented Young Girl*, Bilingual Vietnamese-English. Ha Noi: The Gioi Publishers, Kindle locations 613, 727–1228, 4130, 4486.

[129] Macbeth saved kingdom, King grant, Macbeth killed, coverup. Shakespeare, W. & Craig, W.J. ed. (1936). *The Complete Works of William Shakespeare*, NY: Oxford University Press, "MacBeth," Act 1, Scene 2 (rebellion, invasion) Kindle location 69245–87; Act 1, Scene 3 to Scene 7 (King), Kindle location 69428–69601; Act 2, Scene II, Kindle location 69715–69952, and Act III, Scene I, Kindle location 70020–70177, 70227–70273; Act III, Scene VI Forres. The palace, Kindle location 70458–70490; Act IV, Scene III Kindle locations 70776–70970 (people fight back). Macbeth year 1606. Shakespeare, W. & Pierce, J. ed. (2010). *Macbeth : With Contemporary Criticism.* San Francisco: Ignatius Press, Kindle location 32.

130. Wanting independence 500 million; leaders. Economic and Financial Group (1944, June 24). "The United States And The Colonial Problem, E-B71." *CFR Studies of American Interests in the War and the Peace.* NY: Council on Foreign Relations, Inc., p. 5.
131. Robeson passport revocation, Dulles, testimony. Zinn, *Voices of a people's history of the United States*, Chapter 16, Kindle locations 7551–7607. Robeson passport. Performer, petition. Horne, *Paul Robeson : The Artist as Revolutionary*, pp. 105, 126–28, Kindle location 2025, 2392–2436. Racial wealth gap asset ratio 12-to-1. Baradaran, *The Color of Money*, p. 249, Kindle Location 5243. Racial wealth gap 10-to-1. Hannah-Jones, *The 1619 Project*, p. 471. Racial wealth gap ratio 12-to-1.
132. Disregard elementary moral principles, US. Chomsky, *Who Rules the World?*, pp. 11–15, Kindle locations 194–261.
133. Structures independent of US, great powers excluding US. Drezner, Daniel W. (November 12, 2024). The End of American Exceptionalism: Trump's Reelection Will Redefine U.S. Power. *Foreign Affairs*, November/December 2024, Volume 103, Number 6.
134. CELAC challenges US. Chomsky, Noam; Prashad, Vijay. *The Withdrawal: Iraq, Libya, Afghanistan, and the Fragility of U.S. Power*, p. 147). The New Press. Kindle Edition 1471. Sustainable development cooperation CELAC & EU. Moure Pino, A. M., & Janas, W. (2024). EU-CELAC Strategic Partnership: Fostering Peace, Democracy, and Human Rights Towards the 2030 UN Sustainable Development Goals. *Latin American Journal of Trade Policy, 18*(19). Asian Infrastructure Investment Bank added to Global South. Spektor, Matias (January 2025). "Rise of the Nonaligned: Who Wins in a Multipolar World?" Foreign Affairs: Vol. 104, Number 1, January/February 2025, p. 44. https://www.foreignaffairs.com/united-states/rise-nonaligned-multipolar-world-matias-spektor
135. US foreign policy change is needed. Chivvis, C. & Stephen Wertheim (October 14, 2024). "America's Foreign Policy Inertia: How the Next President Can Make Change in a System Built to Resist It." *Foreign Affairs*, September/October 2024**,** Volume 103, Number 5, NY: Council on Foreign Relations. *Newsweek* says CFR "foreign policy establishment." Shoup, *Imperial brain trust*, pp. 4, 7, citing *Newsweek* issue of Sept 6, 1971.
136. Imperial transgressions. Bacevich, A. (March 30, 2021). Requiem for the "American Century" Consortium News. https://consortiumnews.com/2021/03/30/requiem-for-the-american-century/ American operations catalyst for blowback. Turse, N. (2015) *Tomorrow's Battlefield*, Haymarket Books. Kindle Location 1041. Not overcome nationalism, blowback from erroneous hard power. Falk, R., & Andersson, Stefan.

(2018). *Revisiting the Vietnam War and International Law : Views and Interpretations of Richard Falk*, Cambridge, United Kingdom; New York, NY: Cambridge University Press, (p. 10, xiv), Kindle locations 146–161, 223.

CFR journal article on Middle East, Washington less influence credibility in region. Indyk, Martin (*February 20,* 2024) The Strange Resurrection of the Two-State Solution: How an Unimaginable War Could Bring About the Only Imaginable Peace. March/April 2024. *Foreign Affairs,* NY: Council on Foreign Relations.

". . . and to save our own country from becoming an object of hatred and contempt for civilized mankind." Noam Chomsky — U.S. Interest in Vietnam, New York, 1968. Tannhauser108, Jul 14, 2013 https://www.youtube.com/watch?v=hLsNOEfDrNw , 17:25–17:44 of 17:50.

State terror. Woods, C. (2020). *Freedom Incorporated: Anticommunism and Philippine Independence in the Age of Decolonization.* Cornell University Press, p. 188, Kindle Location 4581.

CHAPTER 7

[137] Pilot Randy Floyd on effort to avoid logical conclusions. Schneider, B., Davis, P., Klingman, L., Martin, S., Westmoreland, W. C. (William C., Clifford, C. M., Fulbright, J. W. (James W., Rostow, W. W. (Walt W., & Ellsberg, D. (2002). *Hearts and Minds* (Widescreen.). Home Vision, 1:47:00–1:47:14.

[138] Cherokee treaty, broken, Trail of Tears. Hannah-Jones, N., Roper, Caitlin, Silverman, Ilena, Silverstein, Jake, & New York Times Company. (2021). *The 1619 Project: A new origin story* (First ed.). New York: One World, pp. Adams on native Americans. Chomsky, N. (2015). *Year 501: The conquest continues.* London: Pluto Press, Preface to 2015 edition, Kindle location 48. Centuries of violence against black slaves; Freed slaves deaths and illnesses, failure of Reconstruction, violence against black citizens. Hannah-Jones, *The 1619 Project,* pp. 9–11, 27–32, 234–36, 279–82, 389–90. Downs, J. (2012). *Sick from freedom: African-American illness and suffering during the Civil War and Reconstruction.* Oxford University Press.

[139] Wallace triumph with China on independence for Indo-China. White, J. T. and Company (1971), *The National Cyclopaedia of American Biography,* v. 53, p. 16. FDR on Wallace trip to China. Wise, J. (1948). *Meet Henry Wallace.* New York: Boni and Gaer, p. 37.

Pauley's coup. Roesch, *Corporate Tsunami in Countryside Paradise,* pp. 167–68. Nomination devious. Ferrell, R. (2000). *Choosing Truman: The Democratic Convention of 1944,* Columbia, Missouri: University of Missouri Press, p. 1, Kindle location 110. "Pauley's coup," Wallace ahead first round, dropped on later ballots. Truman vice-presidential candidate. Pauley background. Jay, P., ed. (2012). "The Coup Against Henry Wallace," *the Real News*, filmed interview of Peter Kuznick, Youtube. Truman elected VP. Ferrell, *Choosing Truman*, p. 97, Kindle location 1860. Almost no international experience. Logevall, *Embers of war*, Chapter 3, p. 87, Kindle location 1707.April 12, 1945, FDR died. Logevall, *Embers of war*, Chapter 2, Kindle location 1326. Interagency committee brief Truman April 13. Logevall, *Embers of War*, Chapter 3, Kindle location 1705–1717. Briefing prep, brief Truman, dander. Isaacson, *The wise men*, pp. 260– 61, Kindle location 4324–4343.

Truman novice foreign policy, others sense opening, none of FDR interest in Indochina future, probably not know of trusteeship. State-War-Navy committee. Logevall, *Embers of war*, p. 87, Kindle location 1708–1718, 473.

Truman knew little or nothing on postwar planning for Viet Nam. Bradley, *Imagining Vietnam and America*, Chapter 3, Kindle location 1517

[140] Briefing prep, brief Truman, dander. Isaacson, *The Wise Men*, pp. 260–61, Kindle location 4324–4343. Interagency committee April 13. Logevall, *Embers of War*, Chapter 3, Kindle location 1705–1717. Grand area, limitation of sovereignty. CFR memo E-B19, "The War and United States Foreign Policy: Needs of Future United States Foreign Policy (October 9, 1940)." Quote on limitation of sovereignty. Shoup, *Imperial Brain Trust*, p. 130.

[141] No war if FDR lived. Buttinger, J. (1977). *Vietnam : the Unforgettable Tragedy*. NY: Horizon Press. p. 24.

[142] Truman low on experience, quote little brains so advisors. Isaacson, *The Wise Men*, pp. 255–56, Kindle location 4208–4709. CFR people 42 percent top foreign policy posts Truman presidency. Shoup, *Imperial brain trust*, p. 62. Obama some knowledge but conciliator. Kloppenberg, James. T. (2012). *The education of Barack Obama* (Princeton Shorts ed.). Princeton University Press.

[143] No mention of country knowledge; called "right-wing zealot." Evans, *The Education of Ronald Reagan*, entire book, and p. 163, Kindle location 2921. Reagan actor, governor, president, style. Gans, *White House Warriors*, p. 63, Kindle Location 1236.

[144] Obama education and thinking. Kloppenberg, James. T. (2012). *The education of Barack Obama* (Princeton Shorts ed.). Princeton University Press, Kindle locations 141–162 (Indonesian influence) and entire short book, Kindle locations 1–970.

[145] CFR 529 members in gov't 2011, Obama advisors. Shoup, *Wall Street's Think Tank*, pp. 95, 98, Kindle Locations 2028, 2096. Drone increase

under Obama. Shoup, *Wall Street's Think Tank*, p. 262, Kindle Location 5812.

[146] A DRV wins battles in 1950, so US alternative plan. Roesch, *Corporate Tsumani in Countryside Paradise*, Chapters 25, 26.

[147] Geneva left Viet Nam one nation, did not mention North or South Viet Nam. Geneva Agreements 20–21 July, 1954. *Agreement on the Cessation of Hostilities in Viet-Nam 20 July, 1954*, (espec Articles 1, 14), and Final Decl. The Avalon Project, Yale Law School, https://avalon.law.yale.edu/20th_century/inch001.asp
https://peacemaker.un.org/sites/peacemaker.un.org/files/KH-LAVN_540720_GenevaAgreements.pdf.

France duty to administer; relations with US, money. Lawyers Committee on American Policy Towards Vietnam. Consultative Council. (1967). *The Vietnam War and international law: The illegality of the United States military involvement (2d ed.)*. Flanders, N.J.: O'Hare Books, pp. 132, 139, 336.

Additional points this section. Roesch, *Corporate Tsumani in Countryside Paradise,*

[148] France duty to administer; pressure on relations with US, US money for French invasion. Lawyers Committee on American Policy Towards Vietnam. Consultative Council. (1967). *The Vietnam War and international law: The illegality of the United States military involvement (2d ed.)*. Flanders, N.J.: O'Hare Books, pp. 132, 139, 336. US pressure, French final withdraw April 28, 1956. Ngo, V. (1989). "Vietnam: The real enemy." Critical Asian Studies, 21 (6–34).

[149] Southern regrouping zone soldiers killing "large numbers" of civilians. Kidder to Secretary of State (February 1, 1955), telegram. Murphy, G., Hydrick, Blair, & United States. Department of State. (1988). *Confidential U.S. State Department central files, Indochina, 1955–1959*. 751G.00/2-155, a8456, Reel 1, Frame 00397.
Nuremberg Judgment, standard of aggression. Falk, *Revisiting the Vietnam War and International Law*, pp. 225, 286, 330–336, Kindle locations 6750, 8475, n. 78, 8954–9165.

[150] US and Diem. Roesch, *Corporate Tsumani in Countryside Paradise*, pp. 218–19, 221, 233–37, 247, 249–59, 260–62, 271–72, 286.

[151] Death penalty if behalf of organization designated Communist. Thayer, C. A. (1989). *War by other means : national liberation and revolution in Viet-Nam 1954-60*. Allen & Unwin, p. 82.

[152] Geneva Accords. Roesch, *Corporate Tsumani in Countryside Paradise*, Chapters 29, 30.

153. Congress for Cultural Freedom a CIA creation, CIA books were published in 1950s. Williams, S. (2021). *White Malice: The CIA and the Covert Recolonization of Africa.* NY: Hachette Book Group, Public Affairs Press, pp. 81–84, Kindle Locations 1111–1148. CIA backed publishing. Price, Ray (Sept. 13, 2020). "The CIA Book Publishing Operations: Fragments of Sol Chaneles' Lost Manuscript" CounterPunch.

154. Rostow background, distinguished professor MIT. Milne, D. (2008). *America's Rasputin : Walt Rostow and the Vietnam War* (1st ed.). New York: Hill and Wang, pp. 6–10, Kindle location 124–197. Rostow MIT, appointment, on NSC, posts. Bird, K. (1998). *The color of truth: McGeorge Bundy and William Bundy, brothers in arms : A biography.* New York: Simon & Schuster. Chapter 9, Kindle locations 4205–4211. Rostow CFR member. Shoup, *Imperial brain trust*, pp. 64, 246–47. Said Vietnam not self-sustained growth, traditional societies "incapable of self-organization." Rostow, *The stages of economic growth*, Title page, Preface to Third Edition, p. 109, Kindle locations 73, 413, 2750.

155. Reason victory over Mongols; later descriptions country. Nguyen Khac Vien, *Vietnam : A Long History*, pp. 57–69. Viet Nam organization and victories. Roesch, *Corporate Tsunami in Countryside Paradise*, Ch 2, 33 & 34.

156. Le Thanh Khoi economic history, available to Rostow. Lê, T. (1955). *Le Viêt-nam : histoire et civilisation.* Paris: Éditions de Minuit, pp. 3, 119, 149–50, 483–84, 487–90, 810. Fighting invasions requires spirit of unity and belief in independence (love of country), community spirit, spirit of autonomy says Tran Ngoc Them. Trần Ngọc Thêm (2001). *Tìm về Bản Sắc Văn hóa Việt Nam: Cái Nhìn Hệ Thống-Loại Hình – Discovering the identity of Vietnamese culture : Typological-systematic views* (In lần thứ 3, sửa chữa và bổ sung, ed.). Việt Nam: Thành Phố Hồ Chí Minh. NXB T.P. Hồ Chí Minh, p. 203.

157. Alsop writings and citations. Ngô, V. (May 2009), From Polarization to Integration in Vietnam. *Journal of Contemporary Asia*, Vol. 39, No. 2, pp. 295–304, especially 296–97. After winter 1954 trip. J. Alsop, "A Man in a Mirror," The Reporter, 25 June, 1955: 35-6.

158. Rostow myopia, life's work to "answer." Milne, *America's Rasputin*, pp. 7, 52, Kindle locations 158, 937.

159. Outsiders changing territory can violate fairness, deep emotions. Bowman, Isaiah. The Strategy of Territorial Decisions. *Foreign Affairs*, 1 January 1946, pp. 177 (nerve center), 178 (fairness, stable peace), NY: Council on Foreign Relations. https://www.foreignaffairs.com/articles/world/1946-01-01/strategy-territorial-decisions. Accessed 29 October 2024. Bowman assistant prof, The Inquiry. Roesch, *Corporate Tsunami in Countryside Paradise*. Chapter 9.

Endnotes

[160] In 1951, JFK colonial trip, in Viet Nam. Logevall, *Embers of war*, Preface, pp. xii–xiii, Kindle location 66–95. JFK newsreel. *Film segment, first floor display*. JFK Presidential Museum, Boston, Mass, 2008 author visit. JFK 1951 realization, ensuing efforts to get out, *Stars and Stripes & NYT* headlines. Douglass, *JFK and the Unspeakable*, pp. 218–85, KL 4404–5540 (news reports pp. 219, 285, Kindle locations 4420, 5549)

[161] News reports on withdrawal. Douglass, *JFK and the Unspeakable*, pp. 219, 285, Kindle Locations 4420, 5549. Diem heard US might withdraw; contacted North, NLF. Ngo, "*Vietnam: The real enemy*," p. 22; Contact North. Ngo, "After the Fall of Saigon," p. 81. North interest. Miller, *Misalliance*, pp. 305, Kindle location 5946–5953. JFK favorable to Diem initiative. Douglass, *JFK and the Unspeakable*, p. 243 (JFK had been there, seen), 260 (want explore mutual disengagement, Kindle location 4844, 5106–5117. Withdrawal orders by JFK, though conditional; Diem settlement proposal, brother on troop withdrawal. Chomsky, *Rethinking Camelot*, Introduction and Chapter 1, Kindle locations 721–734, 1417–1448 (condition); Chapter 1, Kindle location 1430–1460 (Diem proposal goal unification following Geneva Accords.

[162] Some citations of other works showing crossfire on JFK: Experienced trauma doctors at Parkland Hospital Dallas described a small entry wound, with a "large, gaping would," in the back of JFK's head. At the hospital, An autopsy was done in Maryland by a government doctor inexperienced in gunshot wounds. Of 107 witnesses, 77 said from the front. Crenshaw, Charles A., Jens Hansen, & J. Gary Shaw (2013). *JFK Has Been Shot: A Parkland Hospital Surgeon Speaks Out*, Pinnacle Books (entire book), p. 21 (autopsy doctors no experience, 61 (77 of 107), Kindle locations 240. 743. False photo of JFK wounds, Autopsy doctors no expericnce. Crenshaw, *JFK Has Been Shot*, pp. 21, 93, Kindle Locations 240, 1183. Warren fable. Crenshaw, *JFK Has Been Shot*, p. 16, Kindle location 162.

Occipital bone discrepancy Douglass, *JFK and the unspeakable*, pp. 42, 564, 755, Kindle Locations 593, 11771, 15986 16004.

No independent investigators. Marrs, J. (1989). *Crossfire : the plot that killed Kennedy*. Carroll & Graf Publishers, p. 552, Kindle Edition 14369.

Dulles on Warren Commission investigating himself. Douglass, *JFK and the unspeakable*, Kindle Locations 1001–1019. Bay of Pigs invasion, CIA false to JFK ab0ut farmers would rise up, JFK fired Allen Dulles. Talbot, *The Devil's Chessboard*, pp. 45– 51, Kindle locations 941–1067. CIA intent to deceive JFK so he would have to send in Marines. Douglass, *JFK and the unspeakable*, pp. 64–66 (Bay of Pigs) Kindle locations 962–981. JFK seen as weak after Bay of Pigs. Talbot, D. (2007). *Broth-*

ers: *The Hidden History of the Kennedy Years.* NY: Free Press, Chapter 2, Kindle location 930–1073. Allen Dulles, John J. McCloy, and David Rockefeller CFR Directors in 1963. Fifield, R., & Council on Foreign Relations. (1963). *Southeast Asia in United States policy.* (1st ed.). New York: Published for the Council on Foreign Relations by Praeger, p. v.

McCloy fame ten-year investigation, Bethlehem Steel, proved Germans 1916 blew up "Black Tom" munitions plant in New Jersey. Sleuthing in Europe among high Nazi officials and in the US for that case, McCloy won a reversal in 1939 in the European Claims Commission. Isaacson, *The Wise Men,* 119-20 (law), 122-124 (investigation) 336.

[163] JFK battle Natl Sec State on détente Cuba, USSR. Douglass, *JFK and the Unspeakable,* pp. 218–85, 510 (Alliance for Progress), KL 4404–5540, 10853. Anger at steel price roll back, JFK try ease inflation rate, apple cart quote. Marrs, *Crossfire,* pp. 245, 255, 548–49, Kindle locations 6463, 6696, 14269–14289. Alliance for Progress change US approach, Goodwin & Guevara meet. Talbot, *Brothers,* pp. 38, 45, 56–59, Kindle locations 799, 943, 1158–1221.

[164] December 21, 1963 report signed by McNamara but prepared by CIA. Prouty, L. (2008). *The Secret Team :The CIA and its allies in control of the United States and the world.* NY: Skyhorse Publishing, pp. 12–14, Kindle Location 662–692.

[165] New industrial heartland, Jules Henry, Bernard Fall. Roesch, *Corporate Tsunami,* Ch 40–42.

[166] Bombs and explosives Viet Nam three times over World War II. Miguel, E. & Gerard Roland. (October 2005). "The Long Run Impact of Bombing Vietnam," US: Department of Economics, University of California, Berkeley, p. 2.

[167] British "herbicides" Malaysia said to be precedent. Gilpatric, Roswell; Dept of Defense; National Security Council (Nov. 21, 1961). *National Security Action Memorandum No. 115 Defoliant Operations in Vietnam,* 30 November 1961. (NSAM 115). United States Government https://www.jfklibrary.org/asset-viewer/archives/jfknsf-332-017#?image_identifier=JFKNSF-332-017-p0002.

British "herbicides" Malaysia. Tilles, G. (2018). *The History of Chloracne and Dioxin,* Kindle location 2384.

[168] Number of people sprayed estimate; other hamlets numbers not available. Stellman, Jeanne Mager and Steven D. Stellman (Published online: May 09, 2018). "Agent Orange During the Vietnam War: The Lingering Issue of its Civilian and Military Health Impact." https:/ajph.aphapublications.org/doi/full/10.2105/AJPH.2018.304426.

[169] News reports, photos deformities, late 1967, face like duck. Wilcox, F. (2011). *Scorched Earth : Legacies of chemical warfare in Vietnam* (A Seven Stories Press 1st ed.). New York: Seven Stories Press, pp. 156–157, Kindle location 1959–1965. In 1967 new birth defects Sai Gon, coincide increased Agent Orange. Schuck, P. (1986). *Agent Orange on Trial : Mass toxic disasters in the courts.* Cambridge, Mass.: Belknap Press of Harvard University Press, p. 22.

[170] USAF study "deteriorating situation" high civilians directed USAF in spraying in Viet Nam. Buckingham, *Operation Ranch Hand*, pp. iv, 7–8. Chief scientist, USAF, spraying dioxin frightened people. Sills, *Toxic war*, Chapter 8, Kindle location 1746–1753.

[171] ARPA and NSC. Roesch, *Corporate Tsunami,* Chapter 34.

[172] Kennan on 50 percent, that is freedom to rob, exploit. Chomsky, *The Chomsky reader*, pp. 306–07, Kindle location 6464–6489.

[173] Kassel on cessation of dioxin. Roesch, *Corporate Tsunami,* Chapter 34.

[174] *Pentagon Papers* not mention early entry. United States. Department of Defense, *United States-Vietnam relations, 1945–1967, study prepared by the Department of Defense* (Pentagon Papers), Bk 1, pp. A-1–A-21.

[175] 1973 agreement, 1973 peace agreement. "Agreement on ending the war and restoring peace in Viet-Nam. Signed at Paris on 27 January, 1973." https://treaties.un.org/doc/ Publication/UNTS, volume-935-I-13295-English. Nixon letter prom- ise billions in aid. Lee Lescaze, L. & Washington Post (May 20, 1977). Nixon Note on Aid to Hanoi Disclosed. https://www.washing- tonpost.com/archive/politics/1977/05/20/nixon-note-on-aid-to-ha-noi-disclosed/88206081-016d-4e85-8d49-2c45fa0d9ad6/

Peace talks resume after US losses, agreement signed; Willbanks, *Vietnam War Almanac*, pp. 432–434, Kindle location 9470–9508Cites for embargo: Trade embargo after war. PORTER, G. (1977). "The U.S. and Vietnam: Between War and Friendship." *Southeast Asian Affairs*, 325–338. http://www.jstor.org/stable/27908325.

Cockburn, P.(1994, Feb 4) "US Finally Ends Trade Embargo." https://www.independent.co.uk/news/world/us-finally-ends-vietnam-embargo-1391770.html.

US uses several thousand military technicians who enter as civilians carrying on technological warfare after 1973 agreement. Ngo, Vinh Long with Laderman, Scott & Edwin A. Martini, editors (2013). *Four Decades on Viet Nam, the United States and the Legacies of the Second Indochina War.* Chapter 1: "Legacies Foretold: Excavating the Roots of Postwar Vietnam." Durham NC and London: Duke University Press, pp. 16–43, espec. 32–34.

Viet Nam agrees to pay "debt." "Hanoi Agrees to Pay Saigon's Debts to U.S." (1997). *New York Times (Online)*. Pay 145 million. https://www.nytimes.com/1997/03/11/world/hanoi-agrees-to-pay-saigon-s-debts-to-us.html

[176] Congressional testimony 2009 on dioxin victim needs in Viet Nam. US HOUSE OF REPRESENTATIVES, (4 June, 2009). "AGENT ORANGE: WHAT EFFORTS ARE BEING MADE TO ADDRESS THE CONTINUING IMPACT OF DIOXIN IN VIETNAM." SUBCOMMITTEE ON ASIA, THE PACIFIC AND THE GLOBAL ENVIRONMENT, COMMITTEE ON FOREIGN AFFAIRS, Washington, DC: USGPO.

[177] For Viet Nam victims, US requires each victim prove individual causation from dioxin to the disease; Dioxin victims at home, severe, await funding. Bailey, C., & Son, Le Ke (2017). *From Enemies to Partners: Vietnam, the U.S. and Agent Orange.* Chicago, IL: Anton Publishing, Introduction Kindle Location 178–184, 2124–2159. For US veterans, IOM presumes causation dioxin to some diseases. Sills, *Toxic War*, pp. 224, Kindle locations 5539.
Disabled dioxin victims. Photojournalism websites:
https://widerimage.reuters.com/story/legacy-of-agent-orange
https://www.globalresearch.ca/vietnams-horrific-legacy-the-children-of-agent-orange/5451862
https://www.businessinsider.com/paula-bronsteins-photos-of-disabled-agent-orange-vietnamese-2014-7.

[178] *Come Mister tally man.* https://genius.com/Harry-belafonte-banana-boat-song-lyrics

[179] *Lift Every Voice and Sing.* https://genius.com/James-weldon-johnson-lift-every-voice-and-sing-annotated

CHAPTER 8

[180] Not accept moral assumption that Palestinians do not belong to Palestine. Carim, Ashfaaq (March 15, 2024). "Ilan Pappe - how he became an Israeli dissident and on why Zionism will fail soon." UNAPOLOGETIC, Middle East Eye, 17:41–17:50 of 49:29.
https://www.youtube.com/watch?v=Bu1_OFUcd0g

[181] Elinor Ostrom quote.
https://www.goodreads.com/author/quotes/130561.Elinor_Ostrom
Elinor Ostrom, Governing the Commons: The Evolution of Institutions for Collective Action
Elinor Ostrom, Nobel Prize. https://www.nobelprize.org/search/?s=Elinor+Ostrom&nonce=1737244500000

[182] Sukarno opening address at Bandung. Pham, Q., & Shilliam, Robbie. (2016). *Meanings of Bandung : Postcolonial orders and decolonial visions*

Endnotes

(Kilombo (Series)). London ; New York: Rowman & Littlefield International, p. 14, Kindle location 508.

[183] Report postwar Thailand and Indo-China no great problems, market for Japan in US system, Japan lead region after defeat. Council on Foreign Relations, *The War and Peace Studies of the Council on Foreign Relations, 1939–1945*, " The Economic Organization of Peace in the Far East" June 20, 1941, War and Peace Studies, E-B33, p. 4.

[184] Bases in Thailand used in 1960s bombing Viet Nam. Colby, *Thy Will be Done*, pp. 550, 557. USAF Thailand WW II and after. Glasser, Jeffrey D. (1995). *The Secret Vietnam War: The United States in Thailand, 1961-1975*, McFarland & Company, Inc., North Carolina, p. 16. Thailand in proposed hydroelectric system with Viet Nam. Colby, G. & Dennett, Charlotte (1995). *Thy will be done : The conquest of the Amazon : Nelson Rockefeller and Evangelism in the age of oil* (1st ed.). NY: HarperCollins, pp. 548–62.

[185] Thailand in World War Two and 1950s, backing coup general, dummy company, 1976 coup. Fineman, D. (1996). *A Special Relationship: The United States and Military Government in Thailand*, 1947–1958. Honolulu, HI, USA: University of Hawaii Press, pp. 22, 115–133.

[186] Post WW-II US air force advisors, etc, stayed in Thailand, addition 1961 combat recon. Glasser, Jeffrey D. (1995). *The Secret Vietnam War: The United States in Thailand, 1961-1975.* McFarland & Company, Inc., North Carolina, p. 16.

[187] US backed military rulers and coups in Thailand during 1947–1976. Chomsky, N., & Herman, E. S. (1979). *The Washington connection and Third World fascism* (1st ed.). South End Press, p. 247–261, Kindle locations 4108–4341 (quote on CIA at 4209). US $10 million aid strengthens, Phibun disregard Foreign Ministry. Fineman, *A Special Relationship*, p. 115.

[188] Willis Bird, Sea Supply, and CIA. Fineman, *A Special Relationship*, p. 133.

[189] Phibun crackdown 1951–52. Fineman, *A Special Relationship*, pp. 165–68.

[190] Report countryside not involved in democracy; quislings with Japan not liked by most Thais. Council on Foreign Relations, *The War and Peace Studies of the Council on Foreign Relations, 1939–1945*, "Thailand, T-B65", (August 2, 1943), pp. 1–4 recent constitution gov't, little countryside participation; p. 6 quote "conciliatory and even indifferent," most live in rice paddies, p. 12 quislings.

[191] During 1954–59, Thai military spending 250 percent, per capita decrease. Chomsky, *The Washington connection and Third World fascism*, p. 249 Kindle location 4157

[192] US no support for Thai 1973–76 democracy; mil aid up, econ aid down. Chomsky, *The Washington connection and Third World fascism*, p. 257, 259 (no support demo), Kindle locations 4286, 4316.

[193] Oil drum burnings 1975–76 in Thailand. Bangkok Post (30 March 1975). "untitled article". Peagam, Norman (14 March, 1975). "Probing the 'Red Drum' Atrocities." Far Eastern Economic Review. The Guardian (7 Oct, 1976). "Brutal Thai Coup." https://www.theguardian.com/theguardian/1976/oct/07/fromthearchive.
Communist Suppression Operations Command in 1975. Montesano, *After the Coup*, pp. 267–68, 299 n. 2, Kindle locations 3672–3680, 4121 n.2.

[194] Thailand coups, 1976 massacre, *khana*, vs democracy, anti-communism, history of military & gov't characteristics. Montesano, *After the Coup*, pp. intro, 14, 39–41, 118–120, 212–213 (1976 coup & succeeding coups), 240–257, 270–74 Kindle locations 107–154, 572–609, 1744–1773, 3359–3389, 3952–4076, 4298–4366.

[195] Open rejection, major export markets. Montesano, *After the Coup*, pp. 47 (rejection), 478 (export markets), Kindle locations 610, 6714.

[196] Palestine and Israel issues. Council on Foreign Relations. *War and peace studies of the Council on Foreign Relations, 1939-1945*, T-B76 "Palestine: A Solution of Its Immediate Problem" (December 19, 1944), pp. 1–4 (p. 4, quote Decl), 5, 13–15 (problems of Arab Palestine nation) 17–18.

On Palestine, US calls freedom efforts "terrorism." Davis, Angela Y. (2016). *Freedom Is a Constant Struggle: Ferguson, Palestine, and the Foundations of a Movement*. Haymarket Books, Chicago, p. 79, Kindle location 1128.

Oil and US and others arming Israel during attacks. Malm, Andreas (2024, 8 April). "The Destruction of Palestine Is the Destruction of the Earth**.**" Verso Books Blog Post, pp. 2, 32. https://www.versobooks.com/en-gb/blogs/news/the-destruction-of-palestine-is-the-destruction-of-the earth

[197] Post-WW II possible policing Middle East with proxy force. CFR, The Oil Situation in the Middle East, March 25, 1944, A-B103, p. 8.War and Peace Studies, 1939–45, CFR Armaments Group, NY: Council on Foreign Relations.

[198] Chomsky, Noam. Who Rules the World? (American Empire Project) (p. 44 45). Henry Holt and Co.. Kindle Edition 784 793.

[199] Palestine, 1840 British conquest, start of Zionism, British wish for Jewish capitalism there. Andreas Malm, Andreas (8 April 2024). "The Destruction of Palestine Is the Destruction of the Earth." Verso blogpost. https://www.versobooks.com/en-gb/blogs/news/the-destruction-of-palestine-is-the-destruction-of-the-earth

[200] Zionism, Balfour decl causes "racial opposition". Council on Foreign Relations, *War and Peace Studies of the Council on Foreign Relations, 1939–1945, T-B68 "The New Zionism and a Policy for the United States,"* October 19, 1943, Territorial Group, pp. 1, 3 ("racial opposition"), 4–5 (US position), 6–8; Post-WW II policy on foreign oil. CFR, *War and Peace Studies*, 1939–45, CFR Territorial Group, T-B74, "Elements to be Considered in an Oil Policy for the United States" (May 16, 1944), Studies of American Interests in the war and the peace, pp. 1, 5–9; US interest in Israel is for access to Middle East oil and gas. Shoup, *Wall Street's Think Tank*, pp. 255–56, Kindle locations 5658–5670. Robert D. Blackwill and Walter B. Slocombe, Israel: A Strategic Asset for the United States (Washington, D.C.: Washington Institute for Near East Policy, 2011), 2–3. https://www.washingtoninstitute.org/policy-analysis/israel-strategic-asset-united-states-0

[201] One suggestion is Palestine should be required to bargain with new Israel. Council on Foreign Relations, *War and Peace Studies of the Council on Foreign Relations, 1939–1945*. "Future of the Jews in Europe with Special Relation to Palestine," EN-A25, May 31, 1943, Peace Aims Group, p. 1.

[202] Tribal culture Arabs, Palestine and Israel issues. Council on Foreign Relations (1946). *War and peace studies of the Council on Foreign Relations, 1939-1945*, T-B76 "Palestine: A Solution of Its Immediate Problem" (December 19, 1944), pp. 1–4 (pp. 2 & 4, quote Decl), 5, 13–15 (problems of Arab Palestine nation) 17–18.

[203] "Quote, "no inherent 'promise' of an independent Jewish state in Palestine can be evoked out of the wording of the 1917 Balfour Declaration itself." Council on Foreign Relations (1946). *The war and peace studies of the Council on Foreign Relations, 1939-1945*, T-B76 "Palestine: A Solution of Its Immediate Problem" (December 19, 1944), pp. 2 and 4.

[204] In 2024, 149 nations recognize Palestine. Shira Efron and Michael J. Koplow (July 17, 2024). The Palestinian Authority is Collapsing. *Foreign Affairs*, November/December 2024, Volume 103, Number 6. NY: Council on Foreign Relations. https://www.foreignaffairs.com/palestinian-territories/palestinian-authority-collapsing?

[205] The "reputational damage to the United States. . ." Miller, A. (Sept 29, 2024). America Needs a New Strategy to Avert Even Greater Catastrophe in the Middle East: Shuttle Diplomacy Must Be Backed by Meaningful Pressure. *Foreign Affairs*, November/December 2024, Volume 103, Number 6. NY: Council on Foreign Relations. https://www.foreignaffairs.com/israel/america-needs-new-strategy-avert-even-greater-catastrophe-middle-east

206 Nakba in 1948. Carim, Ashfaaq (March 15, 2024). "Ilan Pappe - how he became an Israeli dissident and on why Zionism will fail soon." UNAPOLOGETIC, Middle East Eye. https://www.youtube.com/watch?v=Bu1_OFUcd0g, 1:25–1:53, 2:43–3:34 of 49:29. https://www.youtube.com/watch?v=Bu1_OFUcd0g

207 Obama calls Palestine situation intolerable. Zeleny, Jeff; Adam Cowell (4 June 2009). "Addressing Muslim World, Obama Pushes Mideast Peace". *The New York Times.* Archived from the original on 21 November 2011. Retrieved 5 June 2009. In 2009, about 130 nations for Palestine statehood. Boyle, Francis A. *(1 September 2009). Palestine, Palestinians and International Law. Clarity Press. p. 19. ISBN 978-0-932863-37-9.* "As I had predicted to the PLO, the creation of [a] Palestinian State was an instantaneous success. Palestine would eventually achieve *de jure* diplomatic recognition from about 130 states. The only regional hold-out was Europe and this was because of massive political pressure applied by the United States Government."

208 Mossadegh elected PM April 1951, nationalized oil. Abrahamian, Ervand (2013). *The coup : 1953, the CIA, and the roots of modern U.S.-Iranian relations.* The New Press, p.1, Kindle location 262. Iran coup forty percent oil to US oil companies; and Dulles development deal, shah CFR dinner, tanks; torture. Talbot, *The Devil's Chessboard,* pp. 229–231, 240, Kindle locations 4244–4267, 4424. Iran coup poverty, torture, executions. Blum, *Killing hope,* Chapter 9, Kindle location 2283. Brutal SAVAK police repression. Kinzer, *Overthrow,* pp. 199–201, Kindle locations 3629. Iran coup background. Roesch, *Corporate Tsunami in Countryside Paradise,* p. 251.

209 Forty percent to US oil; and Dulles development deal, coup, tank attack; torture. Talbot, *The Devil's Chessboard,* pp. 229–236, 239, Kindle locations 4244–4359. Iran coup poverty, torture, executions. Blum, *Killing hope,* Chapter 9, Kindle location 2283. SAVAK created in 1957. Abrahamian, Ervand (2013). *The coup : 1953, the CIA, and the roots of modern U.S.-Iranian relations.* The New Press, p. 214, Kindle location 3496. Brutal SAVAK police repression. Kinzer, *Overthrow,* pp. 199–201, Kindle locations 3629. Iran coup background. Roesch, *Corporate Tsunami in Countryside Paradise,* p. 251.

Iran oil 40 percent to US companies, names and percents. Abrahamian, Ervand (2013). *The coup,* p. 207, Kindle location 3423.

210 Ideological moral assumption; ridiculous assumption on Palestinians. Carim, "Ilan Pappe - how he became an Israeli dissident and on why Zionism will fail soon," 16:47–17:50 of 49:29. https://www.youtube.com/watch?v=Bu1_OFUcd0g

Endnotes

211 Genocide in Gaza including children. Sidhwa, Feroze & J. Mark Perlmutter (April 11, 2024). "As Surgeons, We Have Never Seen Cruelty Like Israel's Genocide in Gaza. Cover photo Gaza 2024 after indiscriminate airstrike by Israel. Photo by Jaber Jehad Badwan, 2024. See also Gaza in Index. Use permission granted through photographer's notice to Wikipedia. https://en.wikipedia.org/wiki/Gaza_Strip
Genocide in 2023 2024, worse than 1948 Nakba. Carim, Carim, "Ilan Pappe - how he became an Israeli dissident and on why Zionism will fail soon," 10:26–12:05 of 49:29. https://www.youtube.com/watch?v=Bu1_OFUcd0g

212 Control of thought in Israel. Carim, "Ilan Pappe - how he became an Israeli dissident and on why Zionism will fail soon,"18:44 –19:05, 21:34–24:30 of 49:29.

213 Israel pursue natural gas Eastern Mediterranean Sea. Piette, Betsey (Nov. 14, 2023). "Behind Israel's 'end game' for Gaza: Theft of offshore gas reserves". International Action Center. https://iacenter.org/2023/11/15/behind-israels-end-game-for-gaza-theft-of-offshore-gas-reserves/

214 The "reputational damage to the United States. . ." Miller, A. (Sept 29, 2024). America Needs a New Strategy to Avert Even Greater Catastrophe in the Middle East: Shuttle Diplomacy Must Be Backed by Meaningful Pressure. NY: *Foreign Affair*s, NY: Council on Foreign Relations. https://www.foreignaffairs.com/israel/america-needs-new-strategy-avert-even-greater-catastrophe-middle-east

215 All African People's Conference but no US message. Williams, *White Malice*, pp. 54–59, Kindle locations 702–793.

216 Ghana independence, support movements. Williams, *White Malice*, pp 175–187, Kindle locations 2533–2725.

217 US 1950s concern for its imports of Congo uranium. Williams, *White Malice*, p. 115, Kindle location 1644.

218 CIA fronts starting in 1950s, CIA secrecy, difficult to know what was done. Williams, *White Malice*, pp. 71–120 (CIA fronts), 591 (CIA secrecy), Kindle locations 973–1731, 8658; Angola and Stockwell on Africa. Stockwell, J. (1978). *In search of enemies : a CIA story* (1st ed.). Norton, pp. 34–43.

219 CIA fronts starting in 1950s, CIA secrecy, difficult to know what was done. Williams, *White Malice*, pp. 71–120 (CIA fronts), 591 (CIA secrecy), Kindle locations 973–1731, 8658.

220 Independence to 17 nations 1960. Mwakikagile, G. (2019). *Post-colonial Africa; A General Survey*, Amazon Digital Services LLC, Chapters Two, Seven, Kindle locations 1155, 1327 (mineral rich) 6078–6222, 6436, 9500.

[221] Indep Day, Lumumba counters Belgian king's paternalizing speech. Africa News Network (July 18. 2023). "The Speech that Got Patrice Lumumba Killed." https://www.youtube.com/watch?v=ouXas0XYHxM Lumumba and Katanga secession, Americans invested in minerals and others, fatal mistake. Colby, *Thy Will be Done*, pp. 325–27. Lumumba, "We will make sure that our country's land truly benefits its children." Witte, *The assassination of Lumumba*, pp. 5–6.

[222] Ghana effort to develop Congo. Williams, *White Malice* p. 219, Kindle Edition 3185.

[223] NSC on nil chance, Africans in trees, Military strong men. Williams, *White Malice*, pp. 168–169, Kindle locations 2429–2441. Eisenhower and others see mad dog, Eisenhower authorize kill. 1959, Meredith, M. (2011). *The fate of Africa : a history of the continent since independence* (Revised and updated ed.). Public Affairs, pp. 105–06, Kindle locations 1780–1788. Special Group on Lumumba. Colby, *Thy will be done*, p. 327.

[224] Gottlieb carries poison into Congo to kill Lumumba, Eisenhower orders him killed. Kinzer, S. (2019). *Poisoner in chief : Sidney Gottlieb and the CIA search for mind control* (First ed.). New York: Henry Holt and Company, pp. 175– 179, Kindle locations 3103–3175. 1960 Congo coup; Bissell ordered CIA agent to kill Prime Minister Lumumba. Agent testified "inconceivable . . . without the personal permission of Allen Dulles." United States. Congress. Senate. Select Committee to Study Governmental Operations with Respect to Intelligence Activities. (1976). *Alleged assassination plots involving foreign leaders : An interim report of the Select Committee to Study Governmental Operations with Respect to Intelligence Activities, United States Senate : Together with additional, supplemental, and separate views* (1st ed.). New York: Norton. (original **Publisher:** Washington : U.S. Govt. Print. Off.) Church Committee), pp. 37–39. Lumumba to Washington. Kinzer, *The Brothers*, Chapter 9 The Tall, Goateed Radical, Kindle location 4707–4730.

Congo. Elements of Counter-Guerrilla Warfare Task Force, US Central Intelligence Agency, *Elements Of US Strategy To Deal With "Wars Of National Liberation,"* December 8, 1961, reviewed by NSC, approved for release May 23, 2002, p.3. Bissell, R., Lewis, Jonathan E., & Pudlo, Frances T. (1996). *Reflections of a cold warrior : From Yalta to the Bay of Pigs*. New Haven: Yale University Press, p. 204. The Special Group". . . any particular activity which might contribute to getting rid of Lumumba." Colby, *Thy Will be Done*, pp. 327. Blum, W. (2003). *Killing hope : U.S. military and CIA interventions since World War II*. London: Zed, Kindle location 5115–5353. Congo coup CIA approval. Van Reybrouck, D., & Garrett, Sam. (2014). *Congo : The epic history of a people*

(First ed.). New York, NY: Ecco, an imprint of HarperCollins, p. 304, Kindle location 5799. Ghana facts and coup. Africa Reloaded (March 23, 2025). "Ghana President Reveals How CIA Orchestrated Coup That Overthrew Kwame Nkrumah." Video on Youtube. https://www.youtube.com/watch?v=yN_Cd7r_uG8

[225] US-France mutual support in Viet Nam and Africa. Former representative African Union to US, Arikana Chihombori-Quao, says African resources support France but no development in Africa, ex Niger uranium Al Jazeera (7 Sept, 2023). "Is it time for a 'reset' of the US strategy in Africa?" | The Bottom Line, https://www.aljazeera.com/program/the-bottom-line/2023/9/7/is-it-time-for-a-reset-of-the-us-strategy-in-africa, 0:00–4:41. US military missions in Niger 2023. The New Africa Channel (15 Sept, 2023). "Niger Releases French Official, Us Bases Resume Operations, EU Call To Counter Russia In Africa." https://www.you-tube.com/watch?v=H4_KpldXxvs

US-France mutual, Viet Nam and Africa. Roesch, *Corporate Tsunami in Countryside Paradise.* Niger parachute regiment 2007 training by US military. Wikipedia Public Domain photo, U.S. Navy photo by Mass Communication Specialist 1st Class Michael Larson - U.S. Navy News Service image 070406-N-6901L-018 https://commons.wikimedia.org/w/index.php?curid=5910468.html#a=search&s=322nd%20Parachute%20Regiment&n=90&guid=b3feba8b8d594b98b11ac0da741e776e62c4d095, Public Domain; http://www.defenseimagery.mil/imagery.

Kissinger US humiliation in Vietnam, to Angola; warning to public. Stockwell, *In Search of Enemies*, pp. 43 (Kissinger), 213 (independence), 254, 269-75.

[226] By 1978 bases & stations in Africa. Stockwell, *In search of enemies*, p. 254. CIA fronts starting in 1950s, CIA secrecy, difficult to know what was done. Williams, *White Malice*, pp. 71–120 (CIA fronts), 591 (CIA secrecy), Kindle locations 973–1731, 8658. AMSAC CIA front, meetings, pursue American foreign policy. Williams, *White Malice*, pp. 77–80, Kindle locations 1053–1103.

[227] France controls in former colonies, like US. Vallin, V-M (2015). "France as the Gendarme of Africa, 1960-2014." *Political Science Quarterly*, Vol. 130, No. 1 (Spring 2015), pp. 79-101 (23 pages), espec 80– 84 pillars; 84 like US; espec. 85–88. https://www.jstor.org/stable/43828515

[228] France less policing of Africa in late 1990s. Vallin, V-M (2015). "France as the Gendarme of Africa, 1960-2014." *Political Science Quarterly*, Vol. 130, No. 1 (Spring 2015), pp. 79-101 (23 pages), espec 85–88. https://www.jstor.org/stable/43828515

[229] Church Committee on CIA and Lumumba. United States.*Alleged Assassination Plots Involving Foreign Leaders*, Kindle Location 570.
[230] NSC on nil chance, Africans in trees. Williams, *White Malice*, pp. 168–169, 2429–2441. Congo copper 1959, Meredith, M. (2011). *The fate of Africa : a history of the continent since independence* (Revised and updated ed.). Public Affairs, p. 96, Kindle location 1628. US- VN War copper prices, Congo income from the war in Viet Nam. Van Rey Brouck, D., & Garrett, *Congo : the epic history of a people*, pp. 345–47, 356, 358.
[231] Independence to 17 nations 1960. Mwakikagile, Post-colonial Africa, Chapters Two, Seven, Kindle locations 1155, 6078–6222, 6436, 9500. West 1960–65 responsibility. Gondola, C. (2002). *The history of Congo* (Greenwood histories of the modern nations). Westport, Conn.: Greenwood Press, p. 115. Avery of CIA on Mobutu screwing up the Congo. *In search of enemies*, pp. 96–97.
[232] Congo coup to destroy continent, Lumumba bar way so he had to go, 1960–65 killings; 1960 Congo coup. Witte, L. (2001). *The assassination of Lumumba*. London; New York: Verso, pp. xvii, xxv, 177–78.
[233] Congo conflicts over five minerals. Eichstaedt, Peter (2011). *Consuming the Congo: War and Conflict Minerals in the World's Deadliest Place.* Chicago Review Press, Kindle Location 24.
[234] West profits from Africa that remains poor. Mwakikagile, *Post-colonial Africa*, p. 351, Kindle locations 6074.
[235] Stockwell on US in Congo. Stockwell, *In search of enemies*, pp. 38, 53 (million dollars a day). pp. 96–97, 137, 187–88, 203, 249–54, 269–75.
[236] Kissinger US humiliation in Vietnam, to Angola; warning to public. Stockwell, *In Search of Enemies*, pp. 43 (Kissinger), 213 (independence), 254, 269-75.
[237] Stockwell resigned and reported on CIA lies. Stockwell, *In Search of Enemies*, p. 10.
[238] Cabinda area; Angola civil war start; MPLA to US to plead friendliness. Business deals in Angola, CIA & Boeing plea in Washington, Kissinger oppose Angola right to deal with USSR as well as with US. Stockwell, *In Search of Enemies*, pp. 163 (Cabinda), 203–06.
[239] Angola civil war start; Angola to US to plead friendliness. Business deals in Angola. Stockwell, *In Search of Enemies*, pp. 192–93 (civil war, MPLA to Washington), 203–06, 208 (station chiefs).
[240] Business deals in Angola, plea in Washington by Luanda CIA station chief Temmons and Boeing. Stockwell, *In Search of Enemies*, p. 205.
[241] Kissinger oppose Angola right to deal with USSR as well as with US. Stockwell, *In Search of Enemies*, pp. 203–06.
[242] France delivery of weapons to CIA for Congo. Stockwell, *In Search of Enemies*, pp. 190–91.

243 Congo war 1996–2005 and 5 million deaths. Eichstaedt, P. H. (2011). *Consuming the Congo : war and conflict minerals in the world's deadliest place.* Chicago Review Press, Kindle location 62.

244 ACRI & ACOTA; Africom open. Turse, *Tomorrow's Battlefield*, Kindle locations 402– 480, 930, 1340–1353. *"Fact Sheet-African Crisis Response Initiative (ACRI)",* The White House Office of the Press Secretary, April 1, 1998. Archived from the original on March 8, 2013. Retrieved September 2, 2013. https://clintonwhitehouse4.archives.gov/Africa/19980401-20179.html

245 French-US mutual security 1996. Vallin, V-M (2015). "France as the Gendarme of Africa, 1960-2014." *Political Science Quarterly*, Vol. 130, No. 1 (Spring 2015), pp. 79-101 (23 pages), espec 89. https://www.jstor.org/stable/43828515

246 Vallin, V-M (2015). "France as the Gendarme of Africa, 1960-2014." *Political Science Quarterly*, Vol. 130, No. 1 (Spring 2015), pp. 79-101 (23 pages)

Political Science Quarterly, Vol. 130, No. 1 (Spring 2015), pp. 79-101 (23 pages) espec 89–90 (interventions). https://www.jstor.org/stable/43828515

247 US and China in Africa. Vallin, V-M (2015). "France as the Gendarme of Africa, 1960-2014." *Political Science Quarterly*, Vol. 130, No. 1 (Spring 2015), pp. 79-101 (23 pages), espec 92–93 (Africom, US and China). https://www.jstor.org/stable/43828515

248 Africom open 2007, war on terror. Vallin, V-M (2015). "France as the Gendarme of Africa, 1960-2014." *Political Science Quarterly*, Vol. 130, No. 1 (Spring 2015), pp. 79-101 (23 pages), espec 92–93 (Africom).

249 Boko Haram newsletter. African Arguments weekly newsletter (Nov. 9. 2011). "African Arguments Editorial – Boko Haram in Nigeria : another consequence of unequal development." Royal African Society. https://africanarguments.org/2011/11/african-arguments-editorial-boko-haram-is-another-consequence-of-unequal-development-in-nigeria/

250 Wikipedia Public Domain photo, U.S. Navy photo by Mass Communication Specialist 1st Class Michael Larson - U.S. Navy News Service image 070406-N-6901L-018 https://commons.wikimedia.org/w/index.php?curid=5910468.
html#a=search&s=322nd%20Parachute%20Regiment&n=90&guid=b3feba8b8d594b98b11ac0da741e776e62c4d095, Public Domain; http://www.defenseimagery.mil/imagery.

251 Africom, train local armies, joint training exercises in 2012. Turse, *Tomorrow's Battlefield*, Kindle locations 294 (joint) 399 (train), 411 (Africom 2008).

252 France control former colonies. Caspian Report (Feb 24, 2023). "France secretly owns 14 countries." https://www.youtube.com/watch?v=_-u1Pjce4Lg Niger_coup US training locals to fight insurgencies, air operations from Niger for intelligence for France in other countries. Turse, *Tomorrow's Battlefield*, Kindle Locations 402, 480, 1041 (blowback).

France topple or kill leaders. Motasem A Dalloul (August 25, 2023 at 8:57 am) "Africa will not allow France's exploitation to continue." Middle East Monitor https://www.middleeastmonitor.com/20230825-africa-will-not-allow-frances-exploitation-to-continue/

253 West profits from Africa that remains poor. Mwakikagile, *Post-colonial Africa*, p. 351, Kindle locations 6074.

254 Predatory states Mwakikagile, *Post-colonial Africa*, p. 372, Kindle Location 6440.

255 France pay 1/250 for uranium, France in Niger, world's 7th largest uranium producer, under- paid value of uranium The New Tourist (8 Sept, 2023). Niger Raises Its Uranium Prices From €0.80 per kilo to €200 per kilo. 2:16–2:21 of 5:17 (value amount France steals per year). US in Niger, drone bases strategic location, intvw of Stephanie Savell of Brown Univ. Costs of War project. Democracy Now. (1 Aug, 2023). "Did Western Military Presence Help Foster Coup in Niger, Where U.S. Has Drone Base & 1,000+ Troops?" https://www.democracynow.org/2023/8/1/ Niger_coup US training locals to fight insurgencies, air operations from Niger for intelligence for France in other countries. Turse, *Tomorrow's Battlefield*, Kindle Locations 402, 480, 1041 (blowback). Mwakikagile, *Post-colonial Africa*, p. 453, Kindle location 6093.

256 Traore says Africa resources but among poorest continents; Africa unite, collaborate. Africa Reloaded (27 August, 2023). "The Youngest President In Africa Ibrahim Traoré Shocked The World," 5:50–6:12, 654–705, 7:40–46 of 11:43. https://www.youtube.com/watch?v=pkfem43I6a4.

Pentagon orders US troops from Niger. Politico (May 10, 2024). "Pentagon orders all US combat troops to withdraw from Niger." https://www.politico.com/news/2024/05/10/pentagon-orders-all-us-combat-troops-to-withdraw-from-niger-00157329

257 Need for Africa. Mwakikagile, *Post-colonial Africa*, p. 553, Kindle location 9610–9620.

258 Burkina Faso and Ghana Oct 2024 efforts. InterVlog Oct 31, 2024. "IBRAHIM TRAORE; Ghanaian President sends delegates to meet IBRAHIM TRAORE for peace talks." https://www.youtube.com/watch?v=cy7y5nzlWK0

Endnotes

[259] Oil difficulties. Council on Foreign Relations, *War and Peace Studies of the Council on Foreign Relations, 1939–1945,* "Afghanistan and the War, T-B46" (February 20, 1942), p. 2. US purposes in Afghanistan, facts. Chomsky, N., pp. 2–6, 50–54, Kindle locations 97–129, 499–540.

[260] US purposes in Afghanistan, facts. Chomsky, *The Withdrawal,* pp. 2–6, 50–54, Kindle locations 97–129, 499–540.

[261] Wolfowitz position. Bacevich, Andrew (March 2013). Harper's Magazine. "A Letter to Paul Wolfowitz, occasioned by the tenth anniversary of the Iraq war." https://harpers.org/archive/2013/03/a-letter-to-paul-wolfowitz/?single=1

[262] Drone increase under Obama. Shoup, *Wall Street's Think Tank,* p. 262, Kindle Location 5812.

[263] Drone increase under Obama. Shoup, *Wall Street's Think Tank,* p. 262, Kindle Location 5812.

[264] US killing Afghan civilians. Chomsky, *The Myth of American Idealism,* p. 92, Kindle Location 1663.

[265] Condemn US aggression. Chomsky, *The Myth of American Idealism,* p. 93, Kindle location 1686.

[266] US failure in Afghanistan. Herd, Graeme (August 2021). "The Causes and the Consequences of Strategic Failure in Afghanistan?" The George C. Marshall European Center for Security Studies. Security Insights, Number 068.
https://www.marshallcenter.org/en/publications/security-insights/causes-and-consequences-strategic-failure-afghanistan-0

[267] Corruption, gallery of greed. Chomsky, *The withdrawal* pp. 4–5 Kindle locations 109–118.

[268] Lynch, Marc (December 8, 2020). The Arab Uprisings Never Ended: The Enduring Struggle to Remake the Middle East. *Foreign Affairs*: January/February 2021
https://www.foreignaffairs.com/articles/middle-east/2020-12-08/arab-uprisings-never-ended

[269] Lynch, Marc (December 8, 2020). The Arab Uprisings Never Ended: The Enduring Struggle to Remake the Middle East. *Foreign Affairs*: January/February 2021
https://www.foreignaffairs.com/articles/middle-east/2020-12-08/arab-uprisings-never-ended

[270] American Hemisphere; recognizing regional spheres with USSR; US in Pan American Union, PAU ineffective. Council on Foreign Relations. (July 5, 1944) "The Inter-American System in the Postwar World P-B84, pp. 5. 9–10. Poor state of our region is critique of American role in world. Mead, *Power, Terror, Peace, and War,* p. 204, Kindle Location 2709. Ecuador foreign use of resources, poverty. Shaner, A.,

Counterpunch (April 17, 2024). "Ecuador is Not For Sale." https://www.counterpunch.org/2024/04/17/ecuador-is-not-for-sale/. US support right wing in hemisphere; Kirkpatrick attempt justify support dictators. Modeste, Denneth M. (2020). *The Monroe Doctrine in a Contemporary Perspective.* NY, Routledge Studies in the History of the Americas, pp. i, 136–37, 174, Kindle locations 17, 3850–3865, 4745. Support right wing though abuses and Santa Fe report of Kirkpatrick. Smith, Joseph. (2005). *The United States and Latin America : a history of American diplomacy, 1776-2000.* Routledge. https://doi.org/10.4324/9780203004531, pp. 248–49, Kindle Locations 3633–3652 (citing *A New Inter-American Policy for the Eighties*, known popularly as the *Santa Fe Document.*).

[271] Short summary US in Latin America 1960–1990. Chomsky, *Who Rules the World?*, pp. 11–15, Kindle locations 202–261.

[272] Briefest sketch of terrible crimes. Chomsky, *Who Rules the World?*, p. 15, Kindle location 261.

[273] Recent opposition in hemisphere. Chomsky, *The Withdrawal*, p. 12, Kindle Location 189.

[274] Dictator 1885 friendly to US. Vaughn, L. (2007, 2008). *Guatemala—Culture Smart: The Essential Guide to Customs & Culture.* London: Kuperard, p. 34, Kindle location 390. Stilwell mapping Guatemala. Tuchman, B. (1971), *Stilwell and the American Experience in China, 1911-45,* The MacMillan Company, New York, pp. 21–22.

[275] United Fruit control of railroad and electric company 1920s, 1922 coup, quote. Dosal, P. J. (Paul J. (1993). *Doing business with the dictators : a political history of United Fruit in Guatemala, 1899-1944.* US: Wilmington, DE, Scholarly Resources, Inc. SR Books, p. 97 109 (quote on 109).

[276] Dulles contracts for United Fruit, McCloy and other leaders with United Fruit. Colby, *Thy Will be Done,* p. 849, n.10.

[277] McCloy and other leaders with United Fruit; Dulles contracts for United Fruit. Colby, *Thy Will be Done,* p. 849, n.10.

[278] Guatemala control by US, United Fruit 1920s, 1930s, dictators, 1944 rev, 1954 coup, to 1980s violence. Vaughn, L. (2007, 2008). *Guatemala—Culture Smart: The Essential Guide to Customs & Culture.* London: Kuperard, pp. 34–40, Kindle locations 390–445. Domination of Guatemala. Schlesinger, S., & Kinzer, Stephen. (1982). *Bitter fruit : The untold story of the American coup in Guatemala* (1st ed.). Garden City, NY: Doubleday. Guatemala coup decision, CFR members 15 of 22, Altschul; McCloy CFR board 1953–1972; McCloy CFR chairman. Shoup, *Imperial brain trust,* pp. 107, 197, 301–02. JF McCloy World Bank denied loans, Dulles 99-year lease. Colby, *Thy Will Be Done,* p. 849, n.10. Dulles and Guatemala, late 1920s, Kinzer, *The Brothers,* Kin-

dle locations 2563–2576. JF Dulles at Versailles on Viet Nam. Roesch, *Corporate Tsunami in Countryside Paradise*, Chapter 8. Estimated 1,000 machine-gunned. Forster, C. (2012). *The Time of Freedom: Campesino Workers in Guatemala's October Revolution.* University of Pittsburgh Press, pp. 203–04.

[279] Guatemala coup, scorched earth, quota killings. Koonings, K., & Kruijt, D. (1999). *Societies of fear : the legacy of civil war, violence and terror in Latin America.* Zed Books, pp. 44, 48, 51–52. Rios Montt dictator, violence. Vaughn, *Guatemala—Culture Smart*, pp. 37–38, Kindle locations 417–430. Reagan into office, international terrorism. Chomsky, N. (2015). *The culture of terrorism.* Chicago: Haymarket Books, Kindle locations 48–66.

[280] American hemisphere 1950s dictators, savage torture, and US claim of anti-communism.

Talbot, *The Devil's Chessboard*, pp. 315–320, Kindle locations 5687–5743. Coups, Roesch, *Corporate Tsunami in Countryside Paradise*, App III

[281] Called "right-wing zealot." Evans, *The Education of Ronald Reagan*, p. 163, Kindle location 2921.

[282] Reagan speech style and topics; critics say actor. Evans, *The Education of Ronald Reagan*, pp. 18, 111, Kindle Locations 380, 2030. Education on "foreign ideologies," evil communism. Evans, *The Education of Ronald Reagan*, pp. 24, 117–125, Kindle Locations 489, 2150–2301. Evans, *The Education of Ronald Reagan*, pp. 163, 2915.

[283] Reagan actor, governor, president, style. Gans, *White House Warriors*, p. 63, Kindle Location 1236.

[284] Ratio top officials Reagan in CFR, George H.W. Bush CFR. Shoup, *Wall Street Think Tank*, pp. 94–95, Kindle location 2023–2046. George H.W. Bush CIA director. https://en.wikipedia.org/wiki/George_H._W._Bushl

[285] Reagan wars in Central America, American southern hemisphere. Chomsky, *The Myth of American Idealism*, pp. 27, 29–32, 40–41, Kindle locations 547, 566–626, 772–782.

[286] El Salvador 1932, State Dept coffee prices and other farm exports and investments or loans will stop and others, US warships, Martinez killed 10,000. Lauria-Santiago, A. & Binford, Leigh (2004). *Landscapes of Struggle: Politics, Society, and Community In El Salvador* (Pitt Latin American series). Pittsburgh, Pa.: University of Pittsburgh Press, p. 52 (revolt, 1923 treaty), p. 53 (warships and message, 10,000) El Salvador 30,000 killings for business. Clements, C. (1984). *Witness To War: An American Doctor in El Salvador.* Toronto: NY: Bantam Books, 4, says 30,000, an old village fighter Miguel told Clements; later Miguel was tortured to death).

[287] Undersecretary of State Nelson Rockefeller signed the 1945 Act Of Chapultepec, Mexico, US for militaries for rich elites, sometimes against poverty-ridden majorities. US generals at the conference advocated this pact, relation of Pan Amer Union to OAS, Chapultepec. Colby, *Thy Will Be Done*, pp. 92, 165-172. Military pact aspect of Chapultepec. Notter, H., & United States. Department of State. Office of Public Affairs., (1949). *Postwar Foreign Policy Preparation, 1939–1945*, (Department of State Publication : 3580). Washington: For sale by the Supt. of Documents. : U.S.G.P.O, p. 406; Colby, *Thy Will Be Done*, p. 169. Postwar effort to keep the southern hemisphere's production of raw materials which Rockefeller had led during World War Two. *Thy Will Be Done*, p. 115. McCloy and Rockefeller companies, congruent with national interest. Schulzinger, *The wise men of foreign affairs*, pp. 336, 573. In 1946, McCloy join Rockefeller Foundation board of directors. Colby, *Thy Will Be Done*, p. 221. Haiti and US support right wing in hemisphere; Kirkpatrick attempt justify support dictators. Modeste, *The Monroe Doctrine in a Contemporary Perspective*, pp. i, 136–37, 174, Kindle locations 17, 3850–3865, 4745. Outside causes of Haiti poverty, US occupation and businesses, central power, racism. Dubois, L. (2012). *Haiti : the aftershocks of history* (1st ed.). NY: Metropolitan Books, pp. 265–71, 285–86, 365 Kindle locations 82, 4292–4293, 4236–4640 (racism), 5948 (continued foreign control). US in 2024 on Haiti. Democracy Now! (April 3, 2024). "Haitians Resist Foreign Intervention as U.S. Pushes for Unelected 'Transition Council' to Rule Island." https://www.democracynow.org/2024/4/3/haiti_crisis_pierre_ives?utm_source=Democracy+Now%21&utm_campaign=6dead4d411-Daily_Digest_COPY_01&utm_medium=email&utm_term=0_fa2346a853-6dead4d411-192432413. Ecuador foreign use of resources, poverty. Shaner, A., Counterpunch (April 17, 2024). Ecuador is Not For Sale. https://www.counterpunch.org/2024/04/17/ecuador-is-not-for-sale/.

[288] Haiti and US support right wing in hemisphere; Kirkpatrick attempt justify support dictators. Modeste, *The Monroe Doctrine in a Contemporary Perspective*, pp. i, 136–37, 174, Kindle locations 17, 3850–3865, 4745. Outside causes of Haiti poverty, US occupation and businesses, central power, racism. Dubois, *Haiti : the aftershocks of history*, pp. 265–71, 285–86, 365 Kindle locations 82, 4292–4293, 4236–4640 (racism), 5948 (continued foreign control). US in 2024 on Haiti. Democracy Now! (April 3, 2024). "Haitians Resist Foreign Intervention as U.S. Pushes for Unelected 'Transition Council' to Rule Island." https://www.democracynow.org/2024/4/3/haiti_crisis_pierre_ives?utm_source=Democracy+Now%21&utm_campaign=6dead4d411-Daily_

Endnotes

Digest_COPY_01&utm_medium=email&utm_term=0_fa2346a853-6dead4d411-192432413

[289] Chiquita company liable for Colombia killings 1990s and 2000s. National Security Archive (June 10, 2024). "National Security Archive Schedule of Chiquita's Paramilitary Payments Evidence at Trial Jury Awards Banana Company Victims $38.3 Million in Landmark Human Rights Case."
https://nsarchive.gwu.edu/project/chiquita-papers.

[290] Not curb climate change, not to affect capitalism growth. Shoup, *Wall Street's Think Tank*, pp. 292–93, Kindle Locations 6490–6497.

[291] Two years to save world, UN Stiell says. The Energy Mix staff (April 10, 2024). "Just 2 Years to 'Save the World' as UN Climate Secretary Urges New Deal on International Finance." https://www.theenergymix.com/just-2-years-to-save-the-world-as-un-climate-secretary-urges-new-deal-on-international-finance/?utm_source=The+Energy+Mix&utm_campaign Not curb climate change, not to affect capitalism growth. Shoup, *Wall Street's Think Tank*, pp. 292–93, Kindle Locations 6490–6497.

[292] Children more likely to suffer death. UN Convention on the Rights of the Child. Committee on the Rights of the Child, General comment No. 26 (2023), on children's rights and the environment, with a special focus on climate change, Paragraph 73. Children on adults' bad decisions, lives at stake, destroying planet, Paragraph 26.
https://www.ohchr.org/en/documents/general-comments-and-recommendations/crccgc26-general-comment-no-26-2023-childrens-rights

[293] Children's views on adult failures on climate. UN Convention on the Rights of the Child. Committee on the Rights of the Child, General comment No. 26 (2023), Paragraph 3.

[294] The 2018 Paris Climate Agreement.
https://unfccc.int/process-and-meetings/the-paris-agreement
The 2025 ICJ ruling.
https://www.juancole.com/2025/07/historic-imperils-polluters.html
Warning of 12 years. IPCC (2018). Summary for Policymakers. In: *Global Warming of 1.5°C. An IPCC Special Report on the impacts of global warming of 1.5°C above pre-industrial levels. . . . World Meteorological Organization, Geneva, Switzerland, 32 pages.* Climate change risks, extensive discussion. IPCC (20 March, 2023). "Multiple risks interact, generating new sources of vulnerability to climate compounding overall risk (high confidence)." Synthesis Report of the IPCC Sixth Assessment Report (AR6) (IPCC AR6 SYR) Longer Report, pp. 1–85; p. 16, https://www.ipcc.ch/report/sixth-assessment-report-cycle/

[295] That 99 percent of climate scientists say climate change is real, humans are a cause, and it could be curbed; a 2013 study had said 97 percent. Meissner, Martin/AP (2021). The Conversation (October 28, 2021)
https://theconversation.com/the-97-climate-consensus-is-over-now-its-well-above-99-and-the-evidence-is-even-stronger-than-that-170370.

[296] Santa Ana winds worse with "high-emission scenario." "The results suggest an end-of-century shift in SAOs from September and October to November and December that are greater under a high-emission scenario (A2)". Miller, Norman L. & Schlegel, Nicole J. (Aug 15, 2006). "Climate change projected fire weather sensitivity: California Santa Ana wind occurrence." Geophysical Research Letters, Volume33, Issue15, August 2006.https://doi.org/10.1029/2006GL025808. "Hellscape" on Southern California fires in 2025. Democracy Now! (January 10, 2025). "Climate Scientist Peter Kalmus Fled L.A. Fearing Wildfires. His Old Neighborhood Is Now a Hellscape". https://www.youtube.com/watch?v=mMYvuY_MLMQ.

[297] Worse drought a cause of S. Cal. Fires. Bland, Alistair (January 15, 2025). "'Literally off the charts': LA's critically dry conditions stun scientists as fires rage." Cal Matters: Nonprofit & Nonpartisan News.

[298] Climate change and inaction. Hayes, C. & MSNBC (July 22, 2021) "Extreme Weather Is 'New Normal' Thanks To Decades Of Climate Inaction."
https://www.msnbc.com/all-in/watch/chris-hayes-says-decades-of-climate-inaction-makes-extreme-weather-the-new-normal-117149253785.o

Climate change fingerprints. DW News (Oct 10, 2024). "How is climate change turbocharging Hurricane Milton?" | DW News. https://www.youtube.com/watch?v=E7Y2Aw-3L-o

[299] Ocean warming record in 2023. BBC News (August 4, 2023). Ocean heat record broken, with grim implications for the planet. https://www.bbc.com/news/science- environment-66387537. Seas warmer than thought. BBC Future 21 July, 2023 "There's a heatwave in the sea and scientists are worried."
https://www.bbc.com/future/article/20230720-theres-a-heat- wave-in-the-sea-and-scientists-are-worried.
Sea ice cover. J. C. Comiso, C. L. Parkinson, R. Gersten, A. C. Bliss, and T. Markus (2024), "Current State of Sea Ice Cover./ NASA, https://earth.gsfc.nasa.gov/cryo/data/current-state-of-sea-ice-cover, last access: 11-07-2024.

Summer 2024 US climate change heat, fires, and tropical storm. BBC News (June 20, 2024). "New Mexico wildfires burn out of control as US battles under heat alerts." https://www.youtube.com/watch?v=oDXc9zWqhQM

[300] Hurricane Milton exploded. Schlanger, Zoe (Oct 8, 2024). "Milton Is the Hurricane That Scientists Were Dreading". The Atlantic.
https://www.theatlantic.com/science/archive/2024/10/hurricane-milton-climate-change/680188/

DW channel on climate change turbocharge Milton. DW News (Oct 10. 2024). How is climate change turbocharging Hurricane Milton? | DW News https://www.youtube.com/watch?v=E7Y2Aw-3L-o&t=36s.

Climate change and hurricanes. Bergen, Peter; CNN (Oct 11, 2024). "Monster storms Helene and Milton prove climate change is a national security issue." CNN. https://edition.cnn.com/2024/10/11/politics/climate-change-national-security-issue/index.html

[301] Earliest Cat. 5 hurricane, developed nations not taking seriously. Democracy Now (July 3, 2024). Science, "Not Scare mongering: St. Vincent & Grenadines PM on Hurricane Beryl & Climate Crisis STORY."
https://www.democracynow.org/2024/7/3/hurricane_beryl_pm_ralph_gonsalves

[302] US oil and gas expansion under Biden; actions despite IRA, boon for fossil fuel industry, hypocritical in quote of Bill Hare. Chomsky, *The Myth of American Idealism*, pp. 228–229, Kindle locations 4033–4077.

[303] Climate change and energy in Inflation Reduction Act. https://en.wikipedia.org/wiki/Inflation_Reduction_Act

Reuters, Timothy Gardner (July 29, 2022) WASHINGTON, July 27 (Reuters) "U.S. Senate climate deal 'transformative', backers say".
https://www.reuters.com/world/us/us-senate-climate-deal-thin-details-praised-by-clean-energy-backers-2022-07-28/

Climate change and energy total about $800 billion. Wikipedia, Inflation Reduction Act (retrieved 9 Sept, 2023) https:// en.wikipedia.org/wiki/Inflation_Reduction_Act

Estimates $135 to $150 billion damage January 2025 S. Cal fires.
https://www.accuweather.com/en/press/media-advisory-accuweather-increases-estimate-of-total-damage-and-economic-loss-as-catastrophic-wildfires-in-southern-california-continue-to-ravage-the-los-angeles-area-updated-preliminary-estimate-i/1732268

[304] Chomsky quote on IRA. Chomsky, Noam; Polychroniou, C.J. (2024). *A Livable Future is Possible: Confronting the Threats to Our Survival.* Haymarket Books. Kindle Edition, pp. 58–60, Kindle locations 718–740.

[305] Climate change Atlantic Council, national security resource control approach to climate change. Engelke, *Climate Change and US National Security : Past, Present, Future*, pp. 13, 15.

306 Pentagon biggest on global warming. https://www.motherjones.com/environment/2022/10/pentagon-climate-change-neta-crawford-book/
307 Children in sinking Sewol Ferry. https://en.wikipedia.org/ wiki/Sinking_of_MV_Sewol
308 Bedjaoui on clean-slate theory. Penet, *Sovereign Debt Diplomacies*, pp. 213–216, Kindle locations 5739–5799.
309 ICJ found detachment of archipelago from Mauritius violated free will. Penet, *Sovereign Debt Diplomacies*, p. 216, Kindle location 5815.
310 Opposition to G77 debt restructuring or moratoriums. Penet, *Sovereign Debt Diplomacies*, pp. 238–239, Kindle locations 6401–6424.
311 Argentina debt increase. Penet, *Sovereign Debt Diplomacies*, p. 276, Kindle Location 7403.
312 Puerto Rico debt. Penet, *Sovereign Debt Diplomacies*, pp. 304–331, Kindle locations 8130–8860.
313 Holdout creditors gain vs Peru. Penet, *Sovereign Debt Diplomacies*, pp. 265–266 Kindle locations 7145–7176.
314 In sub-Saharan Africa, 19 countries unable or at risk on pay debt. Suzman, Mark (July 11, 2024). "Debt Is Dragging Down the Developing World: How to End the Current Crisis—and Avoid the Next One." Foreign Affairs, NY: Council on Foreign Relations. https://www.foreignaffairs.com/africa/debt-dragging-down-developing-world

Independence to 17 nations 1960. Mwakikagile, G. (2019). *Post-colonial Africa; A General Survey*, Amazon Digital Services LLC, Chapters Two, Seven, Kindle locations 1155, 6078–6222, 6436, 9500.
315 West profits from Africa that remains poor. Mwakikagile, *Post-colonial Africa*, p. 351, Kindle location 6074.
316 View on lender largesse on debt relief. Suzman, Mark (July 11, 2024). "Debt Is Dragging Down the Developing World: How to End the Current Crisis—and Avoid the Next One." Foreign Affairs, NY: Council on Foreign Relations. https://www.foreignaffairs.com/africa/debt-dragging-down-developing-world

Independence to 17 nations 1960. Mwakikagile, G. (2019). *Post-colonial Africa; A General Survey*, Amazon Digital Services LLC, Chapters Two, Seven, Kindle locations 1155, 6078–6222, 6436, 9500.
317 Tripartite cooperation in East Europe a benefit. Council on Foreign Relations, "Russia and an East European Federation (October 26, 1942), T-B55", p. 5. NATO Russia security concern WW 2 Invasion route through Ukraine. By C. BROOKS PETERS By Telephone to

Endnotes

THE NEW YORK TIMES. (1941). "CONSTANT ADVANCE REPORTED BY NAZIS: Fortified Russian Lines Are Declared Broken in Drives Along Entire Front BIG BATTLE IS HELD NEAR Soviet Air Force Already Has Lost 1,200 Planes, German News Agency States." *New York Times (1923-)*, 4–. Quote of Baker, "not one inch"; cooperation possibility, 1989 opportunity, shift by 1994. Sarotte, M. E. (2021). *Not One Inch: America, Russia, and the Making of Post-Cold War Stalemate.* Yale University Press, pp. 1 (not one inch), 3, 4, 14, 56, 110, 342, Kindle locations 172 (not one inch), 219, 255, 475, 359, 2619, 8042.

[318] Big play in Europe. Sarotte, *Not One Inch*, p. 15, Kindle location 479.
[319] US coups. Roesch, *Corporate Tsunami in Countryside Paradise*, Appendix III.
[320] Baker on not extending NATO. Sarotte, *Not One Inch*, p. 1, Kindle location 172.
[321] NATO expand to 28 members, by years. Campbell, Horace (2013). *Global NATO and the Catastrophic Failure in Libya: Lessons for Africa in the Forging of African Unity.* NY: Monthly Review Press, p. 39, Kindle location 509. Bush "to hell with that." Sarotte, *Not One Inch*, p. 3, Kindle location 209.
[322] 2008 Bucharest Declaration breaking point. Sarotte, *Not One Inch*, p. 348, Kindle location 8156.
[323] Quote Sestanovich on trouble if democracy in Russia fails. Sarotte, *Not One Inch*, p. 348, Kindle location 8166.

CHAPTER 9

[324] Combination equal stakes, empire. Mead, *Power, Terror, Peace, and War*, p. 157, Kindle location 2080.
[325] The first Red Scare. Woods, *Freedom Incorporated*, p. 9, Kindle location 325.
[326] Standard profits 1886–89, Rockefeller investments. Prins, Nomi (2014). *All the President's Bankers: the hidden Alliances that drive American Power*, NY: Nation Books, member of Perseus books Group, pp. 2–3, Kindle locations 334–341. Standard Oil 1885, 70 percent abroad. Smith, *On His Own Terms*, p. 11, Kindle location 719. Foreign markets. Rockefeller, J., *Random Reminiscences of men and events*, pp. 10, 121.
[327] Standard profits 1886–89, Rockefeller investments. Prins, *All the President's Bankers*, pp. 2–3, Kindle locations 334–341. US- VN War copper prices, Congo income from the war in Viet Nam. Van Rey Brouck, D.,& Garrett, *Congo : the epic history of a people*, pp. 345–47, 356, 358, Kindle locations 6601–6638, 6812–6819, 6859
[328] Early US business in Viet Nam. United States Consulate (1957). *Despatches from United States consuls in Saigon, 1889–1906*. Washington:

National Archives and Records Service, General Services Administration, Reel 1, Format one microfilm reel.

United States. Department of State. (1971). *Records of the Department of State relating to internal affairs of France, 1919–1929*. (National Archives microfilm publications: M560). Washington, D.C.: National Archives and Records Service, General Services Administration, Reels 150–152. Format 162 microfilm reels.

[329] Presidents have waged illegal wars for decades. Hathaway, O. (July 16, 2024). "For the Rest of the World, the U.S. President Has Always Been Above the Law: Americans Will Now Know What A Lack Of Accountability Means." *Foreign Affairs*. NY: Council on Foreign Relations. Over 80 election interferences. Chomsky, *The Myth of American Idealism*, p. 27, Kindle location 534. Partial list of coups. Roesch, *Corporate Tsunami in Countryside Paradise*, Appendix III.

[330] Grand area, limitation of sovereignty. CFR memo E-B19, The War and United States Foreign Policy: Needs of Future United States Foreign Policy (October 9, 1940).

[331] Post-WW II policy on foreign oil. CFR, *War and Peace Studies*, 1939–45, CFR Territorial Group, T-B74, "Elements to be Considered in an Oil Policy for the United States" (May 16, 1944), NY: Council on Foreign Relations.

[332] Chomsky, Noam. Who Rules the World? (American Empire Project) (p. 44 45). Henry Holt and Co.. Kindle Edition 784 793.

[333] Opposition to G77 debt restructuring or moratoriums; Puerto Rico debt. Penet, *Sovereign Debt Diplomacies*, pp. 238–239, 304–331, Kindle locations 5401–6424, 8130–8860.

[334] Early slave laws allowed maim and kill, etc. Hannah-Jones, *The 1619 Project*, p. 103, Kindle location 2263. Burning, beating veteran to death. Ginzburg, *100 years of lynchings*, Kindle location 1740–1807. Economic domination; soldiers lynched. United States. National Advisory Commission on Civil Disorders. (1968, 2016). *Report of the National Advisory Commission on Civil Disorders*. The James Madison Library in American Politics. Princeton University Press. Kindle Edition (*Kerner Commission Report*), pp. 220, 222, Kindle locations 7429, 7456. Extensive discussions of race and economic purpose. Roesch, *Corporate Tsunami in Countryside Paradise*.

Nixon's promise against Civil Rights Act; racism voting strategy; continues in 2019. Maxwell, Angie and Shields, Todd (2019). *The Long Southern Strategy : How Chasing White Voters in the South Changed American Politics*. NY: Oxford University Press., pp. 3–4, 6, 37–41, 105–06, and 323, Kindle Locations 353–373, 416–421 (Nixon promise), 1101–1217, 2608–2621 (resentment), and 7195–7202 (continues in

Endnotes

2019). Chairmen on Southern Strategy continuing; welfare queen; immigrants as criminals; overt racists and racial fears. Haney-López, I. (2014). *Dog whistle politics : How coded racial appeals have reinvented racism and wrecked the middle class.* Oxford; New York: Oxford University Press, pp. 1–5, 58, 157, Kindle locations 162–247, 1296, 3253. Racist voters and Republican Party. Chomsky, N., with Amy Goodman (Apr 20, 2019). "Chomsky perfectly Explains Trump and Russiagate," 0:00–5:27 of 10:10. https://www.youtube.com/watch?v=sLyS0E91H1o.

[335] Attempts to ban books due to history of race. USA Today (Sept 19, 2024). "Florida Attorney General's Office heading out of state to defend Texas library book bans". "Proponents say that some lessons blame children for actions of generations past or make them feel guilty for being white." Alfonseca, K. (Dec. 3, 2021). "Authors of color speak out against efforts to ban books on race." ABC News. https://abcnews.go.com/US/authors-color-speak-efforts-ban-books-race/story?id=81491208.
www.usatoday.com › story › newsFlorida to argue for Texas book bans in federal court out of state. Racial wealth gap asset ratio 12-to-1. Baradaran, *The Color of Money*, p. 249, Kindle Location 5243. Racial wealth gap 10-to-1. Hannah-Jones, *The 1619 Project*, p. 471. Racial wealth gap ratio 12-to-1.

Murder of George Floyd. https://en.wikipedia.org/wiki/Death_of_George_Floyd.

Murder of Ahmaud Arbery. NBC News (Nov. 5, 2021). "Jury Finds All Three Defendants Guilty In The Murder of Ahmaud Arbery." https://www.youtube.com/watch?v=IOPbuGssS7A

[336] Robeson, Dulles, race. Robeson overseas opera star, passport canceled, Dulles. Horne, *Paul Robeson : The Artist as Revolutionary*, pp. 5, 126–28, Kindle locations 2025, 2392–2436. Robeson passport revocation, Dulles, testimony. Zinn, *Voices of a people's history of the United States*, Chapter 16, Kindle locations 7551–7607.

Race terms. Bradley, *Imagining Vietnam and America*, pp. 46–49, Kindle location 687–734. Gook, slant, etc. Turse, *Kill anything that moves*, pp. 27–28, 39, 49–50, Kindle locations 424–443, 637, 827–855. Intersectionality of struggle of blacks in US, of Palestine; common struggle of blacks in US, Africa, and vs military aggression in Viet Nam. Davis, *Freedom is a Constant Struggle*, pp. 45 (US blacks, Palestine), 52–53 (US, Africa, & Viet Nam), Kindle locations 707, 780–789

[337] King Duncan grant to Macbeth, who wanted more, killed. Shakespeare, *The Complete Works of William Shakespeare*, "MacBeth," Act I, Scene 2 (rebellion, invasion) Kindle location 69245–87; Act I Scene

Betrayed by Foreign Policy Fault Line

      3 to Scene 7 (King), Kindle location 69428–69601; Scene VI. Forres. The palace, Kindle location 70458–70490.

[338] Petition points. Viet Nam National Museum of History (April 2018). Revendications du Peuple Annamite. *Colonial Exhibits*, Room 3. Moderate tone, delivers in Paris and Peace Conference. Duiker, *Ho Chi Minh*, Chapter 2, Kindle location 1399–1407.

[339] Early 1945 Ho OSS agent, reports. Bradley, *Imagining Vietnam and America*, Chapter 4, Kindle location 1792–1803.

[340] USIA report, want gear to US, emulate. Pettit, C. (1975). *The Experts*. Secaucus, N.J.: L. Stuart, pp. 20–21. Call for US businesses, US businesses in Ha Noi after war, movies. Bradley, *Imagining Vietnam and America*, Chapter 4, Kindle location 1941–49.

[341] Ho letters to US 1945, 1946, unanswered. United States. Department of Defense, United States-Vietnam relations, 1945–1967, study prepared by the Department of Defense (Pentagon Papers), Bk. 1, p. A-3. Ho eight letters October 1945, February 1946, none answered. Ngo, "Vietnam: The real enemy," p. 16. Ho to Sec'y Byrne, Nov. 1, 1945. Pettit, *The Experts*, pp. 24–25.

[342] Ho-France agreement, *Suffren* attack. Roesch, *Corporate Tsunami*, Ch 20–22.

[343] DRV written offers of tax-free monopolies including rice. Bradley, *Imagining Vietnam and America*, Chapter 5, Kindle location 2141–2203. Logevall, *Embers of war*, Chapter 8, Kindle location 3562–3574.

[344] Diem heard US might withdraw; contacted North, NLF. Ngo, "Vietnam: The real enemy," p. 22; Contact North. Ngo, "After the Fall of Saigon," p. 81. North interest. Miller, *Misalliance*, pp. 305, Kindle location 5946–5953.

[345] Ho Chi Minh on tea with US. https://vietnamwardv.weebly.com/ho-chi-minh.html

[346] Iran coup forty percent to Standard Oil; and Dulles development deal, shah CFR dinner, tanks; torture. Talbot, *The Devil's Chessboard*, pp. 229–231, 240, Kindle locations 4244–4267, 4424. Iran coup poverty, torture, executions. Blum, *Killing hope*, Chapter 9, Kindle location 2283. Brutal SAVAK police repression. Kinzer, *Overthrow*, pp. 199–201, Kindle locations 3629. Iran coup background. Roesch, *Corporate Tsunami in Countryside Paradise*, p. 251.

[347] 1945 Brazil coup. Colby, G., *Thy will be done*, pp. 181–190, espec p. 189. not accept "the theory of operations restricted only to the nationals of any given country." The world order. Roesch, *Corporate Tsunami*, Ch 19.

[348] Outsiders changing territory can violate fairness, deep emotions. Bowman, Isaiah. "The Strategy of Territorial Decisions." *Foreign Affairs*, 1

January 1946, pp. 177 (nerve center), 178 (fairness, stable peace), NY: Council on Foreign Relations. https://www.foreignaffairs.com/articles/world/1946-01-01/strategy-territorial-decisions. Accessed 29 October 2024

349 Ho Chi Minh childhood experiences molding his view. Roesch, *Corporate Tsunami in Countryside Paradise,* Ch 7.)

350 Quote JCS nationalism cannot be crushed or reversed; Army planners estimate 80 percent. Chomsky, *Rethinking Camelot,* Chapter 1, Kindle location 1946–1959.

351 Outsiders changing territory can violate fairness, deep emotions. Bowman, Isaiah (1946). "The Strategy of Territorial Decisions." *Foreign Affairs,* 1 January 1946, pp. 177 (nerve center), 178 (fairness, stable peace), NY: Council on Foreign Relations. https://www.foreignaffairs.com/articles/world/1946-01-01/strategy-territorial-decisions. Accessed 29 October 2024

352 Death penalty if behalf of organization designated Communist. Thayer, *War by other means,* p. 82. Imprisonment if danger to state. Gruening, E., & Beaser, Herbert Wilton. (1968). *Vietnam folly.* Washington: National Press, p. 174. "Denounce the Communists" sessions; denounce Ho, DRV, Party. Communist denunciation sessions, five-family leaders. Hickey, G. C. (1964). *Village in Vietnam.* Yale University Press, pp. 93 n.8, 205.

Innumerable crimes and suppression. Buttinger, *Vietnam : A Dragon Embattled,* pp. 975–77. Murderous terrorist state 1950s by US. Chomsky, *Rethinking Camelot,* Introduction and Chapter 1, Kindle locations 140, 888. Killings 1956, 1957 by Southern regrouping zone, beheadings, disembowelment. Logevall, *Embers of war,* p. 655, Kindle location 11432.

Against Viet Minh all political views. Gillespie, R. (2011). *Black Ops, Vietnam : The Operational History of MACVSOG.* Annapolis: Naval Institute Press, p. 3, Kindle location 288. Arrested people implicated, searched houses, forced divorces. Lê, H., Vietnam. Quân Đội nhân dân. Tổng cục chính trị, & Đảng cộng sản Việt Nam; Tỉnh ủy Bến Tre. (2010). *Bến Tre Đồng khởi anh hùng.* Hà Nội: NXB Quân Đội nhân dân, pp. 13, 24. Military often no trials; torture, brutality, summary killings in villages. Buttinger, *Vietnam: A Dragon Embattled,* pp. 975–76; Duiker, *Sacred War,* p. 109. Resistance people's families fined or imprisoned. Appy, C. (2003). *Patriots: The Vietnam War remembered from all sides.* New York: Viking, pp. 54–59, 735.

353 Misery and millions in revolution, driving force. Nguyen Khac Vien, *Vietnam: A Long History,* pp. 170–72 (172, "driving force"). Land to collaborators Catholics, landless class. Ham, *Vietnam : the Australian*

War, Chapter 2, Kindle location 491; Carter, *Inventing Vietnam,* p. 38, Kindle location 750. Frenchman on destruction. Lamb, *Vietnam's Will to Live,* p. 48.

354 Ho Chi Minh appealed nationwide September 26, 1945. *Ho Chi Minh Museum,* Ho Chi Minh City, First Floor, photograph and caption, author visit 4 May, 2015. September 1945, Ho organizing, "sense of justice," unity, decrees and duties, starvation effects, dike breaches.

Hội Đồng chỉ Đạo biên soạn. . . ., *Lịch sử kháng chiến chống Pháp khu tả ngạn sông Hồng, 1945–1955, pp. 48–57.* Other than Ho's no other peasant movement worthy, citing Dabezies. Buttinger, *Vietnam : A Dragon Embattled,* pp. 1244, 1263, Appendix VII, pp. 1234–48. Land ownership under French and Japan before 1945 reinvasion. Halberstam, *Ho,* p. 11. Ho set up general election for entire country. Ho Chi Minh Museum, Ho Chi Minh City, First Floor, photograph and caption, from author visit 4 May, 2015.

355 Quote JCS nationalism cannot be crushed or reversed; Army planners estimate 80 percent. Chomsky, *Rethinking Camelot*, Chapter 1, Kindle location 1946–1959.

356 Hau Nghia 98 percent NLF 1965. Chomsky, *Rethinking Camelot*, Chapter 3, Kindle location 1167–74. Hau Nghia location. *Bản Đồ hành chính Việt Nam Cộng Hòa 1967.* https://www.flickr.com/photos/13476480@N07/22408888269.

NLF in Peoples Army. Military Institute of Vietnam, The; Pribbenow, M.L. transl. (2002). *Victory in Vietnam : The official History of the People's Army of Vietnam, 1954–75,* Lawrence, Kan: University Press of Kansas, p. 143, Kindle location 1934.

May 1959 Ho Chi Minh Trail in mountains, later Ho Chi Minh Trail on the Sea. Ban Chấp Hành Đảng Bộ Tỉnh Bà Rịa-Vũng Tàu, *Đường Hồ Chí Minh Trên Biển Bà Rịa-Vũng Tàu,* pp. 9–13. HCM Trail also in Laos. Willbanks, *Vietnam War Almanac,* p. 147, Kindle location 3334.

State White Paper 1961 said communist activity after Geneva mainly "political action. . . ." Herman, E., (1972). *Atrocities in Vietnam: Myths and Realities.* Boston: Pilgrim Press, p. 20. Pike on NLF political only. Chomsky, *Manufacturing Consent,* Chapter 5, Kindle location 4944. Force first by Southern regrouping zone. Buttinger, *Vietnam : A Dragon Embattled,* p. 982.

Interviews of Southerners. Roesch, *Corporate Tsunami in Countryside Paradise,* Ch 40 et al., (Ch 40 on Hau Nghia.) Hai Xuan experiences. Recorded interview of Pham Hai Xuan by author with interpreter June 19, 2017. Dang Hong Nhut experiences. Recorded interviews of Dang Hong Nhut by author with interpreter May 8, 2017, June 4, 2017, and September 5, 2017.

Endnotes

Nguyễn Thị Kim Dung (2017). *Gia Tài của Mẹ*. TP. Hồ Chí Minh: NXB Quân Đội Nhân Dân, pp. 97–99, 142. Recorded interview of Nguyen Thi Kim Dung, 23 June, 2019, by Brian Roesch, with interpreter. Recorded interview of Lê Văn Bé Ba (Le Van Be Ba) by author with interpreter, February, 2017, with recorded interpreting into English July 4, 2017, by author with interpreter, February, 2017. Phan Thi Hue age nine. Recorded interview of Phan Thi Hue (Phan Thị Huệ) by author 4 July, 2019, with interpreter.

Van Can age seven. Recorded interviews of Nguyen Van Can [Nguyễn Văn Cân] by author with interpreter, June 20 and June 22, 2017.

[357] Leadership increase in Army. Military Institute of Vietnam, The (2002). *Victory in Vietnam : The official History of the People's Army of Vietnam, 1954–75*, Lawrence, Kan: University Press of Kansas, p. 328, Kindle location 4492.

[358] Education about aggressors, determined spirit, Military Institute of Vietnam, The (2002). *Victory in Vietnam : The official History of the People's Army of Vietnam, 1954–75*, Lawrence, Kan: University Press of Kansas, pp. 327, 742, Kindle locations 4477, 10174.

[359] Indiscriminate air power lose war; civilians dying every day, indiscriminate aerial bombing villages, napalming village, interview pilot. By CHARLES MOHR Special to The New York Times, "Air Strikes hit Vietcong–and South Vietnam Civilians," New York Times (1923–Current file) 05 Sep 1965: E4. Indiscriminate killing. Turse, *Kill anything that moves*, p.13 Kindle location 234.

[360] Chase Bank announces will open in Sai Gon, 1966 David R. to Sai Gon, Chase reassures investors, SEADAG, cheap labor after destruction, Mekong hydroelectric, corporate activity 1965–68. Colby, *Thy will be done*, pp. 6, 550–51 (diagram), 562 (1965), 559–64.

[361] Global war vs communism. Woods, *Freedom Incorporated*, pp. 9, 15–16, 18 Kindle locations 325–343, 462–481, 522.

[362] Dulles brothers early lessons. Roesch, *Corporate Tsunami in Countryside Paradise*, Chapters 7 & 8.

[363] Nelson, John III, and David Rockefeller joined CFR late 1930s, early 1940s. Shoup, *Imperial brain trust*, pp. 61, 106. Assistant secretary of state conf'd Dec 20, 1944. Smith, *On His Own Terms*, p. 171, Kindle locations 4252–4259. As assistant secretary of state, Nelson Rockefeller signed the 1945 Act Of Chapultepec, Mexico, US for militaries for rich elites, sometimes against poverty-ridden majorities. US generals at the conference advocated this pact, relation of Pan Amer Union to OAS, Chapultepec. Colby, *Thy Will Be Done*, pp. 92, 165–72. Military

pact aspect of Chapultepec. Notter, H., & United States. Department of State. Office of Public Affairs., (1949). *Postwar Foreign Policy Preparation, 1939–1945*, (Department of State Publication : 3580). Washington: For sale by the Supt. of Documents. : U.S.G.P.O, p. 406; Colby, *Thy Will Be Done*, p. 169.

364 Dulles brothers and Eisenhower in CFR; Shoup, *Imperial brain trust*, pp. 235, 289. Guatemala coup decision, CFR members 15 of 22, Altschul; McCloy CFR board 1953–1972. Shoup, *Imperial brain trust*, pp. 107, 197, 301–02. CFR "foreign policy establishment." Shoup, *Imperial brain trust*, pp. 4, 7, citing *Newsweek* issue of Sept 6, 1971

365 Beginning to use word "communist" in 1954 Guatemala. Forster, *The Time of Freedom*, p. 203.

366 Kill the timid. Bevins, V. (2020). *The Jakarta method : Washington's anticommunist crusade & the mass murder program that shaped our world*. PublicAffairs, Hatchette Book Group, p. 215, Kindle location 4240. Guatemala 1954 Guatemala quote on "rounded up and executed." Bevins, *The Jakarta Method*, p. 44 Kindle location 891.

367 Emblematic of the broader-than-communist approach, exterminate Cintas Largas. Colby, *Thy Will Be Done*, pp. 1–5.

368 Alsop writings and citations. Ngô, V. (May 2009), From Polarization to Integration in Vietnam. *Journal of Contemporary Asia*, Vol. 39, No. 2, pp. 295–304, especially 296–97. After winter 1954 trip. J. Alsop, "A Man in a Mirror," The Reporter, 25 June, 1955: 35-6.

369 Brazil 1964 coup "violent dictatorship. Bevins, *The Jakarta method*, p. 1, Kindle locations 66–78. Charles Maechling Jr. in short summary US in Latin America 1960–1990. Chomsky, *Who Rules the World?*, pp. 11–15, Kindle locations 202–261.

370 Nonalignment postcolonial. Williams, *White Malice*, p. 16, Kindle locations 134–41.

371 Kohnert paper on polarization. Kohnert, Dirk (Nov. 12, 2021). "Asean and African Relations: Toward a Renewed Partnership?" Hamburg Institute of African Affairs. https://papers.ssrn.com/sol3/papers.cfm?abstract_id=3962361.

372 Indonesia 1960s bloodbath, Brazil in US camp. Bevins, *The Jakarta method*, p. 1, Kindle locations 66–78.

373 USSR collapse December 1991; unprecedented quote. Gaddis, J. L. (2005). *Strategies of containment : a critical appraisal of American national security policy during the Cold War* (Revised and expanded edition.). Oxford University Press, pp. 379–84, Kindle locations 7273, 7371

374 Unilateralism and loss of US hegemony. Gaddis, *Strategies of containment*, p. 384, Kindle location 7371.

[375] Americans for Kyoto Protocol, Bush rejected. Chomsky, *The Myth of American Idealism*, p. 236, Kindle location 4113. Climate change risks, extensive discussion of. IPCC (20 March, 2023). "Multiple risks interact, generating new sources of vulnerability to climate compounding overall risk (high confidence)." Synthesis Report of the IPCC Sixth Assessment Report (AR6) (IPCC AR6 SYR) Longer Report, pp. 1–85; p. 16, https://www.ipcc.ch/report/sixth-assessment-report-cycle/

That 99 percent of climate scientists say climate change is real, humans are a cause, and it could be curbed; a 2013 study had said 97 percent. Meissner, Martin/AP (2021). The Conversation (October 28, 2021) https://theconversation.com/the-97-climate-consensus-is-over-now-its-well-above-99-and-the-evidence-is-even-stronger-than-that-170370.

CHAPTER 10

[376] Anti-communism doctrine error on US in VN. Ceplair. L. (2011). Anti-Communism in twentieth-century America : a critical history. Santa Barbara, Denver: Praeger, Kindle locations 82–173.

[377] Greeley, Tribune debate includes Marx. Tuchinsky, A. (2011). Horace Greeley's "New-York Tribune" : Civil War-Era Socialism and the Crisis of Free Labor. Cornell University Press, pp. 22–23, 104–08, 122, 213–18.

[378] Greeley, Tribune debate includes Marx. Tuchinsky, A. (2011). Horace Greeley's "New-York Tribune" : Civil War-Era Socialism and the Crisisof Free Labor. Cornell University Press, pp. 22–23, 104–08, 122, 213–18.

[379] Consul report and State Dept distribution. Daily reports. United States. Bureau of Foreign Commerce (1898). Advance sheets of consular reports, Rpt. No. 1-1746, Washington, D.C.: U.S. G.P.O., Report. Briggs, L. (1914, December 16), "Market Conditions," United States. Bureau of Manufactures (1910 et seq). Daily Consular and Trade Reports. Washington, D.C.: U.S. G.P.O., pp. 1169–78.

[380] Rubber companies and Viet Nam. Figart of General Rubber in Viet Nam. Consul Briggs, Lawrence to David M. Figart, March 10, 1917, Records of the Department of State relating to internal affairs of France, 1910–1929, Reel 152, frame 0248–49. General Rubber 1904, for United States Rubber Co. Moody, J. (1927). Moody's Manual of Investments and Security Rating Service: Industrial Securities, 1927, NY: Moody's Investors Service, p. 2666.

[381] U.S. Steel formation and exports. Warren, Kenneth. (2001). Big steel : the first century of the United States Steel Corporation, 1901-2001. University of Pittsburgh Press, Introduction and p. 83, Kindle loca-

tions 743, 2040. Steel exports growth to Europe and South America, discussion of India staying with British steel. Irwin, Douglas A. (May, 2003). "Explaining America's Upsurge in Manufactured Exports, 1880-1913". The Review of Economics and Statistics Vol. 85, No. 2 (May, 2003), pp. 364–376 (13 pages). Published By: The MIT Press https://www.jstor.org/stable/3211586?

[382] Anti-communism growing 1920s, Ceplair. Anti-Communism in Twentieth-Century America, Kindle Locations 286–350.393

[383] Anti-communism in 1930s, Ceplair. Anti-Communism in Twentieth-Century America, Kindle Locations 316–350, 1775.

[384] House Un-American, Rand urgent conflict. Ayn Rand, HUAC, Cold War. 773–784, 925 (Cold War start).

[385] Truman says threat of Russian Conquest, headline in PBS report, "Truman Warns Free World Must Arm to Meet Threat of Russian Conquest." PBS America (2016; June 7, 2025), The Battle of Chosin, 1:21:32 of 1:53:38 https://www.youtube.com/watch?v=2nUfpdDA6w&t=4845s .

[386] 1945 US-USSR agreement, Sheehan, "peace that permitted. . ." says Halberstam, Soviets held Eastern Europe, losing 20 million in war. Halberstam, D. (2012). The Fifties. Open Road Media, Amazon Digital Services LLC, p. 8, Kindle location 180.

[387] Grand area defined. Shoup, Imperial brain trust, p. 130. Grand area largely follow CFR War and Peace Studies; Southeast Asia resources. Chomsky, N. (Nov. 4, 2011). Changing Contours of Global Order, Professor Noam Chomsky, YouTube Video, Publ. by Deakin University (Nov. 11, 2011), 14:08–14:41 (entire Western Hemisphere, entire Far East, former British Empire including W. Asia's Middle East energy sources; W. Europe, S. Europe 15:38–16:35 (Middle East energy sources), 16:53–19:44 of 1:18:00. US Grand Area, areas, US to have economic and political control, not permit sovereignty that challenged control. Chomsky, N. (November 2015). Noam Chomsky—The Untold History of U.S. Hegemony & Influence in Europe. Munich: Published by acTVism, March 1, 2019, 6:01–8:11 of 35:36. Areas for US, source of raw materials, concept includes Third World. Chomsky, N., Barsamian, David, & Naiman, Arthur (2011). How the World Works (Real Story Series). Berkeley, CA : Soft Skull Press : Distributed by Group West, pp. 13–14, Kindle location 247–268. World order closely followed CFR War and Peace Studies unclassified; access to colonies; military and economic supremacy. Wala, The Council on Foreign Relations and American foreign policy in the early Cold War, pp. 38–39. CFR "blueprints;" limit sovereignty, quote. Shoup, Impe-

rial brain trust, pp. 119 (blueprints), 130–31, n. 41, 45. Grand area, limitation of sovereignty. CFR report E-B19, "The War and United States Foreign Policy: Needs of Future United States Foreign Policy (October 9, 1940)." Quote on limitation of sovereignty. Shoup, Imperial Brain Trust, p. 130; "unquestioned power." Chomsky, N. (Nov. 4, 2011). "Changing Contours of Global Order, Professor Noam Chomsky", YouTube Video, Publ. by Deakin University (Nov. 11, 2011), 18:00–18:28, of 1:18:00.

[388] A "world order." McCain, J. (2017, February 19). 'I Worry About the President's Understanding' Some Issues. NBC News, Meet the Press, YouTube video, 00:33–01:07. Theodore "Roosevelt Corollary." US key role post-war system, unfairness. Kissinger, *World Order*, pp. 251, 278–79, Kindle locations 3537, 3906–3918. CFR book refers to world order. Mead, *Power, Terror, Peace, and War*, p. 157, pp. 15, 52 (majority), 54, 69, Kindle locations 230, 729 (majority), 730, 901. World order defending freedom. Isaacson, *The Wise Men*, p. 19, Kindle location 102. An unfolding new world order. Chomsky, *Who rules the world?* Chapter 4, Kindle location 783–822.

[389] Dardanelles friction point. Turkey, Dardanelles. Ambrose, *Rise to globalism*, p. 71 Kindle location 1127

[390] Czech 1948, CIA networks, Soviets crush. Isaacson, *The Wise Men*, pp. 439–444, Kindle location 7561–7655. Czech 1948. Ambrose, *Rise to globalism*, p. 90, Kindle location 1413. Hungary and East Germany crushed. Kinzer, *The Brothers*, Chapter 7, Kindle location 3777–3783.. CIA networks Eastern Europe, Soviet action. Boot, *The Road Not Taken*, p. 152, Kindle location 3133.

[391] Brazil 1954 coup. Colby, *Thy will be done*, pp. 255–62.

[392] US suppress democracy for business, Greece (torture), Italy, Korea, Central America (torture) and using German war criminals in South America (torture). Chomsky, *How the World Works*, pp. 15–20, Kindle location 284–369. German scientists to US to develop weapons. German scientists to US, warning, Hoffmann. Jacobsen, A. (2015). *Operation Paperclip : The secret intelligence program that brought Nazi scientists to America*, New York: Back Bay Books, Little, Brown and Company, Prologue, Chapter 15, Kindle locations 61–90, 4023–4061. Venezuela coup 1948. Colby, *Thy will be done*, pp. 217–19. Ratlines. Talbot, *Devil's Chessboard*, pp. 93–116, Kindle locations 2028–2409.

[393] Viet Nam no help from Soviets, China during first postwar years; cables. Bradley, *Imagining Vietnam and America*, p. 129, Kindle location 1892. Ho talks 1954 with China, Soviets. Logevall, *Embers of war*, Chapter 21, Kindle location 9192–9205.

[394] US power no parallel. US unparalleled power. Chomsky, N. (November 2015). *Noam Chomsky—The Untold History of U.S. Hegemony & Influence in Europe.* Munich: Published by acTVism, March 1, 2019, 8:48–9:59 of 35:36.
[395] US area largely matched blueprints, War and Peace blueprints. Shoup, *Imperial brain trust,* p. 119.
[396] CFR foreign policy establishment. *Newsweek,* September 6, 1971:74; Shoup, Imperial Brain Trust, pp. 4, 7.
[397] Three reports control until deemed. CFR Economic and Financial Group (June 24, 1944), "The United States And The Colonial Problem, E-B71," CFR Studies of American Interests in the War and the Peace. NY: Council on Foreign Relations, Inc., p. 1; CFR Economic and Financial Group (July 29, 1944). "Undeveloped Countries and Exchange Control, E-B72," pp. 2, 11–13; CFR Economic and Financial Group (November 18, 1944). "World Industrialization and International Trade, No. E-B75, pp. 1, 4–9.
[398] Corporate, Lazard and Homburg connection. Cameron, Homburg and Lazard Freres Bank of Wall Street. "Opportunity for Rubber Investments in Indo-China," Records of the Department of State relating to internal affairs of France, 1910–1929, 851g.6176/9, Reel 152, Frames 0350–0353. Ydigoras, United Fruit, Frank Altschul CFR director 1934–72. Shoup, *Imperial brain trust,* pp. 198–99, 289.
[399] CFR, government, United Fruit interlocks, Dulles brothers still in CFR 1954. Shoup, *Imperial Brain Trust* pp. 198–99, 235 (Dulles).
[400] Three reports Viet Nam in postwar regional trade, textiles, colonial. CFR, *The War and Peace Studies of the Council on Foreign Relations, 1939–1945,* "The Economic Organization of Peace in the Far East" June 20, 1941, War and Peace Studies, E-B33, pp. 2–4, 15–19. Hold Da Nang or Cam Ranh Bay. CFR, *The War and Peace Studies of the Council on Foreign Relations, 1939–1945,* "Postwar Security Arrangements in the Pacific Area," September 11, 1942, A-B69, pp. 3–4. Colonial, repression. *War and Peace Studies, 1939–45,* CFR Territorial Group, (November 16, 1943). "The Future Status of Indo-China As An Example Of Postwar Colonial Relationships, T-B69," NY: Council on Foreign Relations, pp. 1–2, 4. Southeast Asia resources and Japan, Europe under Marshall Plan; objectors were called communists. Chomsky, N. (April 21, 1992). Viet Nam "service role." Chomsky, *How the World Works,* p. 14, Kindle location 259.
[401] Bombs and explosives Viet Nam three times over World War II. Miguel, E. & Gerard Roland. (October 2005). "The Long Run Impact of Bombing Vietnam," US: Department of Economics, University of

California, Berkeley, p. 2. Explosives 640 times Hiroshima. Turse, *Kill Anything that Moves*, p. 79, Kindle location 1359.

402 Shaky assumptions. Ceplair, *Anti-Communism in Twentieth-Century America*, Kindle Location 2610.

403 Presidents have waged illegal wars for decades. Hathaway, O. (July 16, 2024). For the Rest of the World, the U.S. President Has Always Been Above the Law: Americans Will Now Know What A Lack Of Accountability Means. *Foreign Affairs*. NY: Council on Foreign Relations. Over 80 election interferences. Chomsky, *The Myth of American Idealism*, p. 27, Kindle location 534. Limitation of sovereignty. CFR memo E-B19, "The War and United States Foreign Policy: Needs of Future United States Foreign Policy (October 9, 1940)." Quote on limitation of sovereignty. Shoup, *Imperial Brain Trust*, p. 130. NSC and others direct illegal coups, destabilizations, and wars. Roesch, *Corporate Tsunami in Countryside Paradise*, Chapters 17–20, 22–23, 29– 30, and Appendix III. Partial list of coups. Roesch, *Corporate Tsunami in Countryside Paradise*, Appendix III.

404 Taylor mystery rebuild units. Chomsky, *Rethinking Camelot*, Kindle location 1913.

405 Tho joined Peoples Army, later was invited to join the Party. *Cuoc Doi Binh Nghiep*, pp 25, 34 35, 88. Percent of armed forces in Party. *Victory in Viet Nam*, p. 329, Kindle location 4494; entire book (courage and heroism in battle).

406 Tram joined Peoples Army, later was invited to join the Party. Đặng, Thùy Trâm birthdate, early life, graduation, joined, trekked south, later was invited to join the Party, Area controlled by Resistance, free-fire zone, US forces by day, extensive writing of emotions and thoughts. Đặng, Thùy Trâm, Nhật Ký Đặng Thùy Trâm, Lời dẫn (preface), p. 127, n. 1, Kindle edition 4503–4561. English language edition. Dang, Last Night I Dreamed of Peace, pp. v–viii, x–xi (Party). Film of events in life of Dang Thuy Tram. Hương Minh., M., Korschi, Mathew, Thạch, Kim Long, Diễm Lộc, Minh Trang, Hãng Phim Hội điện ảnh Vn, . . . Fafilm. (2010). Đừng đốt Don't burn. Vietnam: Fafilm.

407 Korea causes of unrest, rage. Millett, pp. 177–85, Kindle locations 2112–2224.

408 Japan protectorate, annex Korea. Millett, Allan R. (2005). *The War for Korea, 1945-1950: A House Burning* (Modern War Studies). University Press of Kansas, pp. 31–32, Kindle locations 305–310.. In south of Korea, Rhee in confrontational right, mislabel as leftists, suppress in south. Millett, A. (2005). *The war for Korea, 1945–1950 : A house burning* (Modern war studies). Lawrence, Kan.: University Press of Kansas, Introduction, Chapters 1, 2, 4, 5, and 6, Kindle locations 467–528

(espec. 476), 744, 1266–1273, 1412–1423, 2356–3002, 3554–3559, 3913, 4164–4509. Post-WW II political movements sprang up for Korea, popular uprisings 1946, US crushed, 1948 violent war; Clark, D. (2008). The Journal of Asian Studies. 67(2), 735–738. Retrieved from http://www.jstor.org/stable/20203412.

409 Korea, Dulles, Rhee a Christina & US univ grad, popular movement US against. Millett, *The war for Korea, 1945–1950*, pp. 6, 480–83 (Dulles), Chapters 1, 2, 3, 4, 5, and 6, Kindle locations 757, 467–528 (espec. 476), 744–773, 1266–1273, 1412–1423, 2223, 2356–*3002*, 3554–3559, 3913, 4164–4509, 6196–6207.

410 US in China 1784 and onward, *Empress of China*, Treaties of Wanghia and Nanking. Davies, J.P. (1972). *Dragon by the tail : American, British, Japanese, and Russian encounters with China and one another* (First edition.). W. W. Norton & Company, Inc., p. 74. Tolley, K. (1971). *Yangtze Patrol: the US Navy in China*, Naval Institute Press, Kindle locations 225–240.

411 Shimonoseki plot and John Foster quote, John Foster plot to overthrow China; United States influence. Devine, M. (1981). *John W. Foster: Politics and diplomacy in the imperial era, 1873-1917*. Athens, Ohio: Ohio University Press, p.74, 85.

412 US forces in China. "Instances of Use of United States Armed Forces Abroad, 1798-2023" Publication date 06/07/2023 https://www.congress.gov/crs-product/R42738

413 General Butler on gangster for capitalism . . . in China. https://quaker.org/legacy/co/Writings/SmedleyButler.htm

414 Davies on China vs imperialism 1920s onward imperialists against democracy cause of comm power in civil war. Davies, J. P. (1972). *Dragon by the tail : American, British, Japanese, and Russian encounters with China and one another* (First edition.). W. W. Norton & Company, Inc., pp. 74, 414–17. China, Korea, others, Versailles disaster. MacMillan, M. (2002). *Paris 1919 : Six months that changed the world* (1st U.S. ed.). NY: Random House, Chapter 23, 24, Kindle locations 6280, 6499–6877. China 1920s Chiang & Mao among small numbers vs warlords & imperialists. Davies, J. P. (1972). *Dragon by the tail : American, British, Japanese, and Russian encounters with China and one another* (First edition.). W. W. Norton & Company, Inc., pp. 123–133.

415 Chiang vs farmers. Davies, *Dragon by the tail*, pp. 131–33.

416 Davies on 1945–49 civil war Treaty of Wanghia, China; imperialists against democracy, Chiang view, corrupt, civil war. Davies, J. P. (1972). *Dragon by the tail : American, British, Japanese, and Russian encounters with China and one another* (First edition.). W. W. Norton & Company, Inc., pp. 74 (treaty), 414–19, 423 (Stalin to US secy on troops), 424–29

(nationalistic). US did not "lose" China. Ceplair, *Anti-Communism in Twentieth-Century America*, Kindle Location 39. Citation. Truman, being a novice, had no effective policy. Mao and the communist movement won the civil war in 1949.

[417] Chiang view, corrupt, civil war. Davies, J. P. (1972). *Dragon by the tail : American, British, Japanese, and Russian encounters with China and one another* (First edition.). W. W. Norton & Company, Inc., pp. 74 (treaty), 414–19, 423 (Stalin to US secy on troops), 424–29 (nationalistic). US did not "lose" China. Ceplair, *Anti-Communism in Twentieth-Century America*, Kindle Location 39. Citation. Truman, being a novice, had no effective policy. Mao and the communist movement won the civil war in 1949.

[418] Dulles fired insightful diplomats Davies. Davies, *Dragon by the tail*, p. 10, 351. Dulles fired insightful diplomat Davies. Ceplair, *Anti-Communism in Twentieth-Century America*, Kindle Location 1778.

[419] Post-Viet Nam War criticism of US "Left." Ceplair, *Anti-Communism in Twentieth-Century America*, Kindle locations 2492–2518.

[420] Shaky assumptions. Ceplair, *Anti-Communism in Twentieth-Century America*, Kindle Location 2610.

[421] Unilateralism and loss of US hegemony. Gaddis, *Strategies of containment : a critical appraisal of American national security policy during the Cold War*, p. 384, Kindle location 7371.

PART III

CHAPTER 11

[422] US Marine Corps Hymn. US Marine Corps Hymn excerpt. Collins, A. (2003). *Songs Sung Red, White, and Blue*. NY: HarperCollins, p. 123, Kindle location 1567.

[423] VVAW said public had not been told truth; citizen-soldier change to warrior for empire. Moser, R. R. (1996). *The new winter soldiers : GI and veteran dissent during the Vietnam era*. Rutgers University Press, Kindle locations 334– 643 (nature of soldier), 1589 (VVAW & truth). Stacewicz, R., Vietnam Veterans Against the War., & Vietnam Veterans Against the War. (1997). *Winter soldiers : an oral history of the Vietnam Veterans Against the War.* Twayne Publishers.

[424] Sowders desert, testimony. Schneider, *Hearts and Minds*, 51:48–53:48. Desertion rates. Heinl, R.D., Jr., "The Collapse of the Armed Forces," *Armed Forces Journal, June 7, 1971*, vol.8, No. 19. Desertion rates, AWOLS. Rinaldi, *Olive-Drab Rebels*, p. 21; Vietnam Peace Commemoration Committee (August 29, 2017). *Gi Resistance in the Vietnam War.* http:// vnpeacecomm.blogspot.com/2017/08/gi-opposition-to-war.html.

[425] Winter soldiers hurl medals, epithets at leaders, thought connected with public. Moser, R. R. (1996). *The new winter soldiers*, Kindle locations 1704–1741.
[426] Floyd on avoid. Former pilot Randy Floyd on effort to avoid logical conclusions. Schneider, *Hearts and Minds*, 1:47:00–1:47:14.
[427] Niger four US combat deaths 2017. *Kube, Courtney; Dilanian, Ken (8 May 2018). "Leaders of U.S. soldiers killed in Niger filed misleading mission plan". NBC News. Retrieved 20 July 2019.*Niger US training locals to fight insurgencies, air operations from Niger for intelligence for France in other countries. Turse, *Tomorrow's Battlefield*, Kindle Locations 402, 480, 1041 (blowback).
[428] Moore on humiliating defeat. Humiliating defeat on US. Moore, H. & Galloway, Joseph L. (1992). *We Were Soldiers Once . . . and Young : Ia Drang, the Battle that Changed the War in Vietnam*, New York: Random House, p. 374 (humiliating), pp. 42–end of book (battle & aftermath), 385–89 (Tom Metsker & wife), Kindle locations 7098, 1333 to end of book, 6750–6817. Ia Drang battle. Roesch, *Corporate Tsunami in Countryside Paradise*, Ch 40.
[429] Laxer, G. (2021). *Take This War and Shove It! : A Most Unwilling Soldier 1967– 1971*, Unbearable Truth Publications.

BIBLIOGRAPHY

English, Viet language, French

For consul reports, see United States Government Consul reports and papers.

For War and Peace Studies see English Language Reports CFR.

English Language Books

Abrahamian, Ervand (2013). *The coup : 1953, the CIA, and the roots of modern U.S.-Iranian relations.* The New Press

Anderson, I. I. (1975). *The Standard-Vacuum Oil Company and United States East Asian policy, 1933–1941.* Princeton, N.J.: Princeton University Press.

Appy, C. (2003). *Patriots: The Vietnam War remembered from all sides.* New York: Viking.

Atwood, Paul (2015). *War and Empire: The American Way of Life.* Pluto Press.

Bacon, John; John Bendyk; & Jeff Brown (1998). *Sub- Saharan Africa: Pragmatism in the National Interest.* Defense Technical Information Center, National Defense University, National War College

Bailey, C., & Son, Le Ke (2017). *From Enemies to Partners: Vietnam, the U.S. and Agent Orange.* Chicago, IL: Anton Publishing.

Baptist, E. (2014). *The Half has Never Been Told: Slavery and the Making of American Capitalism.* NY: Basic Books, Perseus Book Group.

Baradaran, M. (2017). *The Color of Money: Black Banks and the racial wealth gap.* Cambridge, Mass: The Belknap Press of Harvard University Press.

Bevins, V. (2020). *The Jakarta method : Washington's anticommunist crusade & the mass murder program that shaped our world.* PublicAffairs, Hatchette Book Group.

Bible, New International Version.

Bird, K. (1992) (Kindle ed. 2017). *The chairman : John J. McCloy, the making of the American establishment.* New York ; London ; Toronto ; Sydney ; Tokyo ; Singapore: Simon & Schuster.

Bird, K. (1998). *The color of truth: McGeorge Bundy and William Bundy, brothers in arms : A biography.* New York: Simon & Schuster.

Bissell, R., Lewis, Jonathan E., & Pudlo, Frances T. (1996). *Reflections of a cold warrior : From Yalta to the Bay of Pigs.* New Haven: Yale University Press.

Blum, W. (2014). *America's deadliest export : Democracy—the truth about US foreign policy and everything else.* Halifax, N.S; London; NY: Fernwood Pub., Zed Books.

Blum, W. (2003). *Killing hope : U.S. military and CIA interventions since World War II.* London: Zed.

Bradley, M. (2000). *Imagining Vietnam and America : The Making of post-colonial Vietnam, 1919–1950* (New Cold War history). Chapel Hill: University of North Carolina Press.

Brocheux, P. (1995). *The Mekong Delta : Ecology, Economy, and Revolution, 1860–1960* (Monograph (University of Wisconsin-Madison. Center for Southeast Asian Studies) ; 12). Madison, WI, USA: Center for Southeast Asian Studies), University of Wisconsin-Madison.

Burke, J. (2001). *Origines: the Streets of Viet Nam, a Historical Companion.* Ha Noi: Thế Giới Publishers.

Byrne, M., Gasiorowski, Mark J., Risen, James, & National Security Archive. (2000). *The secret CIA history of the Iran Coup, 1953* (National Security Archive electronic briefing book ; no. 28). Washington, D.C.]: [National Security Archive, George Washington University].

Buttinger, J. (1967). *Vietnam : A Dragon Embattled,* New York: Praeger.

Buttinger, J. (1977). *Vietnam : the Unforgettable Tragedy.* NY: Horizon Press.

Byrne, M., Gasiorowski, Mark J., Risen, James, & National Security Archive. (2000). *The secret CIA history of the Iran Coup, 1953* (National Security Archive electronic briefing book ; no. 28). Washington, D.C.]: [National Security Archive, George Washington University], pp. 2–3.

Carruthers, B., ed. (2011). *The Nuremberg Trials: The Complete Proceedings*, Vol. 22: The Final Judgment. Great Britain: Coda Books Ltd., Introduction and TWO HUNDRED AND EIGHTEENTH DAY Tuesday, 1 October 1946

Ceplair. L.(2011). *Anti-Communism in twentieth-century America : a critical history.* Santa Barbara, Denver: Praeger.

Bibliography

Chomsky, Noam; Polychroniou, C.J. (2024). *A Livable Future is Possible: Confronting the Threats to Our Survival.* Haymarket Books. Kindle Edition, pp. 58–60, Kindle locations 718–740

Chomsky, N., & Herman, Edward S. (2002). *Manufacturing Consent : The Political Economy of the Mass Media.* NY: Pantheon Books.

Chomsky, N. (2015). *Rethinking Camelot : JFK, the Vietnam War, and U.S. Political Culture.* NY: Haymarket Books.

Chomsky, N., & Peck, James. (1987). The Chomsky reader (1st ed.). New York: Pantheon Books.

Chomsky, N. (2015). *Year 501: The conquest continues.* London: Pluto Press.

Chomsky, N. & Nathan J. Robinson (2024). *The Myth of American Idealism: How U.S. Foreign Policy Endangers the World.* NY: Penguin Publishing Group.

Chomsky, N., & Herman, E. S. (1979). *The Washington connection and Third World fascism* (1st ed.). South End Press.

Chomsky, N. (2022). *The withdrawal : Iraq, Libya, Afghanistan, and the fragility of U.S. power.* (Interview by Vijay Prashad), The New Press.

Chomsky, N. (2016). *Who Rules the World?* (First U.S. ed.). New York: Metropolitan Books, Henry Holt and Company.

Christofferson, T., & Christofferson, Michael Scott. (2006). *France during World War II : From defeat to liberation* (1st ed., World War II--the global, human, and ethical dimension; 10). New York: Fordham University Press.

Clements, C. (1984). *Witness To War: An American Doctor in El Salvador.* Toronto: NY: Bantam Books

Cohen, S. F. (2000). *Failed crusade : America and the tragedy of post-Communist Russia* (1st ed.).

Colby, G. & Dennett, Charlotte (1995). *Thy will be done : The conquest of*

the Amazon : Nelson Rockefeller and Evangelism in the age of oil (1st ed.). NY: HarperCollins.

Consultative Council. (1967). *The Vietnam War and international law: The illegality of the United States military involvement (2d ed.).* Flanders, N.J.: O'Hare Books.

Crenshaw, Charles A., Jens Hansen, & J. Gary Shaw (2013). *JFK Has Been Shot: A Parkland Hospital Surgeon Speaks Out*, Pinnacle Books.

Dang, T. and Pham, A (translator). (2007). *Last Night I Dreamed of Peace.* USA: Crown Publishing Group.

Davis, Angela Y. (2016). *Freedom Is a Constant Struggle: Ferguson, Palestine, and the Foundations of a Movement.* Haymarket Books, Chicago.

Dhammananda, K. S. (1987). *What Buddhists believe* (Expanded and rev. ed.; 4th ed.). Buddhist Missionary Society, *Vol. 1*.

Dosal, P. J. (Paul J. (1993). *Doing business with the dictators : a political history of United Fruit in Guatemala, 1899-1944*. US: Wilmington, DE, Scholarly Resources, Inc. SR Books.

Douglass, James W. (2008) *JFK and the Unspeakable: Why he Died and Why it Matters,* Maryknoll, NY: Orbis Books.

Downs, J. (2012). *Sick from freedom: African-American illness and suffering during the Civil War and Reconstruction.* Oxford University Press.

Dubois, L. (2012). *Haiti : the aftershocks of history* (1st ed.). NY: Metropolitan Books.

Duiker, W. (2012). *Ho Chi Minh : A Life,* US: Hyperion.

Duiker, W. (1995). *Sacred War : Nationalism and revolution in a divided Vietnam.* NY: McGraw-Hill.

Duiker, W. (1996). *The communist road to power in Vietnam* (2nd ed.). Boulder, CO: Westview Press, Chapter 2, Kindle locations 714–717, 951.

Eichstaedt, P. H. (2011). *Consuming the Congo : war and conflict minerals in the world's deadliest place.* Chicago Review Press.

Ellsberg, D. (2002). *Secrets: A memoir of Vietnam and the Pentagon papers.* New York: Viking.

Engelke, P., & Chiu, D. Y. (2016). *Climate Change and US National Security : Past, Present, Future.* Atlantic Council

Ennis, T. E. (Thomas E. (1973). *French policy and developments in Indochina.* Russell & Russell.

Evans, Thomas (2006). *The Education of Ronald Reagan: The General Electric Years and the Untold Story of His Conversion to Conservatism* (Columbia Studies in Contemporary American History) . Columbia University Press.

Falk, R., & Andersson, Stefan. (2018). *Revisiting the Vietnam War and International Law : Views and Interpretations of Richard Falk*, Cambridge, United Kingdom; New York, NY: Cambridge University Press.

Fall, B. (1967). *The Two Viet-Nams: A political and military analysis* (2nd rev. ed.). New York: Frederick A. Praeger

Ferrell, R. (2000). *Choosing Truman: The Democratic Convention of 1944*, Columbia, Missouri: University of Missouri Press.

Fifield, R., & Council on Foreign Relations. (1963). *Southeast Asia in United States policy.* (1st ed.). New York: Published for the Council on Foreign Relations by Praeger.

Fineman, D. (1996). *A Special Relationship: The United States and Military Government in Thailand, 1947–1958*. Honolulu, HI, USA: University of Hawaii Press and co.

Foley, B. (1998). *European economies since the Second World War*. New York: St. Martin's Press.

Forster, C. (2012). *The Time of Freedom: Campesino Workers in Guatemala's October Revolution*. University of Pittsburgh Press.

Fox, Stephen (1970). *The Guardian of Boston: William Monroe Trotter*. New York: Atheneum Press.

Gaddis, J. L. (2005). *Strategies of containment : a critical appraisal of American national security policy during the Cold War* (Revised and expanded edition.). Oxford University Press.

Gans, J. (2019). *White House Warriors : how the National Security Council transformed the American way of war* (First edition). Liveright Publishing Corporation, a division of W. W. Norton & Company.

Gillespie, R. (2011). *Black Ops, Vietnam : The Operational History of MACVSOG*. Annapolis: Naval Institute Press.

Ginzburg, R. (1962). *100 years of lynchings*. Baltimore, MD: Black Classic Press.

Glasser, Jeffrey D. (1995). *The Secret Vietnam War: The United States in Thailand, 1961-1975*, McFarland & Company, Inc., North Carolina.

Gondola, C. (2002). *The history of Congo* (Greenwood histories of the modern nations). Westport, Conn.: Greenwood Press

Gonzalez, J. (2022). *Harvest of Empire: A History of Latinos in America*, 2d ed., rvsd. US: Penguin.

Grose, P. (1996). *Continuing the Inquiry : the Council on Foreign Relations from 1921 to 1996*. NY: Council on Foreign Relations.

Grose, P. (1994). *Gentleman spy : The life of Allen Dulles*. Boston: Houghton, Mifflin.

Gruening, E., & Beaser, Herbert Wilton. (1968). *Vietnam folly*. Washington: National Press.

Halberstam, D. (1971). *Ho*. Random House.

Ham, P. (2007). *Vietnam : the Australian War*. NY, Australia: HarperCollins Publishers Australia Pty Ltd.

Hannah-Jones, N., Roper, Caitlin, Silverman, Ilena, Silverstein, Jake, & New York Times Company. (2021). *The 1619 Project: A new origin story* (First ed.). New York: One World.

Haney-López, I. (2014). *Dog whistle politics : How coded racial appeals have reinvented racism and wrecked the middle class.* Oxford; New York: Oxford University Press.

Hickey, G. C. (1964). *Village in Vietnam.* Yale University Press.

Ho Chi Minh Museum (2016). *Ho Chi Minh Biography.* Viet Nam: The Gioi Publishers.

Horne, G. (2016). *Paul Robeson : The Artist as Revolutionary.* London: Pluto Press.

Huu Ngoc, with Lady Borton (ed) (2016). *Viet Nam: Tradition and Change.* Ha Noi: The Gioi, and Athens, Ohio: Ohio University Press.

Huu Ngoc (2004). *Wandering through Vietnamese culture.* Ha Noi: The Gioi.

Ifill, S. (2018). *On the Courthouse lawn : Confronting the legacy of lynching in the twenty-first century.* Revised Kindle Edition. Boston: Beacon Press.

Isaacson, W., & Thomas, Evan (1986). *The wise men: Six friends and the world they made: Acheson, Bohlen, Harriman, Kennan, Lovett, McCloy.* New York: Simon and Schuster.

Kahin, G.M., ed. (1959). *Governments and Politics of Southeast Asia.* NY: Cornell University Press.

Kissinger, H. (2014). *World Order.* New York: Penguin Press.

Koonings, K., & Kruijt, D. (1999). *Societies of fear : the legacy of civil war, violence and terror in Latin America.* Zed Books.

Kinzer, S. (2006). *Overthrow : America's century of regime change from Hawaii to Iraq* (First ed.) NY: Times Books/Henry Holt

Kinzer, S. (2019). *Poisoner in chief : Sidney Gottlieb and the CIA search for mind control* (First ed.). New York: Henry Holt and Company

Kinzer, S. (2013). *The Brothers: John Foster Dulles, Allen Dulles, and their secret world war,* (First ed.), NY: Time Books/Henry Holt and Company.

Kinzer S. (2017). *The true flag : Theodore Roosevelt, Mark Twain, and the birth of American empire* (First ed.). NY: Henry Holt and Company.

Klein, N. (2023). *Doppelganger : a trip into the mirror world* (First edition.). Farrar, Straus and Giroux.

Kloppenberg, James. T. (2012). *The education of Barack Obama* (Princeton Shorts ed.). Princeton University Press.

Koh, Harold Hongju (2024). *The National Security Constitution in the Twenty-First Century.* Yale University Press. Kindle Edition.

Laderman, Scott & Edwin A. Martini, editors (2013). *Four Decades on Viet Nam, the United States and the Legacies of the Second Indochina War.* Chapter 1: "Legacies Foretold: Excavating the Roots of Postwar Vietnam." Durham NC and London: Duke University Press, pp. 16–43.

Lamb, H. B. (1972). *Vietnam's will to live; resistance to foreign aggression from early times through the nineteenth century.* Monthly Review Press.

Lane, C. (2008). *The day freedom died: The Colfax massacre, the Supreme Court, and the betrayal of Reconstruction* (1st ed.). New York: Henry Holt and Co.

Lauria-Santiago, A. & Binford, Leigh (2004). *Landscapes of Struggle: Politics, Society, and Community In El Salvador* (Pitt Latin American series). Pittsburgh, Pa.: University of Pittsburgh Press.

Lenin, V. (1967). *Lenin on the National and Colonial Questions : Three articles.* Peking: Red Star Publishers, www.redstarpublishers.org/leninnatcolq.doc, p. 22.

Logevall, F. (1999). *Choosing war : The lost chance for peace and the escalation of war in Vietnam.* Berkeley: University of California Press.

Logevall, F. (2012). *Embers of war : The fall of an empire and the making of America's Vietnam* (1st ed.). Berkeley: University of California Press.

Mai Luận, Đắc Xuân, and Trần Dân Tiên (2015). *Hồ Chí Minh from childhood to president of Việt Nam.* Viet Nam, Thế Giới Publishers.

Marciano, J. (2016). The American war in Vietnam : Crime or commemoration? New York: Monthly Review Press.

Marr, D. (2013). *Vietnam State, War, and Revolution (1945–1946).* Berkeley, University of California Press.

Marrs, J. (1989). *Crossfire : the plot that killed Kennedy.* Carroll & Graf Publishers.

Martini, E. (2012). *Agent Orange: History, Science, and the politics of uncertainty* (Culture, poli-tics, and the Cold War). Amherst, MA: University of Massachusetts Press

Maxwell, Angie and Shields, Todd (2019). *The Long Southern Strategy : How Chasing White Voters in the South Changed American Politics.* NY: Oxford University Press.

McCoy, A. (2006). *A question of torture : CIA interrogation, from the Cold War to the War on Terror.* NY: Metropolitan Books/ Henry Holt

Mead, W. (2004). *Power, Terror, Peace, and War : America's Grand Strategy in a World at Risk.* NY: Vintage Books. A Council on Foreign Relations Book; Knopf Doubleday Publishing Group.

Meredith, M. (2011). *The fate of Africa : a history of the continent since independence* (Revised and updated ed.). Public Affairs.

Military Institute of Vietnam, The; Pribbenow, M.L. transl. (2002). *Victory in Vietnam : The official History of the People's Army of Vietnam, 1954–75,* Lawrence, Kan: University Press of Kansas, p. 328, Kindle location 4492.

Miller, E. (2013). *Misalliance : Ngo Dinh Diem, the United States, and the fate of South Vietnam.* Cambridge, Mass.: Harvard University Press.

Miller, R. (1990). *The United States and Vietnam, 1787–1941.* Washington, DC: National Defense University Press.

Milne, D. (2008). *America's Rasputin : Walt Rostow and the Vietnam War* (1st ed.). New York: Hill and Wang.

Modeste, Denneth M. (2020). *The Monroe Doctrine in a Contemporary Perspective.* NY, Routledge Studies in the History of the Americas

Montesano, Michael J., Terence Chong, & Mark Heng. C. (editors) (2019). *After the Coup: The National Council for Peace and Order Era and the Future of Thailand.* ISEAS Publishing, Singapore

Moore, H. & Galloway, Joseph L. (1992). *We Were Soldiers Once . . . and Young : Ia Drang, the Battle that Changed the War in Vietnam,* New York: Random House

Morgan, R., Royal Institute of International Affairs., & Harvard University. Center for International Affairs. (1974). *The United States and West Germany, 1945-1973 : a study in alliance politics.* Published for the Royal Institute of International Affairs and the Harvard Center for International Affairs by Oxford University Press.

Moser, R. R. (1996). *The new winter soldiers : GI and veteran dissent during the Vietnam era.* Rutgers University Press.

Mwakikagile, G. (2019). *Post-colonial Africa; A General Survey,* Amazon Digital Services LLC.

Ngo, Vinh Long in: Laderman, Scott & Edwin A. Martini, editors (2013). *Four Decades on Viet Nam, the United States and the Legacies of the Second Indochina War.* Chapter 1: "Legacies Foretold: Excavating the Roots of Postwar Vietnam." Durham NC and London: Duke University Press, pp. 16–43

Nguyen, D., translated by Counsell, Michael (2017). *Kieu: The Tale of a Beautiful and Talented Young Girl,* Bilingual Vietnamese-English. Ha Noi: The Gioi Publishers.

Nguyen Khac Vien (2015). *Vietnam: A Long History (Tenth edition).* Ha Noi: The Gioi Publishers House.

Nguyen Thi Dinh (1976). *No other road to take : memoir of Mrs. NguyenThi Dinh,* Ithaca, NY: translation by Southeast Asia Program, Dept. of Asian Studies, Cornell University.

Nubia, O. (2022). Routledge Handbook of Pan-Africanism, ed. Reiland Rabaka.

O'Donnell, K., & Powers, David F. (1972). *Johnny, we hardly knew ye; memories of John Fitzgerald Kennedy* (1st ed.]. ed.). Boston: Little, Brown.

Bibliography

Penet, Pierre., & Flores Zendejas, J. (2021). *Sovereign Debt Diplomacies: Rethinking sovereign debt from colonial empires to hegemony.* UK: Oxford University Press.

Pettit, C. (1975). *The Experts.* Secaucus, N.J.: L. Stuart.

Pham, Q., & Shilliam, Robbie. (2016). *Meanings of Bandung : Postcolonial orders and decolonial visions* (Kilombo (Series)). London ; New York: Rowman & Littlefield International.

Prins, Nomi (2014). *All the President's Bankers: the hidden Alliances that drive American Power,* NY: Nation Books, member of Perseus books Group.

Prouty, L. (2008). *The Secret Team :The CIA and its allies in control of the United States and the world.* NY: Skyhorse Publishing.

Quinn-Judge, S. (2002). *Ho Chi Minh : The Missing Years, 1919–1941.* Berkely, CA: University of California Free Press.

Roesch, B. (2020) *Corporate Tsunami in Countryside Paradise : 1875–1900 Origin of US War in Viet Nam.* US: Voter Knowledge Press.

Russell, B. (1967). *War Crimes in Vietnam.* London: Allen & Unwin.

Sarotte, M. E. (2021). *Not One Inch: America, Russia, and the Making of Post-Cold War Stalemate.* Yale University Press.

Schlesinger, S., & Kinzer, Stephen. (1982). *Bitter fruit : The untold story of the American coup in Guatemala* (1st ed.). Garden City, N.Y.: Doubleday.

Schuck, P. (1986). *Agent Orange on Trial : Mass toxic disasters in the courts.* Cambridge, Mass.: Belknap Press of Harvard University Press

Schulzinger, R. (1984). *The wise men of foreign affairs: The history of the Council on Foreign Relations.* NY: Columbia University Press.

Scott, R. (1943). *God is my copilot.* New York: Scribner.

Shakespeare, W. & Craig, W. J. ed. (1936). *The Complete Works of William Shakespeare,* NY: Oxford University Press.

Shakespeare, W. & Pierce, J. ed. (2010). *Macbeth : With Contemporary Criticism.* San Francisco: Ignatius Press>

Sheehan, N. (1990). *A bright shining lie : John Paul Vann and America in Viet Nam* (1st Vintage Books ed.). New York: Vintage Books.

Shoup, L. & Minter, William (1977). *Imperial brain trust : The Council on Foreign Relations and United States foreign policy.* New York: Monthly Review Press.

Shoup, L. (2015). *Wall Street's think tank: the Council on Foreign Relations and the empire of neoliberal geopolitics, 1976–2014.* New York: Monthly Review Press, Amazon Digital Services LLC.

Sills, P. (2014). *Toxic war : The story of Agent Orange.* Nashville: Vanderbilt University Press.

Smith, Joseph (2005). *The United States and Latin America : a history of American diplomacy, 1776-2000.* Routledge. https://doi.org/10.4324/9780203004531.

Smith, R. (2014). *On His Own Terms : A Life of Nelson Rockefeller,* NY: Random House.

Stacewicz, R., Vietnam Veterans Against the War., & Vietnam Veterans Against the War. (1997). *Winter soldiers : an oral history of the Vietnam Veterans Against the War.* Twayne Publishers.

Stiglitz, J. E. (2018). *Globalization and its discontents revisited : anti-globalization in the era of Trump.* W.W. Norton & Company.

Stockwell, J. (1978). *In search of enemies : a CIA story* (1st ed.). Norton.

Subtelny, O. (1994). *Ukraine : a history* (2nd ed.). University of Toronto Press.

Talbot, D. (2007). Brothers: The Hidden History of the Kennedy Years. NY: Free Press

Talbot, D. (2015). *The Devil's Chessboard : Allen Dulles, the CIA, and the rise of America's secret government,* NY: Harper, an imprint of HarperCollins.

Thayer, C. A. (1989). *War by other means : national liberation and revolution in Viet-Nam 1954-60.* Allen & Unwin.

Tilles, G. (2018). *The History of Chloracne and Dioxin: A Skin Disease at the Crossroads of Occupational, Environmental and Political Concerns. A Paradigm of Endocrine Disruption.* Amazon Digital Services LLC.

Tuchinsky, A. (2011). *Horace Greeley's "New-York Tribune" : Civil War-Era Socialism and the Crisis of Free Labor.* Cornell University Press

Tuchman, B. (1971), *Stilwell and the American Experience in China, 1911-45,* The MacMillan Company, New York, pp. 21–22.

Turse, N. (2013). *Kill anything that moves : The real American war in Vietnam* (1st ed., American empire project). New York: Metropolitan Books/Henry Holt and Company.

Turse, N. (2015) *Tomorrow's Battlefield : US Proxy Wars and Secret Ops in Africa,* Haymarket Books.

Tyson, T. (2017). *The blood of Emmett Till.* New York: Simon & Schuster, Simon & Schuster Digital Sales Inc.

Van Rey Brouck, D., & Garrett, S. (2014). *Congo : the epic history of a people* (S. Garrett, Trans.; First edition.). Ecco, an imprint of Harper Collins Publishers.

Vaughn, L. (2007, 2008). *Guatemala—Culture Smart: The Essential Guide to Customs & Culture.* London: Kuperard.

Vigneras, M. (1957). *Rearming the French.* Washington, D.C.: Office of the Chief of Military History, Dept. of the Army : [For sale by the Supt. Of Docs., U.S. G.P.O.].

Wala, M. (1994). *The Council on Foreign Relations and American foreign policy in the early Cold War.* Providence: Bergahn Books.

Wilcox, F. (2011). *Scorched Earth : Legacies of chemical warfare in Vietnam* (A Seven Stories Press 1st ed.). New York: Seven Stories Press.

Willbanks, J. (2013). *Vietnam War Almanac: An in-depth guide to the most controversial war in American history.* NY: Skyhorse Publishing.

Williams, S. (2021). *White Malice: The CIA and the Covert Recolonization of Africa.* NY: Hachette Book Group, Public Affairs Press.

Williams, W. (2009). *The tragedy of American diplomacy* (50th anniversary ed.). NY: WW Norton & Company.

Wise, J. (1948). *Meet Henry Wallace.* New York: Boni and Gaer, p. 37.

Witte, L. (2001). The assassination of Lumumba. London; New York: Verso.

Woodmansee, J. (1975). *The World of a Giant Corporation: a report from the GE project.* Seattle: North Country Press.

Woods, C. (2020). *Freedom Incorporated: Anticommunism and Philippine Independence in the Age of Decolonization.* Cornell University Press.

Zinn, H., & Arnove, Anthony (2004, 2014). *Voices of a people's history of the United States* (10th Anniversary edition). NY, Oakland: Seven Stories Press.

English Language Reports in US, other than CFR or government

Civil Rights Congress (1951). *We Charge Genocide: The Historic Petition to the United Nations for Relief from a Crime of the United States Government Against the Negro People (PDF).* Civil Rights Congress, 1952.

Gottmann, Jean, "Raw Materials in the Western Pacific," Institute of Pacific Relations. Conference. (1945). *[Papers presented to the Ninth Conference of the Institute of Pacific Relations, Hot Springs, Virginia,* January 1945]. New York, French Paper No. 1.

Gourou, P. (1945). "The Standard of Living in the Delta of the Tonkin (French Indo-China)" Ninth Conference of the Institute of Pacific Relations, Hot Springs, Virginia, January, 1945, v.5, French, French Paper No. 4.

Stellman, Jeanne Mager and Steven D. Stellman (Published online: May 09, 2018). "Agent Orange During the Vietnam War: The Lingering Issue of its Civilian and Military Health Impact." https:/ajph.aphapublications.org/doi/full/10.2105/AJPH.2018.304426.

Wright, P., Holland, W. L., & Institute of Pacific Relations. International Research Committee. (1935). *Trade and trade barriers in the Pacific.* London: P.S. King & Son, Table 155, pp. 413–415.

Foreign Affairs journal articles, CFR

Bowman, Isaiah. The Strategy of Territorial Decisions. *Foreign Affairs*, 1 January 1946. NY: Council on Foreign Relations. https://www.foreignaffairs.com/articles/world/1946-01-01/strategy-territorial-decisions. Accessed 29 October 2024

Chivvis, C. & Stephen Wertheim (October 14, 2024). America's Foreign Policy Inertia: How the Next President Can Make Change in a System Built to Resist It. *Foreign Affairs*, September/October 2024, Volume 103, Number 5, NY: Council on Foreign Relations.

Drezner, Daniel W. (November 12, 2024). The End of American Exceptionalism: Trump's Reelection Will Redefine U.S. Power. *Foreign Affairs*, November/December 2024, Volume 103, Number 6.

Hathaway, O. (July 16, 2024). For the Rest of the World, theU.S. President Has Always Been Above the Law: Americans Will Now Know What A Lack Of Accountability Means. *Foreign Affairs*. NY: Council on Foreign Relations, NY: Council on Foreign Relations.

Indyk, Martin (*February 20,* 2024) The Strange Resurrection of the Two-State Solution: How an Unimaginable War Could Bring About the Only Imaginable Peace. March/April 2024. *Foreign Affairs*, NY: Council on Foreign Relations. https://www.foreignaffairs.com/israel/palestine-strange-resurrection-two-state-solution-indyk?utm_medium=newsletters&utm_source=fatoday&utm_campaign=The%20Strange%20Resurrection%20of%20the%20Two-State%20Solution&utm_content=20240220&utm_term=FA%20Today%20-%20112017

Miller, A. (Sept 29, 2024). America Needs a New Strategy to Avert Even Greater Catastrophe in the Middle East: Shuttle Diplomacy Must Be Backed by Meaningful Pressure. *Foreign Affairs*, November/December 2024, Volume 103, Number 6. NY: Council on Foreign Relations. https://www.foreignaffairs.com/israel/america-needs-new-strategy-avert-even-greater-catastrophe-middle-east

Murithi, Tim (April 18, 2023). Order of Oppression: Africa's Quest for a New International System. Foreign Affairs: May/June 2023
https://www.foreignaffairs.com/africa global-south-un-order-oppression.

Bibliography

Shira Efron and Michael J. Koplow (July 17, 2024). The Palestinian Authority is Collapsing. *Foreign Affairs*, November/December 2024, Volume 103, Number 6. NY: Council on Foreign Relations. https://www.foreignaffairs.com/palestinian-territories/palestinian-authority-collapsing?

Suzman, Mark (July 11, 2024). "Debt Is Dragging Down the Developing World: How to End the Current Crisis—and Avoid the Next One." Foreign Affairs, NY: Council on Foreign Relations.
https://www.foreignaffairs.com/africa/debt-dragging-down-developing-world

Vinjamuri, Leslie, and Max Yoeli (November 15, 2024). America's Last Chance With the Global South: In an Age of Great-Power Competition, Washington Needs the G-20. *Foreign Affairs*, November/December 2024, Volume 103, Number 6, NY: Council on Foreign Relations.

Winter, Brian (December 10, 2024). Foreign Affairs, Latin America Is About to Become a Priority for U.S. Foreign Policy: Trump Will Disrupt Three Decades of 'Benign Neglect'. *Foreign Affairs*, December 2024, Volume 103, Number 6, NY: Council on Foreign Relation.
https://www.foreignaffairs.com/united-states/latin-america-about-become-priority-us-foreign-

War and Peace Studies, CFR

Council on Foreign Relations (1946). *The war and peace studies of the Council on Foreign Relations, 1939-1945.* New York: The Harold Pratt House.

Readers may wish to try making an interlibrary loan request for any of these reports and memoranda. In general, upon making such a request, this writer received a digital copy within a few days.

On Viet Nam:

"The War and United States Foreign Policy: Needs of Future United States Foreign Policy, War and Peace Studies, E-B19."

"The Economic Organization of Peace in the Far East," War and Peace Studies, E-B33."

"The United States and the Colonial Problem, War and Peace Studies, E-B71."

"Regionalism in Southeast Asia, War and Peace Studies, T-B67."

"The Future Status of Indo-China as an Example of Postwar Colonial Relationships, War and Peace Studies, T-B69."

CFR, *War and Peace Studies, 1939–45,* Steering Committee (December 31, 1943). "List of Memoranda Issued in 1943 with

Recommendations or Conclusions, No. SC-B4," NY: Council on Foreign Relations, p. 14 (to continue French colony.

Other than on Viet Nam:

"Undeveloped Countries and Exchange Control, War and Peace Studies, E-B72."

"World Industrialization and International Trade, War and Peace Studies, E-B75."

"The Inter-American System in the Postwar World (July 5, 1944), P-B84"

"Afghanistan and the War (February 20, 1942), T-B46"

"Russia and an East European Federation (October 26, 1942), T-B55"

"Mineral Resources and the U.S.S.R. as a World Power (May 25, 1944), T-B73"

"Palestine: A Solution of Its Immediate Problem (December 19, 1944), T-B76"

United States Government: Consul reports and papers

The consular reports and memoranda cited in this volume are declassified. To ask for a copy of any consular item, readers may contact the US National Archives and provide citation information from below, along with any more specific information from any endnote citing consul material.

United States Consulate (1957). *Despatches from United States consuls in Saigon, 1889–1906.* Washington: National Archives and Records Service, General Services Administration, Reel 1, Format one microfilm reel.

United States. Department of State. (1971). *Records of the Department of State relating to internal affairs of France, 1919–1929.* (National Archives microfilm publications: M560). Washington, D.C.: National Archives and Records Service, General Services Administration, Reels 150–152. Format 162 microfilm reels.

United States. National Archives Records Administration. (1986). *Records of the Department of State relating to internal affairs of France, 1930–1939.* (National Archives microfilm publications: M). Washington, D.C.: National Archives and Records Service, General Services Administration, Reels 82–87, Format 89 microfilm reels

Murphy, G., Hydrick, Blair, & United States. Department of State (1988). Confidential U.S. State Department central files, Indochina. 1955–1959: Internal affairs, decimal numbers 751G, 751H, and 751J; 851G, 851H and 851J; and 951G, 951H, and 951J: and foreign affairs decimal numbers 651G, 651H, and 651J; and 611.51G, 611.51H, and 611.51J. Frederick. MD: University Publications of America, Reels 1, 14, and 18.

United States Government, other

Barker, P., & United States. Bureau of Foreign Domestic Commerce. (1939). Rubber industry of the United States, 1839–1939 (Trade promotion series ; no. 197). Washington: U.S. G.P.O.

Buckingham, W., & United States. Air Force. Office of Air Force History. (1982). *Operation Ranch Hand : The Air Force and herbicides in Southeast Asia, 1961–1971.* Washington, D.C.: Office of Air Force History, U.S.Air Force.

Byrne, M., Gasiorowski, Mark J., Risen, James, & National Security Archive. (2000). *The secret CIA history of the Iran Coup, 1953* (National Security Archive electronic briefing book ; no. 28). Washington, D.C.]: [National Security Archive, George Washington University].

Congressional Research Services, Library of Congress (1984), *The US Government and the Vietnam War: Executive and Legislative Roles and Relationships, Part I 1945–1961,* US Govt Printing Office, Washington (prepared for the Committee on Foreign Relations United States Senate).

Elements of Counter-Guerrilla Warfare Task Force, US Central Intelligence Agency, *Elements Of US Strategy To Deal With "Wars Of National Liberation,"* December 8, 1961, reviewed by NSC, approved for release May 23, 2003.

Gilpatric, Roswell; Dept of Defense; National Security Council (Nov. 21, 1961). *National Security Action Memorandum No. 115 Defoliant Operations in Vietnam*, 30 November 1961. (NSAM 115). United States Government https://www.jfklibrary.org/asset-viewer/archives/jfknsf-332-017#?image_identifier=JFKNSF-332-017-p0002.

Notter, H., & United States. Department of State. Office of Public Affairs., (1949). *Postwar Foreign Policy Preparation, 1939–1945,* (Department of State Publication : 3580). Washington: For sale by the Supt. of Documents. : U.S.G.P.O.

United States. Congress. Senate. Select Committee to Study Governmental Operations with Respect to Intelligence Activities. (1976). *Alleged assassination plots involving foreign leaders : An interim report of the Select Committee to Study Governmental Operations with Respect to Intelligence Activities, United States Senate : Together with additional, supplemental, and separate views* (1st ed.). New York: Norton. (original Publisher: Washington : U.S. Govt. Print. Off.) (Church Committee).

United States. Department of Defense, *United States-Vietnam relations, 1945–1967, study prepared by the Department of Defense* (Pentagon Papers).

United States. Foreign commerce yearbook / U.S. Department of Commerce, Bureau of Foreign and Domestic Commerce 1926, USGPO.

United States. *Foreign Commerce Yearbook: Trade with the United States by Principal Commodities, 1928* U.S.G.P.O.

United States. *Foreign Commerce Yearbook: Trade with the United States by Principal Commodities, 1929* U.S.G.P.O.

United States. *Foreign commerce yearbook / U.S. Department of Commerce, Bureau of Foreign and Domestic Commerce : 1935. (1935).* .S. G.P.O. : For sale by the Supt. of Docs., 1934-1953

United States. Foreign commerce yearbook / U.S. Department of Commerce, Bureau of Foreign and Domestic Commerce 1937, USGPO.

United States. *Foreign commerce yearbook / U.S. Department of Commerce, Bureau of Foreign and Domestic Commerce : 1938. (1938).* U.S. G.P.O. : For sale by the Supt. of Docs., 1934-1953

United States. Maritime Commission. Division of Research (1923–1935). *Report on Volume of Water Borne Commerce of the United States by Ports of Origin and Destination,* Part 1. Commerce of US ports with foreign ports; Part 2. Commerce of foreign ports with U.S. ports. (CIS US Executive Branch Documents, 1910–1932 ; no. SB7.2-2.12). Washington: U.S.G.P.O.

United States. National Advisory Commission on Civil Disorders. (1968, 2016). *Report of the National Advisory Commission on Civil Disorders.* The James Madison Library in American Politics. Princeton University Press. Kindle Edition (*Kerner Commission Report*).

United States, Office of Chief of Counsel for the Prosecution of Axis Criminality, & International Military Tribunal. (1946). *Nazi conspiracy and aggression.* U. S. Govt. Print. Off.

US HOUSE OF REPRESENTATIVES, (4 June, 2009). "AGENT ORANGE: WHAT EFFORTS ARE BEING MADE TO ADDRESS THE CONTINUING IMPACT OF DIOXIN IN VIETNAM." SUBCOMMITTEE ON ASIA, THE PACIFIC AND THE GLOBAL ENVIRONMENT, COMMITTEE ON FOREIGN AFFAIRS, Washington, DC: USGPO.

International Agreements, Treaties, and reports

Colombo Plan Bureau. (1961). *The Colombo plan story ; 10 years of progress, 1951–1961.* Colombo, Ceylon: Colombo Plan Bureau.

Bibliography

Geneva Agreements 20–21 July, 1954. *Agreement on the Cessation of Hostilities in Viet-Nam 20 July, 1954*, (espec Articles 1, 14), and Final Decl. The Avalon Project, Yale Law School, https://peacemaker.un.org/sites/peacemaker.
un.org/files/KH-LAVN_540720_GenevaAgreements.pdf.

IPCC (2018). Summary for Policymakers. In: *Global Warming of 1.5°C. An IPCC Special Report on the impacts of global warming of 1.5°C above pre-industrial levels. . . . World Meteorological Organization, Geneva, Switzerland, 32 pages.*

IPCC (20 March, 2023). "Multiple risks interact, generating new sources of vulnerability to climate compounding overall risk (high confidence)." Synthesis Report of the IPCC Sixth Assessment Report (AR6) (IPCC AR6 SYR) Longer Report, pp. 1–85. https://www.ipcc.ch/report/sixth-assessment-report-cycle/

UN Convention on the Rights of the Child. Committee on the Rights of the Child, General comment No. 26 (2023) (International treaty), on children's rights and the environment, with a special focus on climate change*, Paragraph 73: "Children are far more likely than adults to suffer serious harm, including irreversible and lifelong consequences and death, from environmental degradation. . ."

https://www.ohchr.org/en/instruments-mechanisms/instruments/convention-rights-child

English Language reference

Britannica Book of the Year, 1969, p. 790, Encyclopaedia Britannica, Inc., William Benton Publisher, Chicago, Toronto, London, Geneva, Sydney, Tokyo, Manila. "Published with the editorial advice of the faculties of The University of Chicago." *See also* Encyclopaedia Britannica, Inc., 1956, p. 733.

White, J. T. and Company (1971), *The National Cyclopaedia of American Biography*, v. 53, p. 16.

Film

Schneider, B., Davis, P., Klingman, L., Martin, S., Westmoreland, W. C. (William C., Clifford, C. M., Fulbright, J. W. (James W., Rostow, W. W. (Walt W., & Ellsberg, D. (2002). *Hearts and Minds* (Widescreen.). Home Vision.

Viet language

Ban Chấp Hành Đảng Bộ Tỉnh Bà Rịa-Vũng Tàu, (1993). *Đường Hồ Chí Minh Trên Biển Bà Rịa-Vũng Tàu*, NXB Chính Trị Quốc Gia.

Bảo Tàng Hồ Chí Minh (2017). *Hồ Chí Minh Tiểu Sử*. Hà Nội: NXB Chính Trí Quốc Gia Sự Thật.

Chương Thâu, Biên Soạn (2012). *Phan Bội Châu (1867–1940) Nhà Yêu Nước Nhà Văn Hóa Lớn*. Việt Nam: NXB Văn Hóa Thông Tin.

Đảng Cộng sản Việt Nam. Tiểu ban nghiên cứu lịch sử Đảng. Tỉnh ủy Nghệ An. Bùi Ngọc Tam, chủ biên (2011). Hồ Chí Minh thời niên thiếu. Nghệ An: NXB Văn Hóa Thông Tin.

Đinh Xuân Lý & Trần Minh Trường, Đồng chủ biên (2013). *Hồ Chí Minh với Cách Mạng Việt Nam : Cuộc Đời, sự nghiệp, và Đạo Đức*. Hà Nội, NXB Đại Học Quốc Gia.

Hồ Chí Minh (NXB Quốc Gia)(1995). *Hồ Chí Minh Toàn Tập*, Hà Nội: NXB Quốc Gia., v. 1912–1924.

Ho, S.K., & Ha M.H., & Vo, V.S (1996). *Lịch Sử Việt Nam 1954–1975*, TP. HCM: Từ Sách Đại Học Tổng Hợp TP. HCM.

Hội Đồng chỉ Đạo biên soạn (2001). *Lịch sử kháng chiến chống Pháp khu tả ngạn sông Hồng, 1945–1955*. Chính trị quốc gia.

Lê, H., Vietnam. Quân Đội nhân dân. Tổng cục chính trị, & Đảng cộng sản Việt Nam; Tỉnh ủy Bến Tre. (2010). *Bến Tre Đồng khởi anh hùng*. Hà Nội: NXB Quân Đội nhân dân.

Nguyễn Lân (2006). *Từ Điển từ và Ngữ Việt Nam*. TP. Hồ Chí Minh: NXB Tổng Hợp TP. Hồ Chí Minh.

Nguyễn, Lan (2014). *Từ Điển thành ngữ và tục ngữ Việt Nam*. Hà Nội, NXB Văn Học.

Nguyễn Q. Thắng và Nguyễn Bá Thế, biên tập (1997) *Từ Điển Nhân Vật Lịch Sử Việt Nam*, Hà Nội: NXB Văn Hóa, pp. 452–453.

Nguyễn, T., & Trần, Hương Nam (1968). *Không còn Đường nào khác : Hồi ký* (Tái bản. ed.). Hà nội: Phụ nữ

Nguyễn Thị Kim Dung (2017). *Gia Tài của Mẹ*. TP. Hồ Chí Minh: NXB Quân Đội Nhân Dân

Nguyễn Văn Dương, sưu tầm & biên soạn (2012). *Nguyễn Sinh Cung– Nguyễn Tất Thành : Giai Đoạn 1890–1911*, Pleiku, Gia Lai, Viet Nam: NXB Hồng Bàng.

Nguyễn, V. S., Phạm, N. T., & Phạm, H. B. (1985). *Cuộc kháng chiến chống Mỹ cứu nước của nhân dân Bến Tre : lược sử*. [Bộ chỉ huy quân sự tỉnh Bến Tre].

Nguyễn Xuân Thủy, Tạ Thị Thanh Hà, & Sở Thông Tin Và Truyền Thông (2010). *Bảo Tàng Xô Viết Nghệ Tĩnh 50 Năm Xây Dựng và Phát Triển.* Nghệ An: Bảo Tàng Xô Viết Nghệ Tĩnh, Sở Văn Hóa và Du lịch Nghệ An.

Pham, V. (1990). *Ho Chi Minh : a Man, a Nation, an Age, and a Cause.* Ha Noi: Foreign Languages Publishing House.

Phan N., Nguyễn Ngọc Cơ, & Nguyễn Thị Côi (2005). *Hồ Chí Minh, những chặng Đường lịch sử.* Hải Phòng: NXB Hải Phòng.

Phan Xuân Thành & Giám Đốc Bảo Tàng, Lê Thị Thu Hằng, biên tập (March 1996). *Kỷ Yếu Hội Thảo Khoa Học: 65 Năm Xô Viết Nghệ Tĩnh*, Sở Văn Hóa Thông Tin, Bảo Tàng Xô Viết Nghệ Tĩnh.

Trần, M. (2001). *Những người thân trong gia Đình Bác Hồ* (Tái Bản.ed.). Vinh: NXB Nghệ An.

Trần Ngọc Thêm (2001). *Tìm về Bản Sắc Văn hóa Việt Nam: Cái Nhìn Hệ Thống-Loại Hình – Discovering the identity of Vietnamese culture : Typological-systematic views* (In lần thứ 3, sửa chữa và bổ sung, ed.). Việt Nam: Thành Phố Hồ Chí Minh. NXB T.P. Hồ Chí Minh.

Văn Thị Thanh Mai (2010). *Hồ Chí Minh : Hành Trình từ Làng Sen Đến Ba Đình (1890–1969).* Hà Nội: NXB Chính Trị Quốc Gia.

French language and reports by French in English language

Banque de l' Indochine. BelleIndochine (1922). *Annuaire des enterprises coloniales, 1922*, No.651. Paris.

Challamel, A. (Editeur) (1898). *Annuaire de la Marine de Commerce Francaise Guide du Commerce d'Importation et d'Exportation.* Paris, Havre Ministere de la Marine.

De la Roche, J. "A Program of Social and Cultural Activity in Indo-China." Ninth Conference of the Institute of Pacific Relations. Hot Springs, Virginia, January 1945, French Paper No. 3.

French Indochina, Direction Des Affaires Économiques. (1925). *Annuaire Économique De L'Indochine, Hanoi:* Impr. d'Extrême-Orient.

Gottmann, Jean, "Raw Materials in the Western Pacific," Institute of Pacific Relations. Conference. (1945). *[Papers presented to the Ninth Conference of the Institute of Pacific Relations, Hot Springs, Virginia,* January 1945]. New York, French Paper No. 1.

Gourou, P. (1945). "The Standard of Living in the Delta of the Tonkin (French Indo-China)" Ninth Conference of the Institute of Pacific Relations, Hot Springs, Virginia, January, 1945, v.5, French, French Paper No. 4.

Lanessan, Jean Marie Antoine de (1895). *La colonization francaise en Indo-Chine.* Paris: F. Alcan.

Lê, T. (1955). *Le Viêt-nam : histoire et civilisation.* Paris: Éditions de Minuit.

Robequain, Charles (1935). *L'Indochine Francaise.* Paris: Libraire Armand Colin

INDEX

Note: Page numbers in this index appear in the print edition of this title, but the page numbers here are unlikely to correspond to the pagination in an e-book reader. However, an e-book reader search feature can be easily used to find terms in this index.

1964 Civil Rights Act, 125
1973 Paris Peace Agreement, 63–64

Advanced Research Projects Agency (ARPA), *see* Defense Advanced Research Projects Agency
Afghanistan, 67, 93–96, 201
Africa, 4, 48, 67, 77–92, 114–16, 121, 126, 140, 184, 187, 200–02
　All African People's sub-Saharan Conference, (AAPC), 78
　Sahel, 77–78, 82, 116, 140,
　South Africa, 85, 90
　sub-Saharan Africa, 77, 78, 82, 85, 114, 116, 140
African American Arbery, Ahmaud, 126
　Black National Anthem, 66
　Civil Rights Congress, 19, 21
　Floyd, George, 21, 126
　Johnson, James Weldon, 66
　King, Martin Luther, 46
　Mann, Joseph, 21
　Negro J. H., 11
　racism, racist, racial, xix, 6–7, 11, 19–22, 35, 37, 46, 51, 62, 73, 76, 81–82, 85, 115–16, 125–27, 131, 151, 159, 177, 179, 182–83, 186–87, 189, 201
　Robeson, Eslanda, 21
　Robeson, Paul, 21–22, 46 *see also*, slave, slavery, enslaved, enslavement
African Arguments, 87–89
African Crisis Response Initiative (ACRI), 86
African Contingency Operations Training Assistance (ACOTA), 86
Africom, 87–90
Agent Orange, *see* dioxin
Al Qaeda, 93
Albania, 155

Algerian, 112
All African People's Conference, *see* Africa
Alsop, Joseph, 58, 138
Alternative Plan, 54, 70, 182, 193
American Exceptionalism, 203, 204
Angola, *see also* MPLA, 82–86
Annam, Annamites, 3, 126, 128, 183
Anti-Ballistic Missile Treaty, 142
Arab, 72–77, 97
Arbery, Ahmaud, *see* African American
Argentina, Argentine, 99, 104, 113, 137, 138
Atlantic Council, 110
Atomic, atomic bombs, 14–15, 37, 56, 61, 158, 192, 196
Amazon, 138
anti-communism, 98, 121, 124, 127, 131, 147–67, 176–78, 180, 182, 186–88
Asian Infrastructure Investment Bank 47
Austria-Hungary, 5
Avery, Bill, 82
axiom on control by force, 45–48, 94, 131–32, 160–61, 164–65, 177, 182, 199, 205, *see also* Golden Rule
Ayittey, George, 91

Bacevich, Andrew, 48
Baker, James, 118
Balfour Declaration, 74
Bandung Conference, 68, 85, 140
Bangkok, 70
Bangkok Post, xiii
Bedjaoui, Mohammed, 112
Belgium, 5, 81
Bill & Melinda Gates Foundation, 114
bin Laden, Osama, 93
Binh Gia, 42, 195–96
Bird, Willis, 70

Black, Hugo, 30
Boeing, 84
Boko Haram, 87–90
Bonnie and Clyde, 61
Botswana, 90
Bowman, Isaiah, 25, 27, 58, 131–32, 133, 181
Brazil, 55, 99, 128, 130–31, 139, 141, 155
BRICS, BRICS+, 47, 200
Britain, British, Great Britain, 5, 61, 73, 74, 76, 112, 117, 130, 154, 163
Bucharest Declaration, 118
Bui Vien, 4, 126, 127
Burkina Faso, 91–92, *see also* Traore, Ibrahim
Bush, George H. W., 103, 118
Bush, George W., 93–94
Butler, Smedley Darlington, 164
Buttinger, Joseph, xix, 38, 52, 129, 134, 195

California, xviii, 7, 27, 76, 107–08, 110, 127, 184
Cameroon, 90
Caribbean, 47, 109, 200
Carleton, Mr., 5
Carter, Jimmy, 103
Catholic, Catholics, 56, 138
CELAC, *see* Community of Latin American and Caribbean States
Central America, 52, 99, 102, 103, 151–52, 200, 202
Central Intelligence Agency (CIA), 56, 57, 60, 62, 70, 76, 79–84, 86, 94, 102, 103, 134, 137, 138, 139, 155, 158
Ceplair, Larry, 148, 152, 160, 165, 166–67, 188
Ceylon, *see* Colombo Plan
Chad, 87

Chapultepec, Act of, 104, 137
Chase Far East, 136
Chase Manhattan Bank, 136
Chattanooga Times, 11
chattel slavery, *see* slave
Chagos Archipelago, 112
Chemical Corps, Army, 40–41, 62, 158, 195, 198, *see also* dioxin
Chiang Kai-shek, 165–66
Chile, 33, 71, 99–100
China, xvi, 4, 13, 15, 36, 47, 52, 71, 87, 110, 128, 138–39, 155–56, 162, 163–66, see also South China Sea
Chiquita Brands International, 104
Chomsky, Noam, xxii, 26, 28, 31, 33, 42, 43, 45, 46, 68, 70, 71, 73, 93, 95, 98–99, 101, 103, 110, 124, 132, 155, 156, 160
Cintas Largas, 138
Civil Rights Congress, *see* African American(s)
Clary, James, 40
climate change, xx, 47, 67, 105, 106–11, 142, 143, 201–02, *see also* global warming
Colby, Gerard, 79–80
Cold War, 15–16, 32, 140–41, 180
Colombia, 104
Colombo Plan, 36, 54, 193
common plan, xix, 62, 67–119, 123–25, 127, 157, 191
communism, xiii, xiv, xvii, xviii, 15, 52, 59, 86, 101, 102, 104, 122–23, 124, 130–31, 136–37, 141–44, 147, 149–50, 151–53, 154, 167, 180, 184, 187, 190, 191, 203
communist, xix, 11–12, 13, 56, 59, 71, 102, 122, 132–33, 134, 135, 137–38, 139, 141, 148, 149, 151, 160, 161, 165–66, 167, 189, 198, 201

Communist Manifesto, 122, 149
Communist Party, 12–13, 133–35, 160–61, 166
Communist Suppression Operations Command, 72
Community of Latin American and Caribbean States (CELAC), 47, 200, 201
Congo, Zaire, 78–92, 114, 116, 122–23, 140, 187
consul, consuls, xv, 5–6, 7, 123, 126, 137, 150, 184–85
  Denis Freres firm, 5–6, 8
  MacVitty, Karl deGiers, 7
  Schneegans, Edouard, 5
  Smith, Leland, 7, 126
  Tonsales, Aimee, 5
Convention on the Rights of the Child, *see* United Nations
copper, 79, 82, 122
cotton, 6–7, 73, 183, 186–87
Council on Foreign Relations (CFR), 14–15, 25–33, 35, 36, 42, 47–48, 52–54, 59, 69–75, 94, 101, 102, 103, 120, 123–24, 133, 137, 153, 156–58, 177–79, 186, 190–93
War and Peace Studies, War and Peace reports, 14–15, 25–27, 29, 32, 35, 36, 56, 59, 67–119, 124, 154, 156–58, 179, 180–81, 188, 191–93, 201
coup, coups, 29, 33, 51–53, 55, 68, 69–72, 75–76, 78–82, 85, 86, 98–104, 114, 117, 122, 124, 128–31, 137–41, 151, 152, 155–59, 160, 199, 200
cruelty to children, xx–xxii, 64–65, 67, 76– 77, 80, 95, 105–11, 124, 159, 176, 180. 181, 182, 198–99, 201–02
Czechoslovakia, 139,

297

Dang Thuy Tram, 161 Dardanelles, the, 154
Davies, John Paton, 164–66
Davis, Angela, xxii, 99, 126
Defense Advanced Research Projects Agency (DARPA), 62, 158
Democratic Party, xxi
Democratic Republic of Viet Nam (DRV) (*see* Viet Nam)
Denmark, 5
depression, 7–8
Devillers, Philippe, 20
Diem, *see* Ngo Dinh Diem
Dies, Martin, 152
dioxin, 38–43, 61–65, 67, 105, 131, 155, 158–59, 180, 181, 195–96, 197, 198–99, 201, 202
    Agent Orange, xx, 64–65, 105, 158–59, 180, 197, 198–99
    Stellman study, 61, 197 *see also* Chemical Corps
ditched, ditching, xix, 25–33, 56–61, 63, 71, 84, 94, 102, 105, 111, 123, 131, 142, 166, 179, 182, 202
Dong Loc, 48, 160
Donilon, Thomas E., 54
Dosal, Paul, 100
Duiker, William, 9, 10, 12, 127, 132, 151, 160, 189
Dulles, Allen, 20–21, 32, 62, 75–76, 80, 102, 130, 136
Dulles brothers, 20–21, 58, 101, 131, 136–37, 155, 156, 163
Dulles, John Foster, 20–22, 25, 45, 75–76, 100–01, 126, 146, 156, 163, 166, 199–200

East Germany, *see* Germany
Eastern Europe, *see* Europe, Eastern
Eastern Sea, *see* South China Sea
Einstein, Albert, 24
Eisenhower, Dwight D., 80, 137
El Salvador, 102, 104
Elliott, Cass (Mama Cass), xxiv, 174
Enquirer, 150
Europe, European(s), 8, 12, 45, 46, 57, 72, 73, 78, 104, 117, 123, 141, 150, 152, 157, 180, 185
Europe, Eastern, 117–18, 153–55
European Union (EU), 47

Falk, Richard, 48
Fall, Bernard, 43, 60
false claim, xv–xxiii, 31, 47, 52, 54, 59, 67–119, 125, 142, 143, 144, 167, 172–73, 175–205
famine, 14, 134
Figart, David, 150
Floyd, George, *see* African American,
Floyd, Randy, 50, 172
Foreign Affairs, xxi, 32, 45, 47–48, 74, 77, 96–97, 114, 160
foreign policy force, 27, 33, 51, 54, 58, 75, 148–52, 156–57, 16–62, 177–79, 182, 187–88, 202
Foster, John, 136–37, 163–64
France, *see* entire book
French Union, 129

G-20, 115
Gabon, 90
Gaddis, John Lewis, 142, 170
Gans, John, 32, 53, 103
Gaza, xx, xxii, 67, 72–77, 105, 181, 201, 202, *see also* Palestine
General Electric Company, 38, 40
General Rubber, 150
Geneva Accords, 1954, xix, 54–55, 56, 59, 129–30, 137, 148, 160–61, 179–80, 193, 194, 198
Georgia (Caucasus Region), 118

Georgia (US), 19–20
Germany, 5, 63, 109, 118, 155, 193
    East Germany, 118, 154
Ghana, 79–82, 92, 116, 140
Global South, xxi, 111–16, 123–25
global warming, 106–11, 143, 181, 201–02, *see also* climate change
Golden Rule, xx, 45–48, 51, 95, 99, 131–32, 148, 167, 175, 177, 181, 182, 183, 188, 199–200, 203, 205, *see also* axiom
Gondola, Didier, 82, 90, 140
Gonsalves, Ralph, 109
Gonzalez, Juan, xxi, 203 gook, gooks, 127, 179
Gottlieb, Sidney, 80
Gourou, Pierre, 14
Grand Area 73, 124, 154, 160, 179
Greece, 155
Greeley, Horace, 149
Grenadines, the, 109
Griffin, R. Allen (Griffin Plan), 54
Guatemala, 52, 55, 100–103, 130–31, 137, 151–52, 156–57, 200
Gulf Oil, 84

Ha Noi, Hanoi, xix, 14, 39, 134, 161, 190
Hai Phong, 20
Haiti, 104
Halberstam, David, 154 Hanoi, *see* Ha Noi Hare, Bill, 110
Harley Davidson Company, 190
harmony, 4, 160, 177, 204
Hartford, John, xxiv, 174
Harvard, 40, 53
Hau Nghia, 134
Hawaii, 53
Heikkala, Tomas, xvi

Henry, Jules, 60
Herd, Graeme, 95–96
Himmler (Himmler's), Heinrich, 99
Hiroshima, 37, 158, 192, 196
Hinduism, 45
Hitler, 28, 29
Ho Chi Minh, Nguyen Sinh Cung, Nguyen Ai Quoc, xxi, 9–14, 33, 38, 127–29, 132–36, 151, 160, 177, 182, 188–90, 198
Hoffmann, Friedrich, 40
Homestead Act, 186
Hoover, J. Edgar, 152
House Select Committee, 59
Human Rights Watch, 95
Hungary, 154
Hurricane Beryl, 109
Hurricane Helene, 108–09
Hurricane Milton, 108–09

Ia Drang, 173
Ifill, Sherilyn, 149, 183, 186
Indians, *see* Native Americans
Indochina, Indo-China, 6, 7–8, 13, 14–15, 29, 37, 60–61, 63, 69, 133, 158, 191–93, 196
Indonesia, 8, 53, 141, 185
Inflation Reduction Act (IRA), 110
Institute of African Affairs, 140
Intergovernmental Panel on Climate Change (IPCC), *see* United Nations
International Criminal Court, 142
International Monetary Fund, 32
Iran, 47, 55, 75–76, 97–98, 130–31
Isaacson, Walter, 26
Islam, Islamic, Islamist, 87, 97
Israel, xx, 18, 67, 72–77, 105, 124, 201
Italy, 5, 130, 155

Jackson Daily News, 11
Jacobs, Lawrence, 31
Japan, 13–15, 36–37, 61, 63, 67–69, 72, 136, 157, 162, 163–64, 191, 201
Jerusalem, 75
Jesus, 44, 200
Jewish, 73–74, 76
Johnson, James Weldon, *see* African American
Johnson, Lyndon B. (LBJ), 42, 60
Joint Chiefs of Staff (JCS), 35, 59, 133, 134
Journal of the American Medical Association, 40

Kassel, Ronald, 40, 62
Katanga Province, 79, *see also* Congo Kennan, George, 28, 62
Kennedy, John F. (JFK), 36, 58–60, 99, 139
kerosene (*see* oil)
Khalidi, Rashid, 73
Kieu, Tale of, see Tale of Kieu
King, Martin Luther, *see* African American
Kinzer, Stephen, 21, 28, 75, 130
Kissinger, Henry, 26, 33, 83–86, 113, 154
Koh, Harold Hongju, 4, 30, 184
Kohnert, Dick, 140–41
Korea, 139, 162–63, *see also* North Korea
Kuomintang, 164–66
Kyoto Protocol, 142, 143

Lansing, Robert (Bert), 20, 136
Latin America, *see* Central America, South America
Laxer, Gregory, xvi
Le Thanh Khoi, 58

Lee, Barbara, 64
Lenin, V.I., 11–12
Lesotho, 90
Lewis, Anthony, 30
Lewy, Guenter, 166
L'Indochine Enchainee, 45, 46, *see also* Malraux, Andre
Luang Phibunsongkhram, see Phibun
Lumumba, Patrice, 79–82
Lynch, Marc, 97–98

Macbeth, see Shakespeare
Maechling, Charles, Jr., 139
Malaysia, 61
Mali, 87
malnutrition, xix, 4, 6, 9, 89, 132, 134, 152, 184
Malraux, Andre, 45, 46, 132, *see also L'Indochine Enchainee,*
Mann, Joseph, *see* African American(s)
Mao Tse-Tung, 165–66
Marine Corps Hymn, *see* United States Marine Corps Hymn
Marshall Plan, 16, 157
Martinez, Maximiliano, 104, 200
Marx, Karl, 12, 149 Matrix, xxiii
Mauritius, 112
Mayan, 101
McCain, John, 26, 154
McCloy, John J., 101, 137, 153, 156
McCray, *see* Metsker McCray
Metsker, Thomas, 173
Metsker McCray, Catherine, 173
McNamara, Robert, 60
Mead, Walter Russell, xxii, 26, 30, 120, 154, 204
Mediterranean, 73, 77
Mekong Basin Development Project (Mekong River Basin), 70, 135

300

Mekong Delta, Mekong River, 60, 70, 135
Michigan Farmer, 4
Middle East, xxi, 26, 48, 67, 72–77, 97–98, 124, 154, 201
Millett, Allan R., 163
Mobil, 84
Mobutu, Joseph, 82, 83
Moffatt, Mr., 5
Mongol Empire, 4, 57
Monsanto, 40
Montt, Rios, 101
Moore, Hal, 173
Morgan Bank, 150
Morocco, 90
Moscow, 12
Mossadegh, Mohammad, 75
MPLA *(Movimento Popular de Libertação de Angola; People's Movement for Liberation of Angola)*, 84–85
Mus, Paul, 35–36
mutual security, 77–92, 114
Mwakikagile, Godfrey, 83, 90–91, 114–15, 125, 140

Nagasaki, 37
Nakba, 75
Nanking, Treaty of, 163
NASA, 108
National Archives, U.S., xv–xviii
National Endowment for the Humanities, 197
National Liberation Front (NLF), 42, 134, 198
national security, 33, 54, 99, 110, 139, 166
National Security Council (NSC); National *Securing* Council, 27–28, 32, 36, 39, 54, 82, 179
national security interests, 110

national security state, 139
Native Americans, 51
Negro J. H., *see* African American
Netherlands, The, 5
New Asian African Strategic Partnership (NAASP), 140–41
NATO, 16, 117–18
New York, 3, 5, 25
New York Courier, 150
New York Times, 3, 19–20, 30, 36, 42– 43, 59, 110, 118, 135, 153, 183, 196
New York Herald Tribune, 138
New-York Tribune, 149
Newsweek, 31, 137, 156, 186
Nghe An, 9
Ngo Dinh Diem (Diem), 37, 55–56, 57, 129, 133–34
Nguyen Ai Quoc, *see* Ho Chi Minh
Nguyen Du, 45, 46, 132
Nguyen Khac Vien, 57, 133
Nguyen Sinh Cung, *see* Ho Chi Minh
Nguyen Sinh Sac, 10
Nguyen Tat Thanh, *see* Ho Chi Minh
Niger, 86–91, 114, 142, 172–73, 200
Nigeria, 87, 90, 91
Nixon, Richard, 80, 125
Nkrumah, Kwame, 80
noncommunist, 123, 138
North Korea, 47, *see also* Korea
North Viet Nam (North Vietnam) never existed, 56, 194, 203
Nuremberg Judgment, Nuremberg Ruling, 55, 64, 77, 96, 130, 131, 148, 155, 163, 176, 180, 188, 199

Obama, Barack, 52, 53–54, 75, 94
October 1917 Revolution, 122

oil, kerosene oil, oils, xviii, 4–7, 71–73, 75–76, 77, 84, 86, 93, 94, 97, 122, 124, 130–31, 139, 155, 164, 184, 185, 190
OPEC (Organization of Petroleum Exporting Countries), 47, 200
Osama bin Laden, *see* bin Laden, Osama
Ostrom, Elinor, 66
Othello, *see* Shakespeare
Overseas Consultants Inc., 75

Pacific Stars and Stripes, 59
Pan African, 79, 92
Pakistan, 96
Palestine, 66, 67, 72–77, 105, 201, *see also* Gaza
Palestinian Authority, 77
Pappe, Ilan, 66, 76–77
Paris, 11–12, 63, 107, 202
Paris Climate Agreement, 107, 202
Paris Peace agreement, *see* 1973 Paris Peace Agreement
Pauley's Coup, 51–52
Pentagon Papers, 30, 63, 143, 204
People's Army of Viet Nam, *see* Viet Nam
Persia, 57
Peru, 57, 114
Pham Van Dong, 12
Phan Boi Chau, 10, 11, 132
Phibun (Luang Phibunsongkhram), 69–71
Pike, Douglas, 42
Poland, 155
Portugal, Portuguese 5, 84
Powell, Lewis, 30
Price, Ray, 57
Puerto Rico, 114
Putin, Vladimir, 116

Qatar, 93

racism, racist, racial *see* African Americans
Rand, Ayn, 153
Reagan, Ronald, 52–53, 101–03, 138
real reason, xvii–xviii, 63, 119, 121, 130, 136, 144, 148, 166, 167 171, 172, 176, 180, 181, 182, 188, 200
Red River Delta, 13
Remington, 8
Republic of Viet Nam proxy for US, *see* South Viet Nam
Republican, xxi, 110, 125, 187, 203
Rhee, Syngman, 163
rice, xix, 3–4, 6, 14, 71, 89, 129, 152, 162, 184, 185, 190
Rice, Susan E., 54
Road of Death, 9
Robeson, Eslanda, *see* African American(s)
Robeson, Paul, *see* African American(s)
Rockefeller banking, 150
Rockefeller, John D., 4–5, 122, 186
Rockefeller, John D. III, 60, 135
Rockefeller, Nelson, 104, 137
Roosevelt, Franklin D. (FDR), 51–52, 104, 153
Rostow, Walt, 57–58
Royal African Society, 87
rubber, 8, 123, 150, 157, 185
Rumbaugh, Elwood P. (Woody), xiii–xv, 171
Rumsfeld, Donald, 93
Russell, Bertrand, 33–34
Russia, Russian, 47, 67, 116–18, 122, 153, 165, 201

Sahara, *see* Africa Sahel, *see* Africa
Sai Gon (Saigon), 3, 5–6, 7, 14, 36, 39, 41, 42, 45–46, 123, 134, 196
Saigon, 39

Santa Ana winds, 107
Sarotte, Mary, 117–18
school shootings, xxi, 182
Sea Supply Company, 70
Senegal, 90
Service John S. 164–66
Sestanovich, Stephen, 118
Sewol Ferry, 111
Shakespeare, William, 22, 45, 46, 127, 132, 198
  Macbeth, 33, 45, 46, 127, 132, 198
  Othello, 22
Shanghai Cooperation Organization, 47
Sheehan, Neil, 154
Shimonoseki, 163–64
Shoup, Laurence, 26, 31–32, 53, 156, 157
Siam, *see* Thailand
Signature Techniques, xix, 51–65, 67–119, 122–44, 165–67, 176, 182
Singapore, 5, 8, 185
slave, slavery, enslaved, enslavement, xix, 6–7, 19, 78, 104, 121, 125–26, 148–49, 177, 182–83, 186
South Africa, *see* Africa
South America, 150, 151, 155, 185, 200–01
South China Sea, 15, 157, 192
South Region, 14, 198
South Viet Nam (illegal enclave) (South Vietnam), Republic of Vietnam), 38, 42–43, 54, 56, 64, 134, 135, 180, 194–97
South Zone, Southern Zone, regrouping zone, 42, 54–56, 64, 133
Southeast Asia 4, 7, 15, 57, 61, 162–63, 192
Soviet Union, Soviets, USSR, 12, 71, 83, 85, 102, 117–18, 136, 138, 139, 141–42, 152, 153–55, 162, 167, 188
Spain, 5

St. Vincent, 109
Standard Oil, xviii, 4–5, 122, 130–31, 150, 155, 164, 184, 185
Stellman study, *see* dioxin
Stiell, Simon, *see* United Nations
Stilwell, Joe, 100, 200
Stockwell, John, 83–84, 85
sub-Saharan Africa, *see* Africa
Suffren, 20
Sukarno, 68
Suzman, Mark, 114, 115
Syria, 67, 96–98

Taiwan, 162, 163, 166
Talbot, David, 32
Tale of Kieu, 45, 46, 132
Taliban, 93, 95–96
Taylor, Maxwell, 161
Temmons, Bob, 84–85
terror, by US & proxies, 48, 52, 75–82, 87 (supposed war on terror), 103–104, 124, 125–26, 186
Thailand, Siam, xiii, 5, 14, 67, 68–72, 123, 141, 162, 191, 201
The Netherlands, *see* Netherlands, *Theses on the National and Colonial Questions,* 11–12
Three-Step Analysis, xx, 67–119, 124, 132, 176, 182, 201
Tilles, Gerard, 40 To Lam, xxii
Tradition Of Heroic Resistance Against Foreign Invasion (TOHRAFA), 4, 132–33, 177
Tran Ngoc Them, 4, 58
Tran Ngoc Tho, 65, 161
Traore, Ibrahim, 91, *see* also Burkina Faso
Truman, Harry, 16, 52, 102, 153, 165
Tuchinsky, Adam-Max, 149–50
Turkey, 57, 154
Turse, Nick, 42, 48, 86, 90, 135, 200

Ukraine, 67, 116–18, 155, 201
United Fruit Company, 100–01, 131, 151–52, 156–57, 200
United Nations (UN), 15, 19, 21, 29, 79, 106, 112, 115, 126, 192
  Climate Secretary Simon Stiell, 106–07
  Convention on the Rights of the Child, 106, 202
  Intergovernmental Panel on Climate Change (IPCC), 107
U.S. Information Agency (USIA), 128
U.S. Steel Export Company, 150, 185
United States, *see* entire book
United States Marine Corps Hymn, 170
United States Steel (U.S. Steel), 150, 185
USSR, *see* Soviet Union

Vallin, Victor-Manuel, 86–87
Vann, John Paul, 42 Venezuela, 155
Versailles, 10, 12, 20–21, 25, 58, 126, 127–28, 136, 151, 164, 178, 186, 189
Viet Cong, Vietcong, 39, 42–43, 134
Viet Minh, Vietminh, 13, 58, 138
Viet Nam (Vietnam), *see* entire book, and Democratic Republic of Viet Nam (DRV), 36, 38, 41–42, 59, 63, 129, 133–34, 196
  People's Army of Viet Nam, 134–35
Viet Nam Independence League, 13–14, 133, 190
Viet Nam Veterans Against the War, 171

voters, voter, xv, xvii–xviii, xxi–xxii, 25–33, 94, 111, 119, 125–26, 127, 175–205
voting bloc, 187

Wala, Michael, xxi, 25, 178–79, 186
Wallace, Henry, 51–52 Wanghia, Treaty of, 163
War and Peace Studies, *see* Council on Foreign Relations
Warren Commission, 59, 199
Warsaw Pact, 117
Washington, George, 3, 45, 47, 174, 183
Wayne, John, 2, 174
We Charge Genocide, 19, 21, 126
Westmoreland, William, 134
Williams, Susan, 57, 79, 80
Wilson, Woodrow, 10, 21, 151
Witte, Ludo de, 82, 90, 140
Wolfowitz, Paul, 94
Woods, Colleen, 48, 122, 136
World Bank, 32, 101, 115
world order, 25–33, 35–43, 52, 53–54, 56, 62, 73, 94, 95, 103. 120, 124, 127, 154, 156, 167, 179, 191
Wright, Quincy, xix, 195

Yalta, 153
Yangtze River, 163

Zaire, *see* Congo
Zionism, 73
Zionists, 75

ABOUT THE AUTHOR

Brian Roesch served in Thailand as a helicopter pilot during 1974 75. After returning to the United States, he began to pursue the real reason for the Viet Nam War. He also worked as a criminal defense lawyer. His two books on Viet Nam explain the early US presence in Viet Nam, the concealment of it from the Us public during 1954 into 2024, the false foreign policy based on that concealment, and the reasons for which the US public has failed to correct the ongoing false foreign policy.

www.ingramcontent.com/pod-product-compliance
Lightning Source LLC
Chambersburg PA
CBHW051559230426
43668CB00013B/1910